EuroDisplay 2015

SID Symposium Digest of Technical Papers Volume 46,
Supplement S1

Ghent, Belgium
21 - 23 September 2015

ISBN: 978-1-5108-3310-4

Printed from e-media with permission by:

Curran Associates, Inc.
57 Morehouse Lane
Red Hook, NY 12571

Some format issues inherent in the e-media version may also appear in this print version.

Printed by Curran Associates, Inc. (2017)

For permission requests, please contact John Wiley & Sons
at the address below.

John Wiley & Sons
111 River Street
Hoboken, NJ 07030-5774

Phone: (201) 748-6000
Fax: (201) 748-6088

info@wiley.com

Additional copies of this publication are available from:

Curran Associates, Inc.
57 Morehouse Lane
Red Hook, NY 12571 USA
Phone: 845-758-0400
Fax: 845-758-2633
Email: curran@proceedings.com
Web: www.proceedings.com

TABLE OF CONTENTS

INTRODUCTION

KEYNOTE ADDRESSES

SESSION 1: LIQUID CRYSTALS BEYOND DISPLAYS

SESSION 2: QUANTUM DOTS I

SESSION 3: LIQUID CRYSTALS: MODELLING & MATERIALS

SESSION 4: MANUFACTURING TECHNOLOGY

SESSION 5: EMERGING LIQUID CRYSTAL TECHNOLOGIES

SESSION 6: BACKLIGHTS

SESSION 7: 3D

SESSION 8: HUMAN INTERACTION

BEST STUDENT PAPER AWARD

SESSION 9: DISPLAY DEVICES

SESSION 10: QUANTUM DOTS II

SESSION 11: METROLOGY

SESSION 12: OXIDE TFTS

ADDITIONAL INVITED TALK

SESSION 13: HUMAN FACTORS AND CHARACTERIZATION

SESSION 14: OLEDS

SESSION 15: AUTOMOTIVE

SESSION 16: NTE

POSTER SESSIONS

Impressum

Organizing Committee

General Chair	Herbert De Smet	Ghent University, IMEC
General Co-chair	Kristiaan Neyts	Ghent University
Executive Chair	Jeroen Beeckman	Ghent University
Advisory Co-chair	Ian Sage	Nottingham Trent University
Program Chair	Dieter Cuypers	Ghent University, IMEC
Program Co-chair	Jan Genoe	KU Leuven, IMEC
Exhibit & sponsorship Chair	Stefan Riehemann	Fraunhofer IOF
Academic Advisor	Youri Meuret	KU Leuven
Industrial Advisor	Joerg Winkler	Plansee SE
SID-ME Chair	Jens Osterodt	Merck
SID-ME Vice Chair	Armin Wedel	Fraunhofer IAP

Scientific Program Committee

Dieter Cuypers (UGent, Belgium)
Jan Genoe (KULeuven, Belgium)
Filip Beunis (UGent, Belgium)
Armin Wedel (Fraunhofer IAP, Germany)
Werner Zapka (KTH, Sweden)
John Kymissis (Columbia University, USA)
Youri Meuret (KULeuven, Belgium)
P. K. Nathan (Brunel University, UK)
Gerrit Oversluizen (Philips, The Netherlands)
Uwe Vogel (Fraunhofer FEP, Germany)
Peter Janssens (Barco, Belgium)
Ian Underwood (University of Edinburgh, UK)
Filip Bruyneel (TP-Vision, Belgium)
Karlheinz Blankenbach (U. Pforzheim, Germany)
Norbert Fr¨uhauf (U. Stuttgart, Germany)
Herbert De Smet (UGent, Belgium)
Kristiaan Neyts (UGent, Belgium)
Jeroen Beeckman (UGent, Belgium)

Gold Sponsors

Preface

We are happy to welcome you to the EuroDisplay 2015 conference.

This biannual conference is supported and coordinated by the Society for Information Display (SID), and its organization is rotated among the different SID chapters in Europe. Following the very successful 2013 edition organized by the UK chapter in London, this year's edition takes place in Ghent, Belgium, and is organized by the Mid-Europe Chapter.

EuroDisplay 2015 is the ideal place for networking between all people involved in display-related research and development. The conference hosts a mixture of presentations by academia and industry, and the integrated exhibition is a showcase of new display technologies and state-of-the-art production and analysis equipment.

The special topics for this conference include subjects that are particularly relevant to European scholars and companies, such as "Display Materials" and "Display Metrology", as well as topics that extend into neighboring research and application areas, such as "Liquid Crystals beyond Displays" and "Displays and Lighting".

We are proud that we were able to attract 2 high-level keynote speakers and 12 carefully selected invited speakers to cover each of the special topics.

In total, the conference counts 98 contributions, 65 of which are oral presentations and 33 of which are posters.

Traditionally, SID offers EuroDisplay authors the opportunity to submit their results also as a full paper to the *Journal of the Society for Information Display*. This time, for the first time in the history of the conference, authors were allowed to submit their full paper prior to the conference, and an expedited review procedure was installed to allow the accepted papers to be available at the time of the conference. The proceedings now consist of a book of one page abstracts plus a collection of full papers, all of which are available in electronic form (online or USB stick) to all conference attendees.

This year, EuroDisplay is held in Ghent, Belgium, and hosted by Ghent University. Ghent is a charming Flemish city that featured in the Lonely Planet's top 10 cities. It has a long and great history and is certainly worth a visit. Its "3 Towers" dominate the skyline of the historic center, which is located less than 300 m away from the conference site. The networking event on Tuesday evening will allow the participants to discover Ghent from an interesting perspective and to enjoy the fine cuisine the city has to offer inside one of its most famous buildings ('De Vooruit'), which has played a major role in the history of the city.

Ghent University features in the top 100 of several world university rankings and is one of the largest universities in the Dutch language region, with more than 41,000 students studying at 11 faculties and 9000 employees. Its Faculty of Engineering & Architecture offers 16 different Master of Science programs, ranging from architecture to biomedical engineering.

The venue for the conference is a former monastery, called "Het Pand" that was purchased and renovated by Ghent University and is located along a channel in the medieval center of Ghent.

On behalf of the organizing committee,

Herbert De Smet

Kristiaan Neyts

Jeroen Beeckman

Dieter Cuypers

Keynote Addresses

Fourth Generation Optics

dr. Nelson Tabiryan (Beam Engineering for Advanced Measurements Co)
Diane Steeves, Brian R. Kimball (US Army Natick Soldier Research, Development & Engineering Center)

Light is an elusive state of matter with only a few opportunities for controlling its propagation. Shaping an optical material such as glass - evidently the first generation of optics - is still the most applied technique for making a lens, a prism, etc. Modulating refractive index instead of shape allows thinner components at the expense of compromised efficiency and bandwidth. Anisotropic materials in the form of liquid crystals made a major breakthrough in optical technologies by introducing two new control parameters. Modern display industry is essentially exploring one of them, variations of the effective modulation of birefringence - the third generation of optics. A recent breakthrough in optics relates to patterning optical axis orientation in the plane of an anisotropic film in conditions of half-wave retardation. Obtained as thin film coatings on any desired substrate, glass, plastic, flat or curved, different optical functionalities are obtained with same materials, same coatings, same processes - just by creating different patterns of the orientation of optical anisotropy axis by a gentle touch of polarization modulated light. The new generation lenses, prisms, vortex waveplates, etc. combine the broadband efficiency of conventional optics with low-cost manufacturing and continuous thin structures no other diffractive optics can match. New optical concepts extend to transparent and flexible displays with no polarizers or color filters.

European Research in Electronic Displays in Context
prof. dr. Ian Underwood (Univ. Edinburgh)

Paper No S1.1: Photoaligned Ferroelectric Liquid Crystals: The New Horizons in Physics and Applications

Vladimir G. Chigrinov

State Key Lab on Advanced Displays and Optoelectronics, Hong Kong University of Science and Technology, CWB, Kowloon, Hong Kong, E-mail: eechigr@ust.hk

Abstract

Photoaligned ferroelectric liquid crystals are described. The new electro-optical modes as well as their new applications in displays and photonics are highlighted. Electrically suppressed helix (ESH) mode was considered as the most promising one.

1. Introduction. New Ferroelectric Liquid Crystal Electrooptical Modes

Fast switching photoaligned ferroelectric liquid crystal (FLC) is a good candidate for the new generation of photonic and display devices, which are better in response time, than usually used nematic LC [1]. Four electrooptic modes in FLC: deformed helix ferroelectric (DHF), electrically suppressed helix (ESH) mode, FLC diffraction mode, and FLC orientational electro-optic Kerr effect were proposed for fast photoaligned FLC display (FLCD) [2].

2. FLC Applications in Displays and Photonics

The photoalignment technology enables to solve the key problems in FLCD applications. FLC is the most advanced technology for a high resolution, field sequential color, advanced color gamut, and low power consumption pico-projectors. Fast switchable FLC E-paper can be done with a possibility of a multi-stable memory states (improved color gamma). Fast responded FLC are envisaged in dense wavelength division multiplexing (DWDM) elements of optical communication systems, such as switches, filters and sensors [2].

3. Further Progress: ESH Mode

The further progress of novel fast ferroelectric LCD will be aimed at: (i) development of new fast responded FLC materials with fast switching and a sufficient number of switchable gray levels (V-shape switching); (ii) implementation of the working prototypes of novel frame-sequential color (FSC) FLC displays, including the three-dimensional version; (iii) investigations of regimes of operation to allow to use efficient addressing of FLCD including TFT drivers enabling a high switching current; (iv) solving the problem of a mechanical stability of FLC layers; and (v) mass production of new FLC materials with optimal characteristics. The most promising mode for FLC applications remains ESH mode, which is mechanically stable, provides an extremely high contrast ratio and transmittance, wide 130% of NTSC color triangle, and high brightness (Figure 1).

4. References

[1] V. G. Chigrinov, V. M. Kozenkov, H. S. Kwok, Photoalignment of Liquid Crystalline Materials: Physics and Applications, Wiley, 2008, p. 248.

[2] V. G. Chigrinov, A. Srivastava, "Ferroelectric liquid crystal cells for advanced applications in displays and photonics", Mol. Cryst. Liq. Cryst., Vol. **595**, pp. 39–49, 2014.

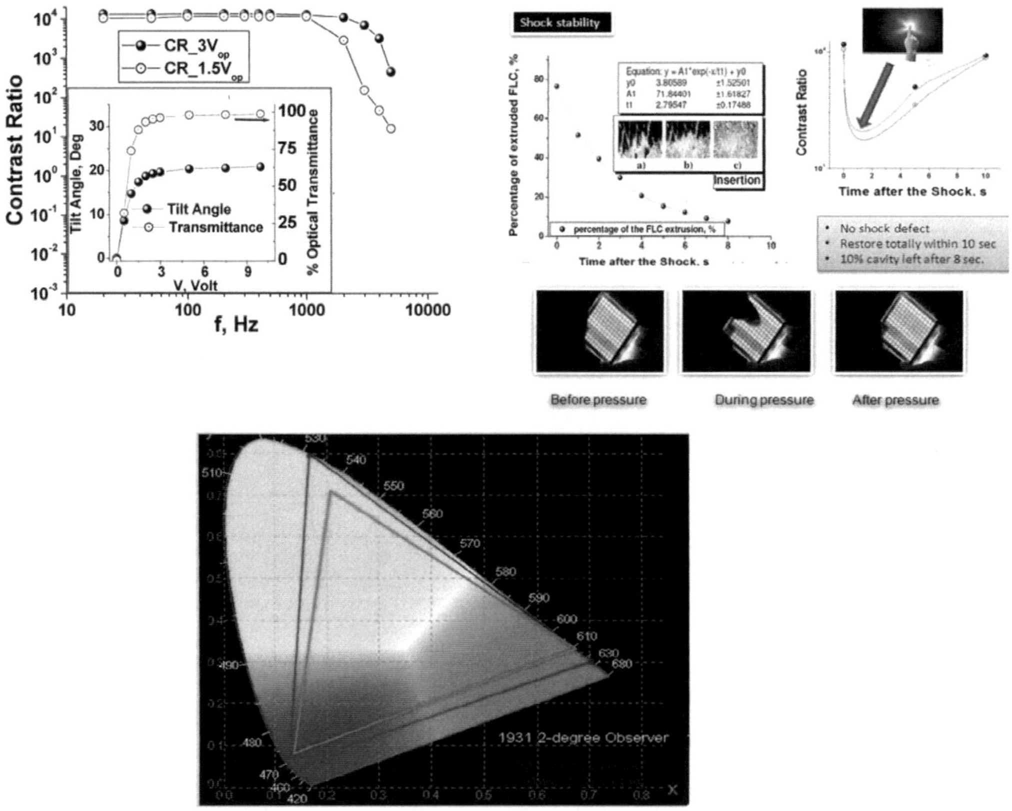

Figure 1. ESH FLC mode: contrast 10,000:1, fast response time 10 μs, color shock stability, 130% NTSC color triangle.

Paper No S1.3: Lead Zirconate Titanate-Based Transmissive Liquid Crystal Lens Approach

Oliver Willekens, John George, Kristiaan Neyts, and Jeroen Beeckman
Department of ELIS, Ghent University, Belgium, E-mail: oliver.willekens@elis.ugent.be

Abstract
We report the design and fabrication of an electrooptical, tunable, liquid crystal-based lens and analysis of its performance. The lens obtains its gradient index (GRIN) profile from multielectrode addressing using a layer with high dielectric constant to extend and smoothen out the horizontal electric field between the large interelectrode distances.

1. Introduction
Since their first report in 1979, many novel electrically tunable liquid crystal (LC) lenses have been proposed [1]. Most are plagued by the inherent polarization dependence of the LC to induce the optical path differences required for a parabolic phase profile, but with the advent of blue phase LC, this problem could also be addressed [2]. The structures can be categorized as either dual-electrode or multielectrode designs. While the latter is more versatile, as defects can be compensated, the driving is more complex. To avoid fringe fields between the electrodes, several designs use a conductive material between the electrodes to generate a gradual potential drop. However, such devices draw a considerable current.

In this paper, we introduce an alternative technique for inducing a gradual voltage drop, by using a layer with a high dielectric constant, $\varepsilon_{\parallel}$, over the substrate containing the addressing electrodes. Such a structure has been proposed earlier [2], but to our knowledge, this is the first report on its successful fabrication. This structure can be manufactured without using the relatively costly transparent conductor indium tin oxide (ITO) and the power consumption is small.

2. Design and Fabrication
LC-based electro-optic devices apply a nonuniform electric field over the liquid crystal to obtain a desired optical path length (OPL) profile. For a lens, the OPL profile should be parabolic. Such a profile could be obtained by using multiple electrodes in a vertical field switching (VFS) configuration. However, when the distance between these electrodes becomes large, the OPL deviates strongly from the desired profile. Our simulations show that these effects can be diminished by applying a layer of high dielectric constant over the electrodes.

Lead zirconate titanate (PZT) is an appropriate material and we have developed a deposition process by spincoating and annealing, which yields a dielectric constant of $\varepsilon_{\parallel} \sim 500$ [3]. We deposited a PZT layer on top of an electrode design made by liftoff. The design consists of 8 metallic concentric rings that are separately addressable. After spincoating the PZT-layer over the electrode pattern, the substrate is pretreated with nylon and subsequently rubbed to set a preferential alignment direction

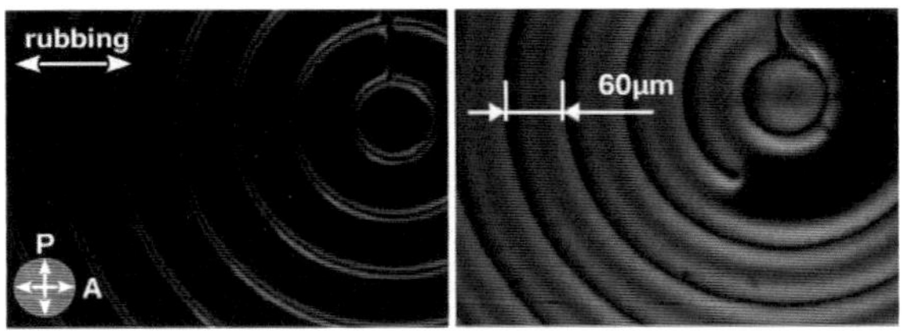

Figure 1. Microscope images with crossed polarizers of a reference device (left) and a device with electrodes covered by 0.84 μm PZT (right). The electrodes are all 3-μm wide and spaced 60 μm apart; they are all at 5.1 V_{rms}.

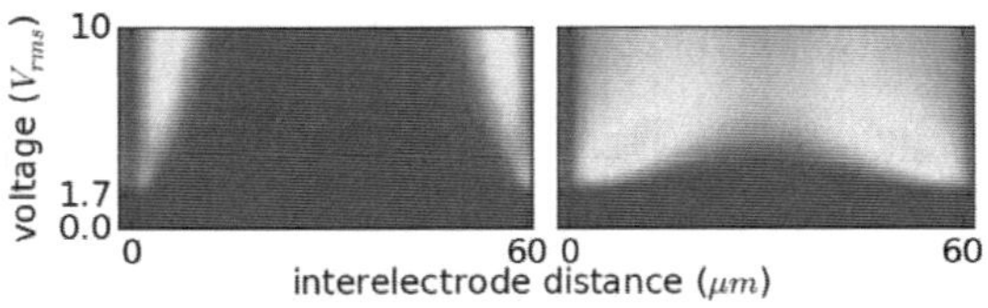

Figure 2. Intensity profile between two neighboring electrodes for the reference lens (left) and the lens with PZT layer (right) at different voltages.

for the LC. This substrate is glued together with another pretreated glass substrate, with a homogeneous ITO layer acting as reference electrode. Both substrates are separated by 5.5 μm spacers and the cavity is filled with the nematic LC mixture E7.

3. Results
Polarizing optical microscopy (POM) is used to analyze the effect of the PZT layer on the electric field distribution indirectly. Figure 1 shows the observed POM images for the device with ring electrodes, with and without the PZT layer, using a green LED light source to simplify the analysis.

The concentric electrodes are all at the same potential with respect to the ground electrode. The rubbing direction is parallel to the analyzer. Because of the mismatch between the rubbing direction and the radial fringe fields, the director does not only tilt with increasing voltage, but also twists, which is the reason why light is transmitted in this configuration.

A series of images was taken for the reference cell and PZT cell at different voltages. These images were then processed to obtain the radial intensity profile between two neighboring electrodes, as a function of the applied voltage, as shown in Figure 2. The comparison shows that PZT is able to bring the applied voltage difference across the gap: even halfway between two electrodes, the LC molecules are reoriented.

A smaller interelectrode distance, a thicker PZT layer or using a layer with an even higher dielectric constant would improve the homogeneity of the electric field and the light transmission.

4. Acknowledgements
This work is partly supported by the IWT through the SBO project SECONDOS, IWT-nr 120019, 2013-2016. The author wishes to thank Steven Verstuyft, Ghent University, INTEC/Photonics, for his assistance during the image reversal.

5. References
[1] H. C. Lin, M. S. Chen, Y. H. Lin, "A review of electrically tunable focusing liquid crystal lenses", Trans. Electr. Electron. Mater., Vol. **12**, pp. 234–240, 2011.

[2] C. T. Lee, Y. Li, H. Y. Lin, S. T. Wu., "Design of polarization-insensitive multi-electrode GRIN lens with a blue-phase liquid crystal", Opt. Express, Vol. **19**, pp. 17402–17407, 2011.

[3] J. P. George, P. F. Smet, J. Botterman, V. Bliznuk, W. Woestenborghs, D. Van Thourhout, K. Neyts, J. Beeckman, "Lanthanide assisted deposition of strongly electro-optic PZT thin films on silicon", ACS Appl. Mater. Interfaces, Vol. **7**, pp. 13350–13359, 2015.

Paper No S1.4: "Continuous" Nanoscale Patterned Photoalignment for Thin Film Pancharatnam-Berry Phase Diffractive Lens

A. M. W. Tam,[1] F. Fan,[2] H. S. Chen,[2] D. Tao,[1] V.G. Chigrinov,[1] H. S. Kwok,[1] and Y. S. Lin[2]

[1]Partner State Key Laboratory (PSKL) on Advanced Displays and Optoelectronics Technologies, Department of Electronic and Computer Engineering, Hong Kong University of Science and Technology, Clear Water Bay, Kowloon, Hong Kong, E-mail: amwtam@ust.hk; [2]Department of Photonics, National Chiao Tung University, 1001 Ta Hsueh Rd, Hsinchu, 30010, Taiwan

Abstract

In this paper, we disclosed the realization of a "continuous" nano-structured alignment patterning for thin film Pancharatnam-Berry phase (PBP) diffractive lens by the use of spatially linear polarized light converter technology. High optical quality thin liquid crystal polymer (LCP) film PBP lens with F number of 45.4 and a diffraction efficiency of 95.5%, operating in blue visible region has been demonstrated. The concave and convex polarization dependent property of the lens can be clearly observed by human eye, which is attractive in many display applications, for example, bifocal lens for eye glasses; camera zoom system; and polarization imaging.

Figure 3. Image display of PBP as (a) convex lens and (b) concave lens.

1. Introduction

Recently, diffractive Pancharatnam-Berry phase optical phase element (PBPOE) plays an important role in the application of polarization imaging and sensing, for which the PBPOE provides a rapid control on the shape of the wavefront and direction of propagation of the light depending on the state of polarization of the incoming optical signal. The PBP lens is an important polarization-sensitive device that consists of a thin layer birefringent material with the optics axis spatially orientated in terms of r^2 on the azimuth plane. It has a remarkable property of behaving as a convex/concave lens given that the incident light is left-/right-handed circularly polarized (LHC/RHC). In this paper, we demonstrate a high-quality LCP thin film PBP lens with stable nanoscopic alignment profile by the use of our pioneered photoalignment patterning technology based on the spatially linear polarized light converter system. A complex alignment pattern of PB lens is established in a single step UV exposure with a simple spatial phase retarder. Unlike the methods introduced in [1], for which the PBOEs profile is quantized that leads to a degradation in optical performance, a nanoscale resolution continuous PBP lens profile is realized from our approach yielding a diffraction efficiency limit close to 100%. The high-quality PBP lens is potentially attractive in many display applications including electrically switchable bifocal lens for eyeglasses correcting for both presbyopia and myopia, reducing the size of zoom camera system, and polarization imaging.

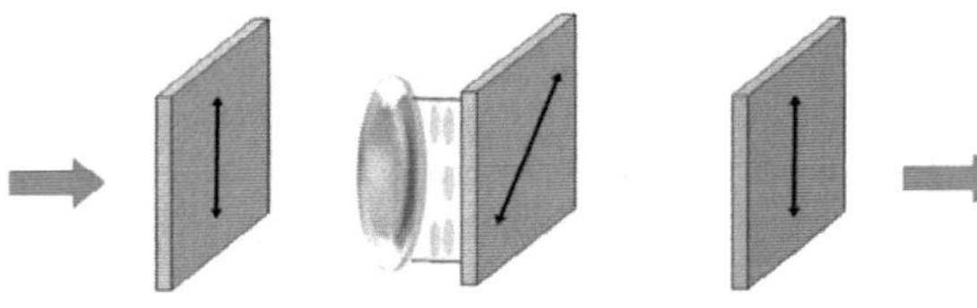

Figure 1. Setup of spatially polarized light converter.

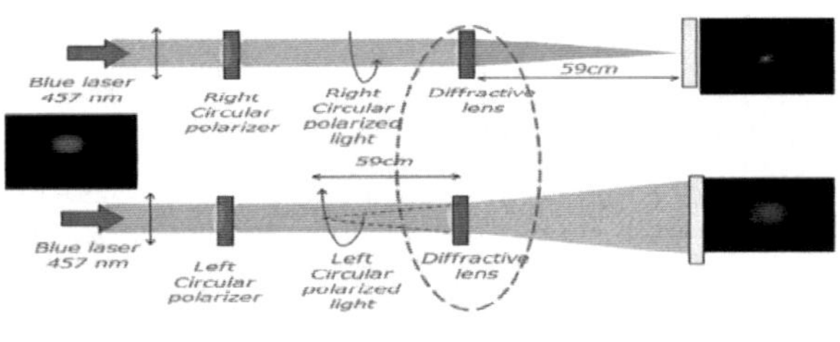

Figure 2. Evaluation of PBP lens from blue laser light.

2. Methods and Fabrication

The PB lens is fabricated beginning by exposing a thin layer of sulfonic azo dye (SD1), which has been spin coated onto the glass substrate, by a 0.3 W/cm^2 450 nm laser for 1 min at the output of the spatial light converter. The spatial light converter, that comprises of a input linear polarizer, followed by a spatially varying phase retarder and a quarter wave plate, as shown in Figure 1, rotates the polarization of the light at an angle of $\Gamma(x,y)/2$, where $\Gamma(x,y)$ is the retardation of the spatial phase retarder. The spatial retarder for PBP lens is realized by sandwiching a LCP birefringent layer in between a plano-convex lens and a glass substrate, so that the rotational angle of the linear polarized light follows the spatial lens profile at the output of the converter. Since the SD-1 molecules are rotated by 90° with respect to the polarization of the output light through rotational diffusion mechanism [2], thus a continuous nanoscopic resolution PBP alignment profile is constructed. A stable PBP lens alignment structure operating at 450 nm is realized by depositing a micrometer thickness UCL017A LCP layer onto the patterned SD1 substrate by spin coating, followed by a photopolymerization process from UV light.

3. Results

The performance of PBP lens is tested by illuminating a 457 nm laser beam through a circular polarizer onto the sample. When a RHC polarizer is placed in front of the PBP lens, the lens behaves as a convex lens that beam is focused into a bright small spot on the screen located at a focal distance away from the lens, as shown in Figure 2(a). Conversely, when a LHC polarizer is inserted, the beam size expands and the intensity of the beam decreases as the PBP lens now behaves as a diverging lens. The focal length of the lens is ±59 cm, and F number of the lens is ±42.4. The diffraction efficiency of the sample is measured to be 95.5% which is close to the 100% diffraction limit. The display performance of PBP lens is demonstrated in Figure 3(a), for which a clear image of the letters "SKL" is magnified when a RHC polarizer is placed in front showing the convex property of the lens. Conversely, when a LHC polarizer is inserted, the letter image "SKL" is minimized showing the concave property of the lens, as shown in Figure 3(b).

4. References

[1] E. Hasman, V. Kleiner, G. Biener, A. Niv, "Polarization dependent focusing lens by use of quantized Pancharatnam-Berry phase diffractive optics", Appl. Phys. Lett. Vol. **82**, pp. 328–330, 2003.

[2] V. Chigrinov, S. Pikin, A. Verevochnikov, V. Kozenkov, M. Khazimullin, J. Ho, D. D. Huang, H.-S. Kwok, "Diffusion model of photoaligning in azo-dye layers", Phys. Rev. E, Vol. **69**, pp. 061713, 2004.

Paper No S2.1: Cathodoluminescence Images and Spectra of Single Nanometer Sized Phosphor Crystals Excited in a Field Emission Transmission Electron Microscope

J. Silver, D. den Engelsen, G. R. Fern, P. Harris, A. Lipman, and T. G. Ireland

Centre for Phosphor and Display Materials, Wolfson Centre for Materials Processing, Brunel University London, Uxbridge, Middlesex, UB8 3PH, United Kingdom, E-mail: jack.silver@brunel.ac.uk

Abstract

In this article, cathodoluminescent images and spectra of a range of single nanometer-sized phosphor crystals and quantum dots are presented to illustrate the power and potential of the technique as an aid to both characterize phosphor materials and assess their homogeneity.

1. Introduction

Two years ago, Brunel University London acquired a scanning tunneling electron microscope (STEM) with a cathodoluminescent attachment that facilitates the study of single nanoparticles of phosphors. In addition, it is possible to obtain cathodoluminescence (CL) spectra from individual crystals. One of the questions that phosphor chemists are often asked is how homogeneous is a phosphor sample? Of course this question is not easy to answer as photoluminescent (PL) or CL spectra collected from phosphor samples are the average spectra of all the particles in the sample. This is true of all samples made either in the laboratory for research or in industrial companies for commercial purpose. We will show that now that it is possible to collect CL spectra from individual nanometer sized particles the question of homogeneity of a sample can be addressed.

The objective of this work is to show examples of a variety of high-angle annular dark-field (HAADF) images and CL images taken in the microscope and to explain what extra information can be gained by overlapping the images. To illustrate this work, we will show images from several studies we have carried out in the last couple of years on $-Y_{2-x}Tb_xO_2S$ (where × has values from 0.001 to 0.05) [1], $Gd_2O_2S:Tb^{3+}$ samples [2], quantum dots (QDs) composed of a CdSe core with a shell of ZnCdS that emit red or green light dependent on the radius of the core material [3–5], $Y_2O_3:Eu^{3+}$ [6], $Y_2O_3:Tb^{3+}$ [7], and $Zn_{0.994}Mn_{0.006}Ga_2O_4$ phosphor.

2. Results and Discussion

All the nanometer-sized phosphor particles were synthesized by procedures described in our earlier work [1, 2, 6, 7], the QDs were supplied by QD Vision Inc. [3–5]. All the phosphors were characterized using X-ray powder diffraction and other appropriate methodologies.

In the cases of the nanometer-sized phosphor particles of both the $Y_{2-x}Tb_xO_2S$ and $Gd_2O_2S:Tb^{3+}$ samples, we collected very good quality HAADF and CL images, as well as very sharp high-resolution emission spectra (at temperatures ranging from 25°C to −170°C). There were no significant differences in the relative intensities of the CL emission spectra between the separate nanometer-sized crystals in each sample showing that the synthetic methodology used in the synthesis led to homogeneous doping in all the crystals produced in any given batch. This was true for both sets of Tb^{3+} phosphors [1,2]. In addition, high-quality light images demonstrate the uniform emission of light from individual phosphor particles.

Both the red and green QDs facilitated high-quality HAADF images, and variations in the size and shape of the individual QDs could be easily seen and commented on. A number of images of the red QDs showed the presence of none uniform dots that were triangular in appearance. Good light images could be collected from the red QDs, and it was possible to see light emitted from individual QDs. Many red QDs appeared not to be emitting, and there was evidence that some QDs were decaying in the electron beam [3–5].

In studies on nanometre-sized crystals of $Y_2O_3:Eu^{3+}$ [6], $Y_2O_3:Tb^{3+}$ [7], and $Zn_{0.994}Mn_{0.006}Ga_2O_4$ phosphor, it was shown that highly detailed CL spectra could give information on the properties of the emission site, and by overlapping HAADF images and CL images taken in the microscope, it was possible to see how well the dopant activator atoms were dispersed.

3. Conclusions

The methodology allowed CL spectra to be collected from a wide variety of down-converting nanometer-sized phosphor crystals along with high-quality light images. The latter shows-uniform emission of light from individual particles/QDS. The techniques used herein to collect CL spectra from nanometer-sized phosphor crystals and QDs could be used to study any such photoluminescent particles. Moreover, any variation observed between such particles in their spectra or light images will aid in the evolution of material science. Overall, such studies could lead to the production of better phosphors for lighting and displays.

4. Acknowledgements

We are grateful to the EPSRC and the TSB for funding the PURPOSE (TP11/MFE/6/I/AA129F; EPSRC TS/G000271/1) and CONVERTED (JeS no. TS/I003053/1) programs.

5. References

[1] J. Silver, X. Yan, G. R Fern, N. Wilkinson, "Cathodolumin-escence spectra of single $Y_2O_2S:Tb^{3+}$ nanometer sized phosphor crystals excited in a field emission scanning transmission electron microscope", Proceedings of the IDW '13, pp. 823–826, 2013.

[2] G. R. Fern, X. Yan, N. Wilkinson, J. Silver, "Cathodolumin-escence spectra of single $Gd_2O_2S:Tb^{3+}$ nanometer sized phosphor crystals excited in a field emission scanning transmission electron microscope", Proceedings of the IDW '13, pp. 820–822, 2013.

[3] G. R. Fern, J. Silver, S. Coe-Sullivan, J. S. Steckel, "Red quantum dots under the electron microscope." 2014 SID International Symposium, Digest of Technical Papers, Vol. XLVI, Books I-III Paper 7.2, SID Digest, pp. 59–62, 2014.

[4] J. Silver, G. R. Fern, T. Ireland, S. Coe-Sullivan, J. S. Steckel, "Images and cathodoluminescent spectra of red and green quantum dots", Proceedings of the IDW '14, pp. 737–740, 2014.

[5] G. R. Fern, J. Silver, S. Coe-Sullivan, "Cathodolumin-escence and electron microscopy of red quantum dots used for display applications", J. Soc. Inf. Disp., in press. doi: 10.1002/jsid.278

[6] G. R. Fern, P. G. Harris, T. Ireland, J. Silver, "Assessing spatial resolution of cathodoluminescence imaging and spectroscopy at the nanoscale for inorganic phosphor powders", submitted to the Fall 2015 ECS Symposium on Luminescence and Display Materials in Phoenix, AZ.

[7] D. den Engelsen, P. G. Harris, T. G. Ireland, G. Fern, J. Silver, "Symmetry-Related Transitions in the Spectrum of Nanosized Cubic $Y_2O_3:Tb_3+$", ECS J. Solid State Sci. Technol., vol. **4**, pp. R105–R113, 2015.

Paper No S2.2: Ecofriendly Quantum Dot Light-Emitting Diode With Inorganic Charge Transport Layer

Min Suk Oh,[1] C. J. Han,[1] B. Yoo,[1] J. Lee,[1] H. Y. Kim,[1,2] Y. J. Park,[1] B. K. Joo,[2] Y. Kim,[3] and A. Wedel[3]

[1]Korea Electronics Technology Institute (KETI), South Korea, E-mail: ohms@keti.re.kr; [2]Korea University, South Korea; [3]Fraunhofer Institute for Applied Polymer Research, Germany

Abstract

Recently, the display technologies using colloidal quantum dot (QD) materials have become one of the most important technologies in the display industry. But, the organic charge transport layer for quantum dot-light-emitting diode (QD-LED) can cause the device stability issues. In this article, we describe the QD-LED devices with inorganic charge transport layer and the solution-based oxide thin-film transistor (TFT) using non-thermal treatment. And we also show the active matrix driving using both technologies simultaneously.

1. Introduction

Colloidal quantum dot (QD) materials are widely used as light-emitting diodes (LEDs) because of the simple solution process, the color tunability by controlling the size of QD, and high color purity. However, QD materials commonly contain toxic materials, such as cadmium, that is harmful to human body, so it is necessary to substitute such materials in QD. Several research groups try to create a stable Cd-free QD-LED devices to overcome this problem. Here, to improve the stability and device properties of Cd-free QD-LED, we fabricated the QD-LEDs using the inorganic charge transport layer and Cd-free QD material.

2. Device Fabrication

After 50 × 50 mm^2 indium tin oxide (ITO)-coated glass substrates were cleaned by the acetone, methanol, and isopropyl alcohol, the ITO electrodes were patterned by the normal photolithography method and wet etching process. Then, for the formation of electron transport layer (ETL), several inorganic nonparticles (ZrO_2 or TiO_2) in the solvent were coated by spin coating in air at room temperature. After ETL coating, the colloidal QDs with eco-friendly materials (InP/ZnSe/ZnS) in solvent were spin-coated on the inorganic ETL layers. After that, the 4,4′-*N,N′*-dicarbazole-biphenyl (CBP) hole transport layer (HTL) layer and MoO_x were deposited by thermal evaporation process. Finally, the Al anode layer was thermally deposited. The fabricated devices were encapsulated by the encapsulation glass using UV sealant in the glove box with nitrogen. The resulting emitting area is 6 × 4 mm^2, which is defined by the overlap of patterned anode and cathode. Our QD LEDs consist of ITO as the cathode, inorganic nano-particles as the ETL, quantum dot with eco-friendly core/shell structure as emitting layer, CBP as the HTL, MoO_x as the charge injection layer, and Al as anode. Figure 1 shows the basic structure for our QD-LEDs.

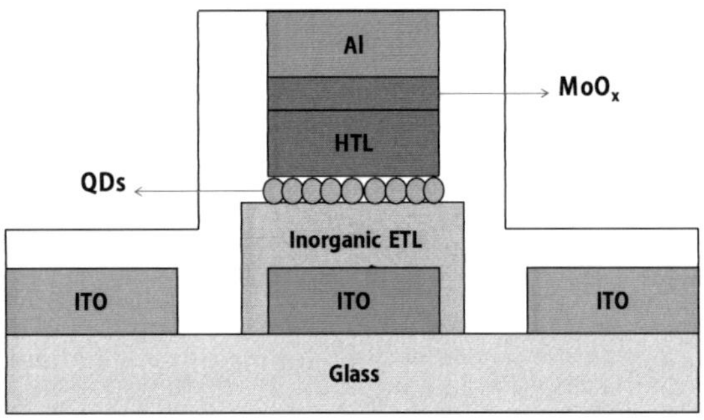

Figure 1. Basic device structure of QD-LED.

3. Results and Discussions

Cd-free QD-LED devices using InP QD for emission layer were fabricated with inorganic ETL. To improve the poor luminance and efficiency, we changed of the concentration the ZrO_2 nanopowder and post-treated them. In case of ZrO_2 layer, the lower concentration and higher postannealing showed better performance (Figure 2). And, after the several post-treatment of ZrO_2 powder at low temperature, we could fabricated the improved QD-LED devices using InP QDs.

4. Acknowledgements

This work was supported by "Development of high performance (>70 cm^2/V s) chalcogenide TFT backplane and cadmium-free highly efficient (>30 cd/A) hybrid EL material/devices (10045145)," "Development of 2G flexible TFT backplane using photo-annealing," and "Core Technology Development of Low-Energy, Visible-Light-Based Photo-Sintering Equipment for TFT Fabrication Process" funded by the Ministry of Trade, Industry and Energy (MOTIE, Korea).

5. References

[1] V. Wood, V. Bulovic, "Colloidal quantum dot light-emitting devices", Nano Rev., Vol. **1**, p. 5202, 2010.

[2] Q. Sun, Y. A. Wang, L. S. Li, D. Wang, T. Zhu, J. Xu, C. Yang, Y. Li, "Bright, multicoloured light-emitting diodes based on quantum dots", Nat. Photon., Vol. **1**, pp. 717–722, 2007.

[3] J. M. Caruge, J. E. Halpert, V. Wood, V. Bulovic, M. G. Bawendi, "Colloidal quantum-dot light-emitting diodes with metal-oxide charge transport layers", Nat. Photon., Vol. **2**, pp. 247–250, 2008.

[4] V. Wood, M. J. Panzer, J. E. Halpert, J.-M. Caruge, M. G. Bawendi, V. Bulović, "Selection of metal oxide charge transport layers for colloidal quantum dot LEDs", ACS Nano, Vol. **3**, pp. 3581–3586, 2009.

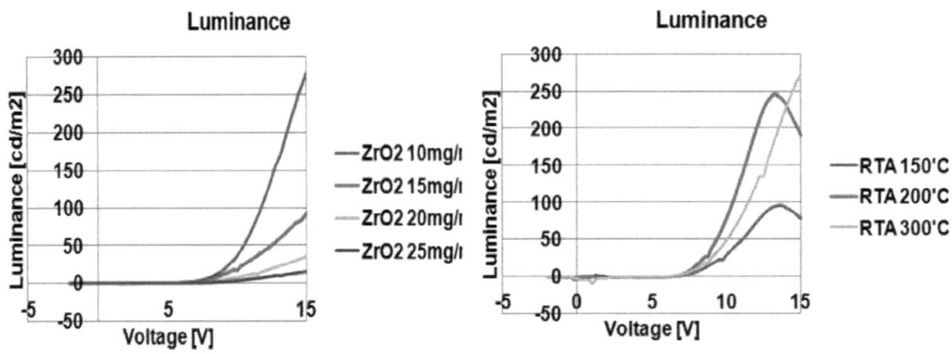

Figure 2. Luminance data of several ZrO_2 concentrations and RTA temperature.

Paper No S2.3: Uniform Quantum Dot Light Emitting Diodes Fabricated by Transfer Mold Method

Masayuki Nakamoto and Jonghyun Moon

Department of Research Institute of Electronics, Shizuoka University, Shizuoka-shi, Japan, E-mail: m-nakamoto@rie.shizuoka.ac.jp

Abstract

Highly uniform quantum dot light emitting diodes (QD LEDs) have been developed by using Transfer Mold method to realize highly efficient and bright displays. The brightness of Transfer Mold QD LEDs is as high as 633 times, being compared with those of QD LEDs by using a flat substrate. Transfer Mold QD LEDs have uniform Mold arrays, QDs in the Molds, and SiO_2 layer patterned on the flat area having no Molds. The SiO_2 layer blocks the leakage current between cathode and anode. Low leakage current due to QDs in the uniform Mold arrays with the patterned SiO_2 layer, improves carrier-injection efficiency. The QD LEDs by using a flat substrate, have non-uniform QD's area due to the QD particle's aggregation, and have low brightness because of the high leakage current. The Transfer Mold QD LEDs can realize the highly efficient QD LEDs.

1. Introduction

QD LEDs are increasing interest as emerging display devices, because of the good color purity and color tunability. However, QD LEDs by using conventional QD formation methods on the flat substrate, such as the spin coating and spray methods, have the issues for QD particle's aggregation and non-uniform arrangement. In the field of vacuum nanoelectronic devices utilizing field emitter arrays (FEAs), Transfer Mold fabrication method has been developed to obtain sharp, uniform, low operation voltage FEAs for the highly efficient and reliable vacuum nanoelectronic devices [1]. Extremely sharp, uniform and 36 nm emitter size FEAs were obtained by using Transfer Mold emitter fabrication method. The 36 nm FEAs are the smallest FEA, ever reported [2]. In this work, highly uniform and high brightness QD LEDs have been developed by using Transfer Mold method to realize highly efficient displays.

2. Experimental

Figures 1(a)-(d) shows the fabrication process of Transfer Mold QD LEDs (TM QD LEDs). TM QD LEDs have uniform Mold arrays, QDs in the Molds, and SiO_2 layer patterned on the flat area having no Molds. Si Mold substrates were prepared by anisotropic Si etching in Figure 1(a). Aluminum as a cathode and SiO_2 layer was deposited in Figure

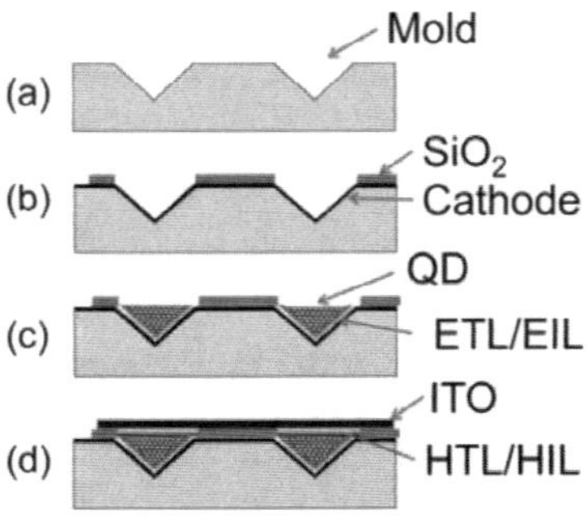

Figure 1. Fabrication process of TM QD LEDs.

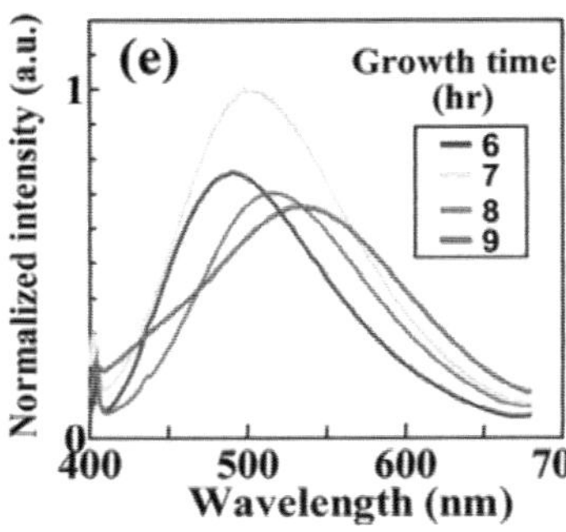

Figure 2. PL spectra as a function of QD growth time.

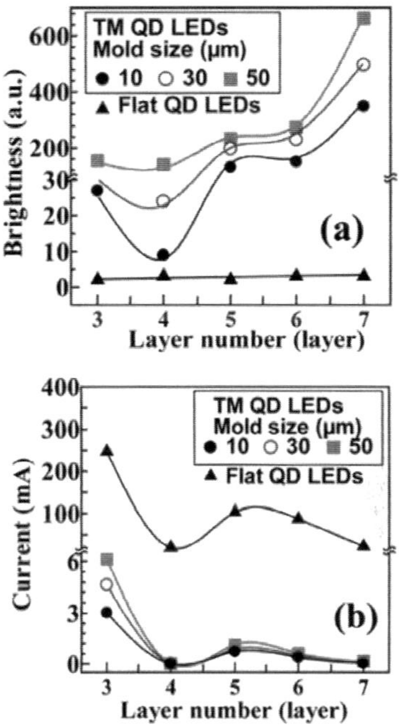

Figure 3. (a) Relation between brightness and layer number, (b) Relation between current and layer number.

1(b). QDs, were formed in the Mold with an electron transport layer (ETL) and an electron injection layer (EIL) layer in Figure 1(c). Lithium fluoride and copper (II) phthalocyanine as a hole transport layer (HTL) and a hole injection layer (HIL), were formed. ITO as an anode, was coated in Figure 1(d). InP/ZnS QDs have been synthesized by the QD growth time for 6–9 h. Brightness and I-V characteristics were evaluated by the comparison with those of QD LEDs by using a flat substrate (Flat QD LEDs). QD LEDs were fabricated with three to seven layers of QDs, ETL/QDs, ETL/QDs/HTL, EIL/ETL/QDs/HTL, and EIL/ETL/QDs/HTL/HIL between cathode and anode.

3. Results and Discussion

Figure 2 shows the PL spectra as a function of QD growth time for 6–9 h. As the increase of QD growth time, PL spectra shifted from 491 to 534 nm due to the quantum size effect. The QD size increases as the increase of the QD growth time.

Figure 3(a) shows the relation between brightness and layer number of TM QD LEDs and Flat QD LEDs. Brightness of TM QD LEDs was as high as 633 times, being compared with those of Flat QD LEDs. Figure 3(b) shows the relation between current and layer number. The current values for Flat QD LEDs were as high as 41-226 times, compared with those of TM QD LEDs. Low leakage current due to QDs in the uniform Mold arrays with the patterned SiO_2 layer, improves carrier-injection efficiency. Therefore, TM QD LEDs can realize the highly efficient QD LEDs.

4. Conclusion

Highly uniform and high brightness QD LEDs have been developed by Transfer Mold method. The brightness of TM QD LEDs is as high as 633 times, being compared with those of Flat QD LEDs. The Transfer Mold method is useful for realizing the highly efficient QD LEDs.

5. References

[1] M. Nakamoto, T. Hasegawa, T. Ono, T. Sakai, N. Sakuma, "Low operation voltage field emitter arrays using low work function materials fabricated by transfer mold technique", Tech. Digest of IEDM'**96**, pp. 297–300, 1996.

[2] M. Nakamoto, J. Moon, "Stable, ruggedized, and nanometer-order size transfer mold field emitter array in harsh oxygen radical environment", J. Vaccum Sci. Technol. B, Vol. **33**, pp. 03C107-1-03C107-8, 2014.

Paper No S2.4: Large–Scale and Electroswitchable Polarized Emission From Semiconductor Nanorods Aligned in Polymeric Nanofibers

Tangi Aubert,[1] Ljiljana Palangetic,[2] Mohammad Mohammadimasoudi,[3] Kristiaan Neyts,[3] Jeroen Beeckman,[3] Christian Clasen,[2] and Zeger Hens[1]

[1]Physics and Chemistry of Nanostructures Group, Ghent University, Gent, Belgium, E-mail: tangi.aubert@ugent.be; [2]Department of Chemical Engineering, University of Leuven, Leuven, Belgium; [3]Electronics and Information Systems Department, Ghent University, Gent, Belgium

Abstract

We demonstrate the fabrication of a large-scale device allowing for electrical switching of polarized light with a polarization ratio of 0.45 over a 1.5 cm^2 area. To achieve this, a film of aligned polymeric nanofibers containing aligned silica-coated semiconductor nanorods was prepared by electrospinning. This film, which can conveniently be processed further, was integrated in a liquid crystal cell with a polarizer where applying a voltage allows switching the emitted light on and off, a property highly relevant for display applications.

1. Introduction

Semiconductor nanostructures such as colloidal quantum dots offer interesting optical properties, including tunable emission spectra and high photoluminescence quantum yield. These characteristics make them very promising candidates as light emitters in the next generation of display technologies. Anisotropic structures such as nanorods (NRs) are of further interest as they also show polarized emission along their long axis [1,2]. To fully take advantage of this unique property in lighting or display applications, these colloidal objects need to be ordered on a large scale. To this end, a very interesting approach has been developed for the alignment of gold NRs in polymeric nanofibers made by electrospinning [3]. This technique has been adapted in this work for the alignment of photoluminescent CdSe/CdS NRs, hence producing flexible films showing large-scale polarized emission. Such a self-supporting film, similar to a foil, can be manipulated and combined with any kind of substrate, which we demonstrate here through its integration in a liquid crystal (LC) cell.

2. Results

CdSe/CdS NRs with a dot-in-rod heterostructures are known to show polarized emission perpendicularly to their long axis with a polarization ratio of 0.75 for an individual NR [2]. These NRs are prepared by hot-injection synthesis through a seeded growth approach in apolar solutions. To make them compatible with the polar polymeric solution required for electrospinning, the NRs were coated with a thin silica layer through a reverse microemulsion process. After silica encapsulation, the NRs were dispersed in a mixture of polyvinylpyrrolidone (PVP) in ethanol, and nanofibers were formed by electrospinning of this solution. Transmission electron microscopy images revealed that the NRs were aligned along the nanofibers, axis due to the strong extensional flow generated in the polymer solution during electrospinning. Uniaxially aligned nanofibers were obtained by simply replacing the standard grounded plate collector with a parallel plate collector, consisting of two free-standing stripes of electrical conductors separated by a gap. Using such a collector resulted in self-supporting films of 1.5 cm^2 consisting of aligned PVP nanofibers containing aligned NRs. These films were observed by fluorescence microscopy with a rotatable polarizer revealing a large-scale polarization ratio of 0.45. An important feature of these flexible and self-supporting films is that they can be manipulated and processed, which allowed us to integrate them in LC cells. In this regards, the aligned nanofibers revealed another important asset of our approach as they act as an alignment layer for the nematic LC, which is demonstrated by fluorescence microscopy. When the polarizer is oriented parallel to the nanofibers, the light emitted by the NRs is blocked due to the 90° rotation of their polarized light following the twist of the LC director. When the polarizer is rotated perpendicularly to the fibers, the light goes through and is collected (ON position in Figure 1). When applying a 50 V AC electric field on the cell, the LC takes a vertical alignment. The polarized light emitted by the NRs is not rotated anymore and is blocked again by the polarizer (OFF position in Figure 1).

3. Acknowledgements

The authors acknowledge BelSPo (IAP 7.35, photonics@be), FWO-Vlaanderen (Project G.0760.12; KaN 1509012N), Ghent University (BOF12/GOA/015), ERC-2007-StG starting grant 203043 NANOFIB, and the SoPPom program of the Flemish Strategic Initiative for Materials (SIM) for financial support.

3. References

[1] T. Aubert, L. Palangetic, M. Mohammadimasoudi, K. Neyts, J. Beeckman, C. Clasen, Z. Hens, "Large scale and electro-switchable polarized emission from semiconductor nanorods aligned in polymeric nanofibers", ACS Photon., in press.

[2] A. Sitt, I. Hadar, U. Banin, "Band-gap engineering, optoelectronic properties and applications of colloidal heterostructured Semiconductor Nanorods", Nano Today, Vol. **10**, pp. 494–513, 2013.

[3] K. E. Roskov, K. A. Kozek, W.-C. Wu, R. K. Chhetri, A. L. Oldenburg, R. J. Spontak, J. B. Tracy, "Long-range alignment of gold nanorods in electrospun polymer nano/microfibers", Langmuir, Vol. **17**, pp. 13965–13969, 2011.

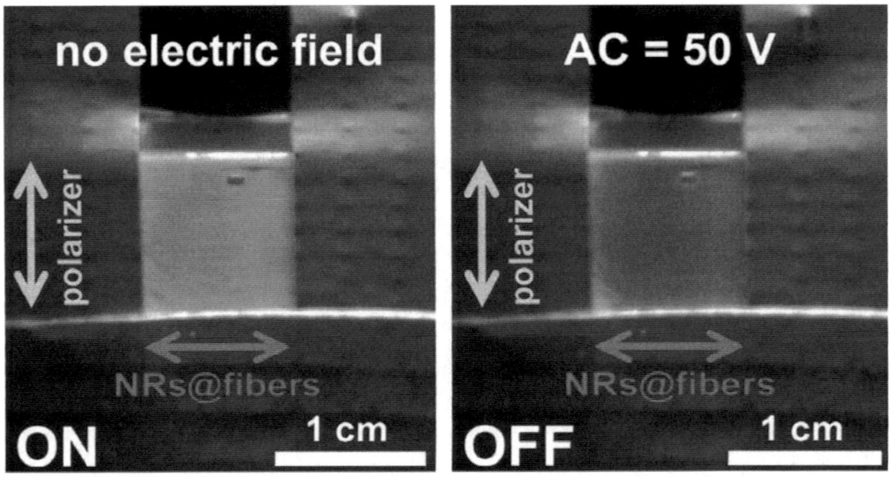

Figure 1. Pictures of the aligned nanofibers containing aligned nanorods and placed in a LC cell. The nanorods are excited using a portable UV lamp and the pictures are taken through a polarizer. The emitted light is switched ON and OFF simply by applying a voltage.

Paper No S3.1: Modeling of Liquid Crystal Structures

Sally E. Day, Zijun Nie, Mengyang Yang, and F. Anibal Fernandez

Department of Electronic and Electrical Engineering, UCL, Torrington Place, London WC1E 7JE, United Kingdom, E-mail: sally.day@ucl.ac.uk

Abstract

Modeling of nematic liquid crystal structures using the tensor method are presented for various configurations. In particular defect formation at the edges of electrodes, which depend on alignment direction have been studied, as well as droplets of cholesteric liquid crystals, where the pitch must adapt to conform to the surface alignment of the droplet and the position of the defects at the poles.

1. Introduction

Modeling has for many years been a valuable tool in the design and optimization of liquid crystal devices. Recent developments in modeling allow the inclusion of not just the elastic and dielectric constants of the liquid crystal, but also defect formation, variable alignment strength as well as surface relief structures, complex electrode configurations and 3-D volumes so that some of the more complex director structures can be modeled.

2. Modeling Method

Modeling methods used have been described in ref. [1] and [2], and allow variable order parameter at defects, as well as alignment strength variation. For large volumes where defects require higher mesh resolution for accuracy an adaptive mesh can be used.

3. Defect Structures at Electrode Edge

At the edge of an electrode the electric field lines curve outwards into the liquid crystal region between the electrodes for an array of electrodes or up to the ground plane at the edge of an isolated electrode edge. If the direction of those field lines is in the opposite direction to the surface alignment pretilt then there can arise a conflict in the direction that the director is switching as the voltage is increased. At high fields this distortion in the liquid crystal director can lead to defect formation or walls of twist, which extend along the length of the electrode. A feature obtained experimentally is a twist-bend distortion, which appear as kinks in the defect wall (Figure 1(a)). Using a 3-D model qualitatively similar results were obtained, Figure 1(b).

The optical properties have been calculated using the Jones' matrix method, but do not include the likely focusing effects that will occur experimentally in these systems.

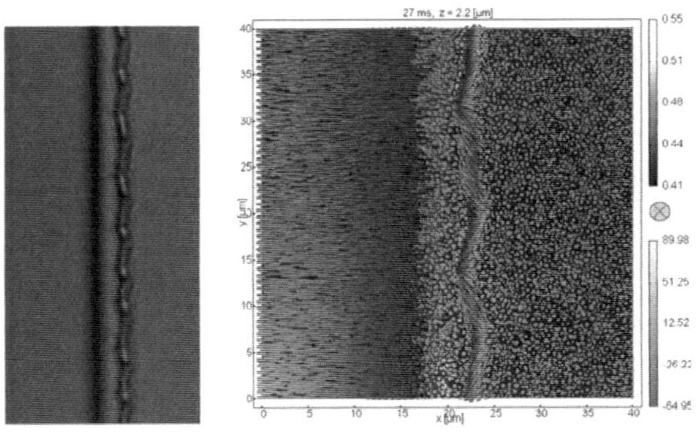

(a) **(b)**

Figure 1. (a) Defect visible in micrograph (b) Modelled director at electrode edge

4. Cholesteric Droplets

The pitch of twisted nematic (or cholesteric) liquid crystals can be defined in the modeling Droplets of such cholesteric have been modeled using the same methods. The alignment at the surface was chosen to be planar degenerate.

Spherical droplets of nematic liquid crystal can form a defect pair at poles of the droplet, which also occurs for the cholesteric configuration. For values of pitch of the order of the droplet diameter the pitch varies across the droplet from the defects at each pole. The pitch is lowest across the middle part of the droplet, furthest away from the pole. As the pitch is decreased the twist increases across the middle part, but can also form in other directions through the droplet and this conflict results in more complex configurations throughout the droplet, shown in Figure 2.

5. Conclusions

Modeling has been used to investigate the defect formation and twist-bend "zig-zag" defect wall that occurs at the edge of electrodes and the same techniques can be used to investigate cholesteric droplets and the twist formation within the drops.

6. Acknowledgements

We would like to thank Prashant Patel for carrying out some of the droplet modeling.

7. References

[1] R. James, E. Willman, F. A. Fernandez, S. E. Day, "Finite-element modeling of liquid-crystal hydrodynamics with a variable degree of order", IEEE Trans. Electron Devices, Vol. **53**, pp. 1575–1582, 2006.

[2] James, R., E. Willman, F.A. Fernandez, S.E. Day Computer Modeling of liquid crystal hydrodynamics. IEEE Trans. ON MAGNETICS, Vol. **44**, pp. 814–817, 2008.

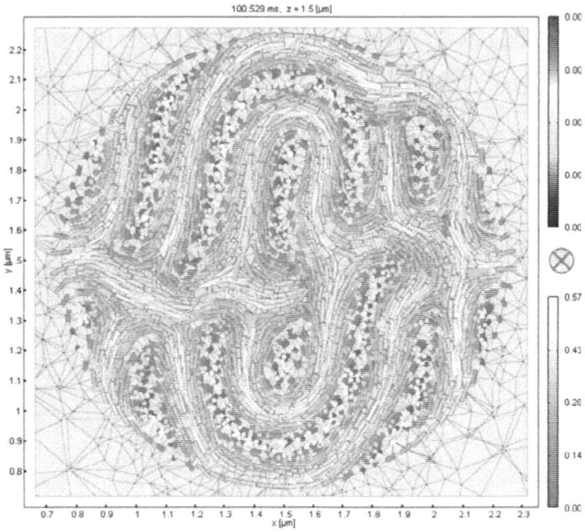

Figure 2. Spherical droplet filled with Cholesteric liquid crystal.

Paper No S3.2: Chiral Mesomorphic Compounds and Materials for Display Applications

V. Bezborodov,[1] V. Lapanik,[2] G. Sasnouski,[2] and W. Haase[3]

[1]Belarusian State Technological University, 220006 Minsk, Belarus, E-mail: v_bezborodov@yahoo.com; [2]Institute of Applied Physics Problems, 220108 Minsk, Belarus; [3]Darmstadt University of Technology, 64287 Darmstadt, Germany

Abstract

In this paper, we describe the effect of the molecular structure of chiral anisotropic compounds and materials on their mesomorphic and physico chemical properties. Modifications of the molecules via cyclic and bridge fragments or via lateral substituents allowed the preparation and optimization of specific mixtures for different display applications. The formation of defect free layers in ferroelectric liquid crystals stable against various mechanical or temperature deformations was studied. A new electro-optic effect based on chiral-nematic mixtures for creating high-speed devices with switching time less than 1 ms was developed.

1. Introduction

A modern liquid crystal material is a specially selected multicomponent mixture consisting of compounds of different chemical classes. The selection of the components of the mixture is important for the creation and optimization of the physicochemical parameters, which determine the electro-optical characteristics and quality of liquid crystal displays (LCDs). At present, the establishment of LCDs with high-performance is limited because of the low-speed reorientation of the nematic liquid crystal materials under the influence of the electric field. Yet, for fast switchable ferroelectric liquid crystals (FLCs), the lack of a stable orientation is limiting.

2. Results and Discussion

2.1 Design of Chiral Compounds

Clearly, there is a close relationship between the molecular structure of the liquid crystalline compounds and their properties. Also, it has been shown that the conformation changes are responsible for the orientation of molecules in the smectic layers, the layer spacing and the mechanical and shock-sensitive FLC alignment in the cells and displays [1]. Taking into account these requirements and the new approach to preparing anisotropic compounds from 3,6-disubstituted cyclohex-2-enones and other similar intermediates [2], we synthesized the mesomorphic chiral poly-*p*-phenylenes (**I-V**) with different lateral substituents and investigated the relevant relationships between their properties and the molecular structure.

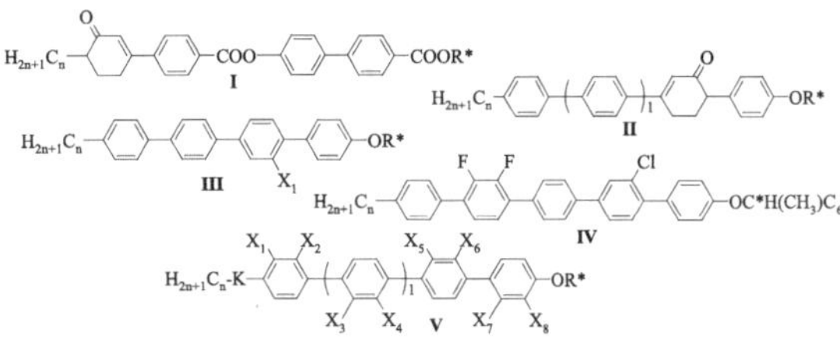

$n = 6$–12; K = cyclohexane, benzene, pyridine or pyrimidine rings; $l = 0$–2; $X_{1\text{-}8}$ = H, F, Cl, CF_3, CH_3; R* = chiral group or fragment

This allowed creating LC compositions with a broad temperature range of the mesophase usable for different well-known and new effects [3].

2.2 "Shock-Free" Ferroelectric Liquid Crystal Displays

The data from detailed investigations of the electro-optical properties of the prepared FLC mixtures have shown that such mixtures have a wide temperature range of Sm C* phase, from < 0 till ±90°C, a value of spontaneous polarization from 9 to 15 nC/cm^{-2}, and switching time around 30–50 ms [3]. These results reveal that the effect on the parameters of the mixtures strongly depends on the chemical structures of their components and that the substituted chiral quaterphenyls and similar other conjugated poly-*p*-phenylenes are favorable for the preparation of FLC mixtures with a wide temperature range for the Sm C* phase, which are characterized by weak dependence conformation changes of the fragments of the molecules from the temperature, pressure, etc., and give the opportunity of preparing of the thermal and the mechanical stable "shock-free" Ferroelectric Liquid Crystal Displays.

It should be noted that the bistable memory capability for the FLC mixtures based upon mesomorphic chiral poly-*p*-phenylenes was also found. For the chiral substituted cyclohex-2-enones (**I, II**) hysteresis, free transmission-voltage curves and V-shaped or thresholdless switching at different temperatures and at different frequencies were observed. The presented results envisage that not only antiferroelectric, but also FLCs can form hysteresis-free transmission-voltage curves.

2.3 Fast-Switching Chiral-Nematic Displays

A new electro-optic effect based on the synthesized mesomorphic chiral poly-*p*-phenylenes and chiral-nematic mixtures for creating high-speed devices was developed [3]. All the boundary conditions necessary for the realization of this effect were experimentally investigated. The cells, which have been prepared using the chiral-nematic mixtures, have several advantages in comparison with the cells containing the commercial LC materials and possess switching time less than 1 ms and the viewing angle 170–180°.

We plan to develop new mesomorphic chiral poly-*p*-phenylenes and hope that new results of our investigations may lead to better understanding of the nature of the anisotropic materials and their practical applications.

3. References

[1] V. S. Bezborodov, V. I. Lapanik, G. M. Sasnouski, W. Haase, "The synthesis and properties of some chiral mesomorphic quaterphenyl and cyclohexylterphenyl derivatives and the FLC compositions based upon them", Liq Cryst., Vol. **40**, pp. 1383–1390, 2013.

[2] V. S. Bezborodov, V. I. Lapanik, G. M. Sasnouski, S. G. Mikhalyonok, "Prospects of the development of new approaches of the preparation of anisotropic compounds and materials", 25th International Liquid Crystal Conference, Dublin, Ireland, S-03.003, 2014.

[3] V. Lapanik,V. Bezborodov, G. Sasnouski, W. Haase, "Unique chiral compounds as part of mixtures with optimized properties for different types of FLCDs", Phase Transitions, Vol. **85**, pp. 900–909, 2012.

Paper No S3.3: Dielectric Properties of Liquid Crystals for Display and Sensor Applications

V. V. Belyaev,[1] D. N. Chausov,[1] A. D. Kurilov,[1] D. O. Rybakov,[1] A. S. Solomatin,[1] A. A. Murauski,[2] A. A. Muravsky,[2] V. G. Chigrinov,[3] and F. Fan[3]

[1]Moscow Region State University, Moscow, Russian Federation, E-mail: vic_belyaev@mail.ru; [2]Institute of Chemistry of New Materials, NAS Belarus, Minsk, Belarus; [3]Hong Kong University of Science and Technology, Hong Kong, China

Read the full article at DOI: 10.1002/jsid.352

Abstract

Temperature dependence of dielectric properties of nematic liquid crystals are investigated for two types of devices: wide temperature range liquid crystal displays and capacitor temperature sensor.

1. Introduction

The paper is devoted to some problems of enhancement of liquid crystal (LC) display applications in extreme ambient conditions and expansion of LC devices functionality.

2. Measurement of Both Real and Imaginary Components of the Dielectric Constant

2.1. Temperature and Frequency Dependences

Both real and imaginary components of the dielectric constant (ε' and ε'') have been measured in wide frequency and temperature range. Results for the dielectric anisotropy $\Delta\varepsilon'$ are presented in Figure 1.

Some physical parameters of the NLC dielectric relaxation (Molecular relaxation frequency, friction coefficient and relaxation time, activation energy) have been determined.

2.2. Dependences on the Angle θ Between the Directions of Both Magnetic and Electric Field

The LC cell was rotated in a magnetic field and dependences of both real and imaginary components of the dielectric constant ($\varepsilon'(\theta)$ and $\varepsilon''(\theta)$) on the angle θ between the directions of both magnetic and electric field have been measured. They are described by equations

$$\varepsilon'(\theta)=\varepsilon'_\perp+\Delta\varepsilon'\cdot\cos^2\theta,$$

where $\Delta\varepsilon'$ and $\Delta\varepsilon''$ is anisotropy of both real and imaginary components of the dielectric constant, respectively.

3. Dielectric Properties of an LC Temperature Sensor With Different Boundary Conditions of the LC

In Ref. 1 a LC capacitor temperature sensor has been proposed that comprises two couples of areas with both planar and vertical alignment.

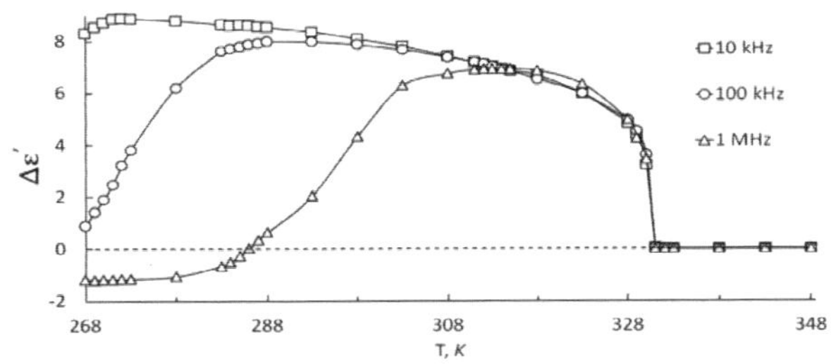

Figure 1. Temperature dependences of the dielectric anisotropy $\Delta\varepsilon'$ for frequencies 0.01, 0.1, and 1 MHz.

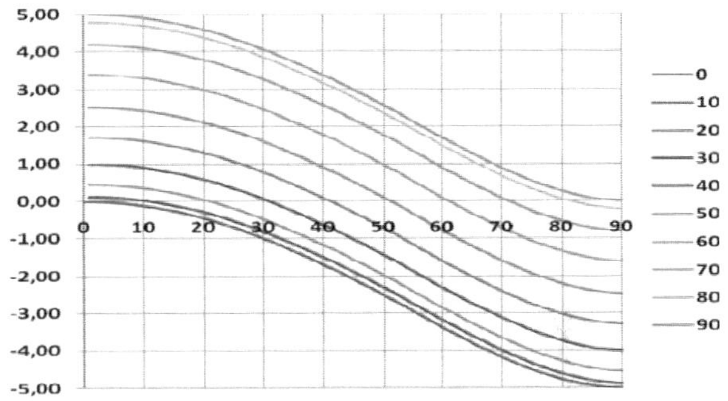

Figure 2. Simulation results of efficient value of the dielectric anisotropy $\Delta\varepsilon^{eff}(\theta_1, \theta_2)$ in the cells investigated. $\varepsilon_{//}=10$, $\varepsilon_\perp=5$. Vertical axis is $\varepsilon(\theta)$, horizontal axis is θ_1 and θ_2 is a parameter.

Its output signal depends on the LC dielectric anisotropy as well as ambient medium temperature.

We have simulated efficient values of the LC dielectric permittivity with different values of the LC pretilt angles in both parts of the LC cell that differ from perfect LC orientation.

Let us suggest that in the "vertical" part of the cell, the pretilt angle is θ_1 and in the "planar" part it is θ_2. Efficient value of the dielectric constant for such case is equal $\varepsilon(\theta)=\left(\varepsilon^2_\perp\sin^2\theta+\varepsilon^2_{//}\cos^2\theta\right)^{1/2}$. Then, the output signal in such cell is proportional to $\Delta\varepsilon^{eff}=\varepsilon(\theta_1)-\varepsilon(\theta_2)$. We varied both θ_1 and θ_2 values from 0 to 90°. In Figure 2 $\Delta\varepsilon^{eff}(\theta_1, \theta_2)$ dependences are presented. Anisotropy of the NLC elastic constants is taken into account.

4. Conclusion

Measurement of the LC dielectric constants demonstrates that in kilohertz frequency range reduction of the dielectric anisotropy is not dramatic for the operation mode. Parameters of the NLC dielectric relaxation have been determined. The simulation can be used for arbitrary LC layers with different boundary conditions. New designs of the LC active matrix displays can be simulated. This method allows also to simulate LC switching in cells subjected to the matrix driving mode that results in small difference of the voltage for neighboring levels of the gray scale.

5. Acknowledgements

The work was supported by grants of the Russian Foundation of Basic Researches 14-07-90009-Bel_a (with Belarusian Republican Foundation of Basic Researches), No. 14-47-03608 (with Moscow Region Government) and by a grant of President of Russian Federation No. MK-2382.2014.9.

6. Reference

[1] An. Al. Murauski, et al., "Liquid crystal capacitor temperature sensor"., Bull. of Moscow Region State Univer. Series Physics and Mathematics., Vol. 1. pp. 40–47, 2014.

Paper No S3.4: Switchable Liquid Crystal Devices for Efficient Light Steering

X. Shang,[1] J. De Smet,[1] P. Joshi,[1] D. Cuypers,[1] J. Tan,[1] O. Willekens,[2] J. Beeckman,[2] K. Neyts,[2] T. Baghdasaryan,[3] M. Vervaeke,[3] H. Thienpont,[3] and H. De Smet[1]

[1]CMST, Ghent University and IMEC, Gent, Belgium, Email: xiaobing.shang@elis.ugent.be; [2]LCP, Ghent University, Gent, Belgium; [3]B-Phot, Vrije Universiteit Brussel, Ixelles, Belgium

Abstract

In this article, we describe an electrically switchable light beam steering component, based on the combination of microprism structures and nematic liquid crystals, which effectively deflects both a laser beam and a collimated white light beam with a controllable steering range of 3°.

1. Introduction

Conventional light steering devices based on mechanical mirrors, prisms and lenses are bulky and require frequent maintenance. Recently, beam steering devices based on liquid crystals (LCs) attract much interest due to their compactness, electrical tunability, and process compatibility with the dominant liquid-crystal display technology [1]. In this work, polymer micro-prism structures are combined with nematic LCs to realize electrically switchable beam steering components for large-area smart lighting applications, autostereoscopic displays, etc.

2. Device Fabrication

For the fabrication of micro-prism structures, soft embossing is adopted to replicate the micro prism structures into a UV curable glue layer on indium tin oxide (ITO) glass substrates. Soft embossing offers a high processing efficiency and is compatible with a large variety of UV curable glues. For more details of the soft embossing process we refer to our previous work [2].

Active LC beam steering devices based on UV micro prism replicas (50 μm pitch, 8.5 μm height, and 10° blaze angle) are fabricated in this work. Figure 1 shows the concept of the device operation. In the off state, the effective refractive index of the LC (E7, Merck) is higher than that of the micro prism material (NOA74, $n_p=1.52$), the linear polarized light incident on the active device undergoes a deflection. When applying a high voltage, the LC molecules reorient parallel to the direction of the electrical field so that the refractive indices of the LC and the prism grating are matched mutually. Hence, no deflection occurs in the propagation of the incoming polarized light beam.

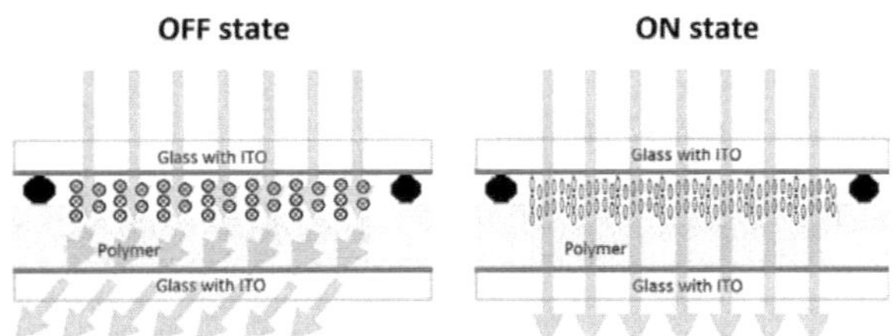

Figure 1. Schematic illustration of LC beam steering device.

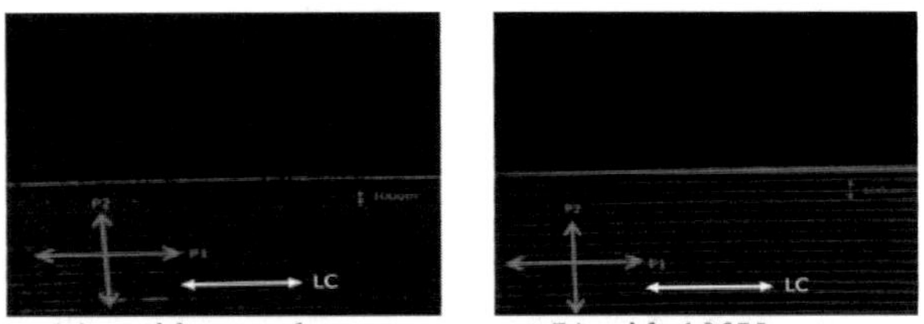

(a) without voltage (b) with $100V_{pp}$

Figure 2. LC alignment assessed using a crossed polarizer microscope.

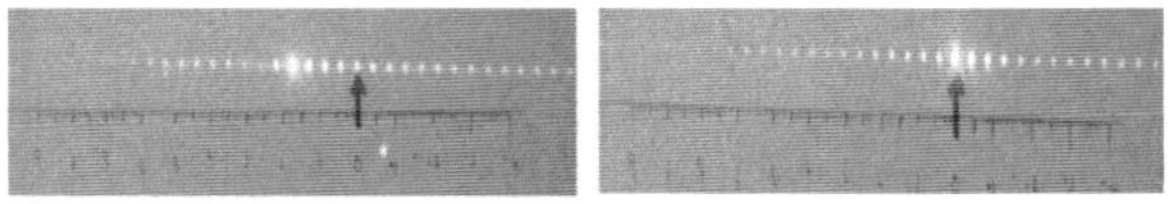

(a) without voltage (b) with $100V_{pp}$

Figure 3. Laser beam steering with the LC device.

(a) without voltage (b) with $100V_{pp}$

Figure 4. Collimated white light steering with the LC device.

In this work, oblique SiO_2 evaporation is applied to both the microprism substrate and the counter ITO glass substrate to implement an antiparallel LC orientation along the prism groove direction. A micrograph made with a crossed polarizer microscope is shown in Figure 2. Without and with applying a high voltage, the dark fields shown in Figure 2(a) and (b) indicate that a good LC alignment along the grooves exists within the LC component.

3. Optical Steering Performance

Both a monochromatic laser beam ($\lambda=543$ nm) and a collimated white light beam are used to characterize the LC beam steering component. The optical steering patterns are projected on a screen, and respectively shown in Figures 3 and 4.

For the polarized laser beam, the maximum intensity shifts to the fourth order without applying a voltage due to the refractive index difference between the LC and the microprism. For the unpolarized white light, the extraordinary ray undergoes a deflection while the ordinary ray remains the same. With 100 V pp, there is no refractive index difference, both the laser beam and the white light keep the initial light-propagating direction. A maximum steering angle of about 2° and a total steering range of 3° (−1° to 2°) are obtained with this LC beam steering component.

4. Acknowledgements

This work was partly sponsored by the IWT (SBO project 120019 "SECONDOS") and partly by the FWO (project G.A047.11N).

5. References

[1] Y. C. Chang, T. H. Jen, C. H. Ting, Y. P. Huang, "High-resistance liquid-crystal lens array for rotatable 2D/3D autostereoscopic display," Optics Express, Vol. **22**, pp. 2714–2724, 2014.

[2] X. Shang, J.-Y. Tan, J. De Smet, P. Joshi, E. Islamaj, D. Cuypers, M. Vervaeke, J. Van Erps, H. Thienpont, H. De Smet, "Replicating micro-optical structures using soft embossing technique", Proc. SPIE, Vol. **9231**, pp. 92310H-1-92310H-7, 2014.

Paper No S4.1: Inkjet Printing in Industrial Applications and Its Use in Display Manufacturing

Werner Zapka

Xaarjet AB, Jarfalla, Sweden, E-mail: Werner.Zapka@Xaar.com

Abstract

Inkjet printing has grown from printing of graphic pattern or nonfunctional features into "printing beyond color." Specifically, the increased knowledge and experience in producing nanoparticle inks has opened up new applications for industrial inkjet printing.

1. Discussion

Printing of functional features, however, requires highest levels of reliability of all processes involved, like high-quality fluids and high-quality printheads. Specifically, an optimum adaptation between the fluid and the printhead is required for high reliability of the drop formation process. Missing drops as well as accidental drops can cause device failure, when functional device layers are inkjet printed. Driving waveforms of the printheads have to be optimized to produce drops with controlled volume, velocity and with the least amount of satellites and misting, and at highest print frequencies.

Industrial inkjet printhead technology will be presented and the process of adaptation between printhead and fluid. Several metrology techniques were developed to evaluate the jetting performance of fluids and to identify promising candidates for inkjet printing. Further metrology was developed to identify causes for failing drop formation or for quantitatively and statistically assessing missing drops under high duty and long-term printing.

Examples of inkjet printing applications in the area of displays or general printed electronics will be discussed.

To reduce the time for implementation of industrial inkjet printing applications, it is necessary to assess the full technology chain from fluids, printheads, substrates, pre/postprocesses, metrology, machine integration, data flow, etc. and to address the interfaces between these individual steps. An approach to establish a group of expert companies and institutes will be presented.

Paper No S4.2: Eighth Generation Linear Source for AMOLED Mass Production

Sungmoon Kim, Daejoon Chi, Hyun Seo, and Eunsang Jung
R&D Center of YAS Co., Ltd, Gyeongi-do, Korea, E-mail: smkim@yasoled.com

Abstract
In this article, we introduce our eighth generation organic linear source for mass production of white organic light-emitting diode (OLED) TV panel (world first OLED TV that you can buy).

1. Background
Recently, the largest active-matrix organic light-emitting diode (AMOLED) substrate size is eighth generation substrate (2200 mm × 2500 mm). YAS developed 8G linear source which is 2400 mm in length. Because of the long length of the linear source, there are several technical problems; deformation problem caused by thermal expansion, temperature variation along the long way of crucible, and how to achieve film thickness uniformity within 2200 mm area repeatedly. We will introduce several ideas to overcome such problems.

2. Introduction of 8G Linear Source
8G linear source in this article is composed by long box-shaped crucible, nozzle assembled with it, and heater surround it. Such a composition is conventional way of linear source which is already applied to 3.5G AMOLED mass production line.

2.1. Crucible and Nozzle
Crucible is divided into two same shaped. Nozzle is also divided into two parts. Total length of nozzle is 2200 mm which is the same as the substrate length. We can make uniform thin film by just same length nozzle because of the special edge nozzle which is filled by many small holes inclined to the outside substrate. Using it, we can make the deposition chamber small and material utilization be maximized.

To be able to adjust various deposition conditions, we made center nozzles can be replaceable. We prepared several nozzle array sets which can be applied to various deposition rates and various deposition conditions using our own flux simulation tool that is based on Monte-Carlo method.

Especially, we put the special inner plate between crucible and nozzle to prevent film thickness uniformity from changing as operation time goes on. Because of long crucible length (>2 m), the temperature along the crucible can be varied. So, when the material in crucible is almost exhausted, the remaining material at each position can be different along the crucible. At that time, the flux distribution and film thickness uniformity can be changed. To prevent from flux change problem, we put the special shaped inner plate (center hole inner plate). It can cancel out any influence of the shape of remaining material in crucible by making neck point of flux at the center of crucible.

Table 1. Basic specifications of 8G linear source

Items	Specifications
Uniformity (%)	<3
Material utilization (%)	>70
Operation time (h)	>336 h
Mixing homogeneity (%)	>95

2.2 Heater and Rate Control
Heater also divided into two parts for individual control of each crucible. Two quartz crystal sensors which detect deposition speed are located at each edge of the linear source. These two sensors are connected with PID controller and heater part at same side. So, heater can control each crucible independently.

As mentioned before, main problem of large size linear source is crucible temperature nonuniformity along the crucible. In general case, if we use uniform density heater, the temperature at center position in long direction is higher than that at edge of crucible. So, we should modify the density of heater by changing the number of filament turns within same area. And we should modify reflectors. Finally, we can make temperature nonuniformity be under 5°C within 2.2 m crucible length. (Nevertheless, the deferent remains problem still happens, so we should use center hole inner plate.)

To provide more flexibility in various deposition conditions, we introduce optional parameter which can change the temperature at the center of crucible be slightly higher or lower than edge by supplying more or less power at center area than edge. By this option, we can change the flux distribution in situ (without venting chamber). It will be useful when you want to change the deposition speed during operation the system because as deposition rate becomes higher, the thickness at the center of substrate becomes lower than edge.

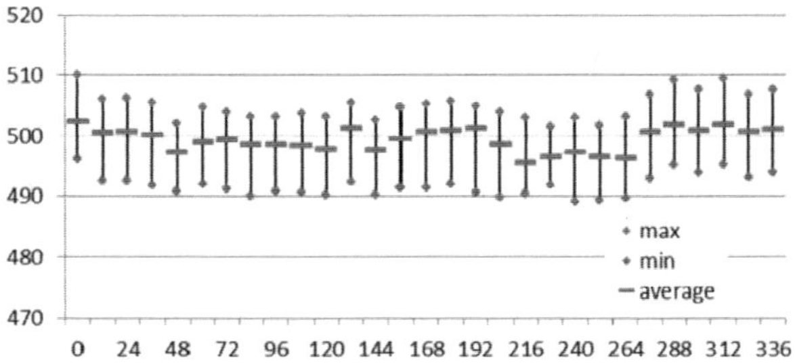

Figure 1. Thickness profile during 336 h operation.

3. Results

3.1. Basic Performance
The basic performance of our 8G linear source is given in Table 1.

3.2. Repeatability
We checked thickness uniformity during 336 h (2 weeks) (Figure 1). During 2 weeks, the thickness uniformity keeps under 3%. Also we checked the difference of thickness distribution under quite abnormal conditions such as we put the material just one side edge and all other regions keep empty. Even in that abnormal case, the thickness uniformity keeps under 3%.

4. Impact
Using our 8G linear source, large size white organic light-emitting diode (OLED) and OLED lighting panel mass production can be successful. And, in our experience, Ninth generation linear source can be possible. But over ninth generation, substrate manufacturing seems not to be possible because at that case, additional quartz crystal sensor which detects flux of center may be needed.

5. Acknowledgement
We thank to LGD for providing inspiration and opportunity to supply our works in mass production system.

Paper No S4.3: Printed Circuit and OLED on Foldable Paper Substrates

Sung Min Jo and Byung Doo Chin

Department of Polymer Science and Engineering, Dankook University, Yongin-si, Korea, E-mail: bdchin@dankook.ac.kr

Abstract

In this article, we describe the fabrication of stable silver-graphene composite electrode pattern and organic light emitting diodes (OLEDs) on the surface-modified paper substrates. Relative conductance and light emission efficiency of OLED was evaluated for folding cycle and angle. In case of inside folding up to 180° and 1000 cycle, more than 85% of initial conductance was remained at nanowire-graphene composite circuits.

1. Introduction

Foldable and flexible electronics are not only an important but also a promising issue for the convenient transportation and diverse deployment of mobile displays. Unlike flexible or simply bendable electronic devices, foldable electronics require substrates and conductors with a very stable flexural strength; this is because, in contrast to bending, which forms a smooth curve, folding generates an edge at the point of the folding, which develops creases, and the deformation remains even after unfolding. Therefore, in order to realize the technology in foldable electronic devices, it is important to develop foldable substrate, conductor (both for semi-transparent and circuits) and study the behavior at substrate-conductor interfaces. Paper is lightweight and foldable, which makes it a promising substrate for various disposable electronic application while it also provides a good testing condition for extreme folding angle. Although the original surface of cellulose-based paper is not suitable for the fabrication of many planar organic devices, lots of surface modification technique with specialty papers are available, which facilitates the transformation of paper-based organic electronics into nonplanar and complex shapes in the near future.

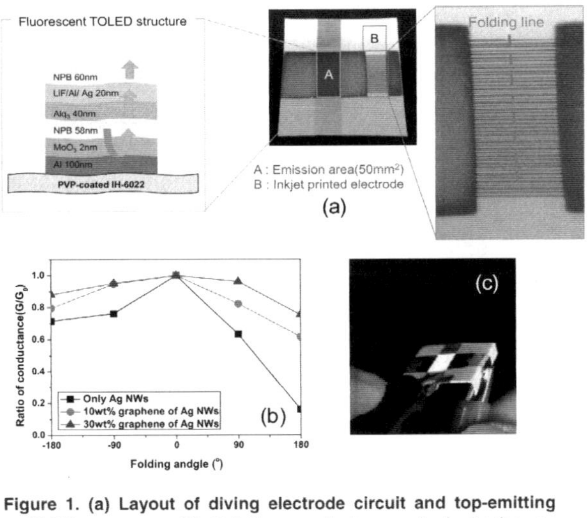

Figure 1. (a) Layout of diving electrode circuit and top-emitting OLED on paper (b) Relative conductance of electrodes on paper with folding angle; AgNW and AgNW-graphene (c) OLED pixel with 50mm2 on paper at +90° folded electrode.

2. Experimental

Various kind of common and specialty papers were tested as candidates of stable foldable substrates; their surface was planarized with several polymeric over-coating layers (polyvinyl alcohol (PVA), poly(4-vinylphenol)(PVP), etc.) in order to reduce the roughness as well as provide a good adhesion condition for vacuum-deposition and printing of electrode patterns. Silver (Ag) electrode was fabricated onto surface controlled paper either by thermal evaporation or inkjet printing. Silver nanowire (AgNW)-graphene composite layers were also formed by suitable jetting and spraying technique. As an OLED pixel, top emitting structure was employed due to the translucent nature of paper used in this study. By a thermal evaporation under 10^{-6} torr, devices with Aluminum(Al)/molybdenum oxide (MoO_3)/N,N-di (naph-thalene-1-yl)-N,N-diphenyl- benzidine (NPB)/Tris-(8-hydroxy-quinoline) aluminum (Alq_3)/LiF/Al/Ag were constructed on surface-planarized paper substrates.

3. Results and Discussion

Composite electrodes with metallic patterns [1] and graphene nanoplate-based circuits prepared on the paper substrate by simple transfer printing [2] showed a unique, small change in conductance under various folding angles, retaining more than 95% of initial conductance at 180° inside folding with 1000 folding cycle in case of graphene-based circuits. However, due to the relatively low current density of graphene-only electrode circuitry, we formed composite electrodes with metallic nanowire networks and graphene nanoplate mixture for OLED-driving circuits, which were prepared on the paper substrate by high-speed jet printing process. The electrode patterns and top-emitting OLED structure driven by this patterns are shown in Figure 1(a). Compared with Ag-only electrode, smaller change in conductance under various folding angles were shown at AgNW-graphene driving electrode, retaining more than 85% of initial conductance at −180° (inside) folding condition. It should be noted that for practical range of folding (−90°∼+90°), stability of electrode against 1000-cycle folding was quite satisfactory. Figure 1(b) and 1(c) showed data of relative conductance with folding angle and image OLED pixel.

4. Conclusion

Driving of OLED either by Ag-based interconnecting circuit or AgNW-graphene composite electrodes were evaluated and characterized in terms of the surface condition of modified paper, relative conductance, and resultant OLED light emitting efficiency and stability. For a practical range of folding (including bending radius 3∼5mm), top-emitting device maintained the stability up to 100 cycle, showing the possibility of its application at disposable electronics and digital signage.

5. Acknowledgements

Authors would like to acknowledge the financial supporting from National Research Foundation of Korea (NRF) grant (2014-005103) funded by the Korea government (MSIP).

6. References

[1] A. C. Siegel, S. T. Phillips, M. D. Dickey, N. Lu, Z. Suo, G. M. Whitesides, "Foldable printed circuit boards on paper substrates", Adv. Funct. Mater., Vol. **20**, pp. 28–35, 2010.

[2] W. J. Hyun, O. O. Park, B. D. Chin, "Foldable graphene electronic circuits based on paper substrates", Adv. Mater., Vol. **25**, pp. 4729–4734, 2013.

Paper No S4.4: Colored OLED With a Multilayered Graphene Electrode for Light-Adaptable Displays

Byoung-Hwa Kwon,[1] Hyunkoo Lee,[1] Jong Tae Lim,[1] Seong M. Cho,[2] Jun-Han Han,[1] Jong-Heon Yang,[3] Sang Hoon Cheon,[2] Tae-Youb Kim,[2] Nam Sung Cho,[1] Byoung-Gon Yu,[1] Chi-Sun Hwang,[3] Seong Chu Lim,[4,5] and Jeong-Ik Lee[1]

[1]Soft I/O Interface Research Section, Electronics and Telecommunications Research Institute, Daejeon 305-700, Korea, E-mail: jiklee@etri.re.kr; [2]Nature-Mimic I/O Interface Research Section, Electronics and Telecommunications Research Institute, Daejeon 305-700, Korea; [3]Smart I/O Control Device Research Section, Electronics and Telecommunications Research Institute, Daejeon 305-700, Korea; [4]Department of Energy Science, Sungkyunkwan University, Suwon 440-746, Korea; [5]IBS Center for Integrated Nanostructure Physics, Institute for Basic Science (IBS), Sungkyunkwan University, Suwon 440-746, Korea

Abstract

In this work, we report reflective colored organic light-emitting diodes (OLEDs) integrated with color-selective reflective filter (CSRF) and transparent OLEDs functioning as the reflective and emissive mode. To fabricate transparent OLEDs with low-reflective anode, the dry bonding technology of graphene anode was developed.

1. Introduction

Emissive displays such as organic light-emitting diodes (OLEDs) are promising as next-generation displays because of high contrast ratio, short response time, and wide viewing angle [1]. However, they are hardly to view in bright ambient lighting situations. Therefore, OLEDs integrated with reflective display such as light-adaptable displays (LADs) are very powerful device because they can show high visibility and low power consumption in any circumstance.

2. Results

Graphene is a two-dimensional sheet of sp^2-hybridized carbon atoms that has extensive attention as a possible transparent electrode in electronic devices [2]. However, there are few reports on their application for devices because of the difficulties to transferring and patterning of graphene [3].

In our works, a multilayered graphene (MLG) was used for top electrode of OLED by dry laminating transfer that makes conformal contact between MLG and the top organic layer. In addition, MLG with high transmittance and low reflectance suppress the distorted optical interference occurring from reflective mirrors in the OLED.

Figure 1(a) illustrates the structure of reflective colored OLED integrated with color-selective reflective filter (CSRF) and transparent organic light-emitting devices (TOLEDs). CSRF designed by the concept of Fabry–Pérot interferometry. An inverted OLED part (indium tin oxide [ITO]/electron-injecting layer [EIL]/emissive layer [EML]/hole-injecting layer [HIL]) was fabricated on glass substrates, and then an MLG part (MLG/bonding layer/supporting layer) was transferred using a dry bonding technology. Last, CSRF was successfully stacked on the supporting layer. Figure 1(b) shows reflective mode image of colored OLED segment panel. Because the MLG top electrode has considerably low optical reflectance and high transmittance, the green reflective color exhibits clearly. In Figure 1(c), the panel uniformly emits the yellowish light exhibiting "ETRI" logo during emissive mode. Therefore, LA OLEDs can display the reflective green color in the daytime and the emissive yellow color at night.

3. Conclusion

We successfully fabricated colored OLEDs integrated with green color RF and yellow-emitting TOLEDs functioning as the reflector and emitter. Our work demonstrated that the dual mode approach is technically realizable for LAD applications.

4. Acknowledgement

This work was supported by Institute for Information & communications Technology Promotion (IITP) grant funded by the Korea government (MSIP) (B0101-15-0133, the core technology development of light and space adaptable energy-saving I/O platform for future advertising service).

5. References

[1] C. W. Joo, J. Moon, J.-H. Han, J. W. Huh, J. Lee, N. S. Cho, J. Hwang, H. Y. Chu, J.-I. Lee, "Color temperature tunable white organic light-emitting diodes", Org. Electron., Vol.**15**, pp. 189–195, 2014.

[2] J. Song, F.-Y. Kam, R.-Q. Png, W.-L. Seah, J.-M. Zhuo, G.-K. Lim, P. K. H. Ho, L.-L. Chua, "A general method for transferring graphene onto soft surfaces", Nat. Nanotechnol., Vol.**8**, pp. 356–362, 2013.

[3] J.-T. Seo, J. Han, T. Lim, K.-H. Lee, J. Hwang, H. Yang, S. Ju, "Fully transparent quantum dot light-emitting diode integrated with graphene anode and cathode", ACS Nano, Vol.**8**, pp. 12476–12482, 2014.

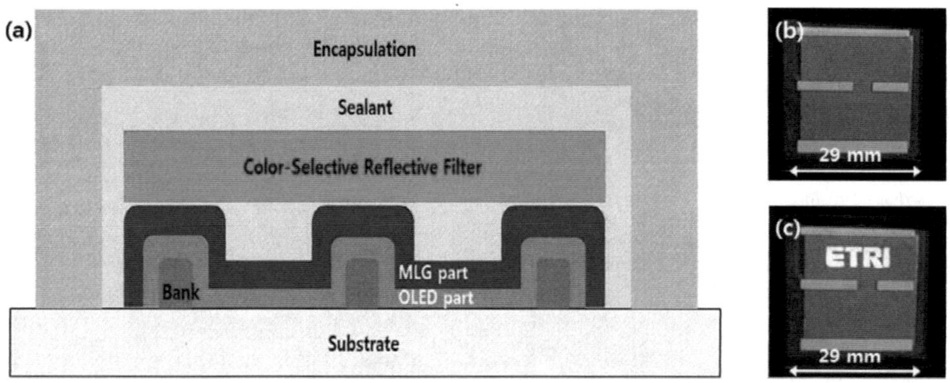

Figure 1. (a) Structure of LA OLEDs, (b) reflective and (c) emissive mode image of colored OLED segment panel.

Paper No S5.1: Fast Bistable Intensive Light Scattering in Helix-Free Ferroelectric Liquid Crystals

Alexander Andreev,[1] Tatiana Andreeva,[1] Igor Kompanets,[1] Huan Xu,[2] Mike Pivnenko,[2] and Daping Chu[2]

[1]P.N.Lebedev Physical Institute, Moscow, Russia, E-mail: kompan@sci.lebedev.ru; [2]University of Cambridge, Centre for Advanced Photonics and Electronics, Cambridge, UK

Abstract

We present results of studying the intensive bistable light scattering in an electro-optical cell filled with a specially designed helix-free ferroelectric liquid crystal (FLC). A stable scattering state can be switched on and off for 70–100 μs and memorized for a few tens of seconds.

1. Introduction

The electrically controlled optical shutters and displays without using polarizer are very desirable in order to obtain high optical efficiency, especially in IR region (up to a few micrometers). One of the approaches to achieve such devices is utilizing an electro-optical response based on the intensive and fast light-scattering phenomena found in ferroelectric liquid crystals (FLCs) [1–3].

In our past work [1,2], we reported the electro-optical response of dynamic light scattering observed in a helical FLC test cell. A scattering texture consisting of microdomains appeared during a nonlinear reorientation process of the FLC molecular director in responding to an alternating electric field $\boldsymbol{E}$. The scattering phenomena was characterized by high speed (scattering on and off times <150 μs under $E = 6$ V/μm), high light-scattering intensity (can be defined as a contrast ratio which is about 100:1), as well as bistable operation mode that was affected by both the amplitude and the duration of the applied electrical pulses. However, the stability of each optical state (scattered or cleared state after an electric field turned off) was rather poor, e.g., only lasting for a few milliseconds [2].

2. Experimental Results and Discussion

We present here a new type of light scattering materials and their optimized electro-optical performances. The materials are specially designed helix-free FLCs with the value of spontaneous polarization P_s less than 50 nC/cm^2. In test cells filled with such FLCs, periodical deformations of smectic layers with a profile characterized in some point by angle Ψ took place in the absence of an electric field.

The basic mechanism of the scattering/clearing bistable operation is described in the following. When frequency f$\geq 1/\tau_m$ (τ_m is Maxwell relaxation time), the dissipative coefficient is shear viscosity γ_Ψ. The interaction of electric field strength $\boldsymbol{E}$ with $\boldsymbol{P_s}$ results in the nonlinear variation ($\Delta\Psi$) of a profile along smectic layers and the appearance of soliton (a steady wave packet with a localized periodic wave vector) accompanied by light scattering. Soliton motion under the electric field causes the reorientation of the molecular director in the entire volume of FLC. If the plane of polarization of the incident light is along the direction of FLC director (along the main optical axis), the light transmittance of an electro-optical cell is maximum. The inversion of the electric field sign (i.e., pulse polarity of the control voltage) again induces the formation of soliton waves that arise an appearance of refraction index gradients along smectic layers and accompanies by intensive light scattering.

Such a bistable electro-optical switching is advanced by some remarkable features. The transition to Maxwellian mechanism of energy dissipation enables a decrease of the electric field down to 2–3 V/μm and thus allows low-voltage driving. Good intensity of light scattering can be achieved (optical contrast ratio >150:l) at high modulation rates (up to 3–5 kHz). The optical response time of FLC can be reduced by increasing frequency, e.g., from about 100 μs (at 100 Hz) to 70 μs (at 3 kHz). Electro-optical characters remain unchanged with temperature over a wide range.

Most importantly, bistable regime and time of memorizing an each stable state is defined by FLC properties and relation between the amplitude and the duration of electric pulses. The maximal memory time reaches a few tens of seconds.

It should be noted that in helix-free FLC with P_s of 70–100 nC/cm^2 and more the efficiency of light scattering connected with forming the ferroelectric domains diminishes [3].

3. Impact

Bistable properties of an electro-optical light-scattering cells filled with a specially designed helix-free FLC are studied. Such a cell can be switched from nonscattering to scattering state or vice-verse by bipolar voltage pulses for 100–70 μs and can store this state so long as a few tens of seconds. These unique properties are due to FLC composition and selected control regime.

4. Acknowledgements

The authors thank the Russian Found of Basic Research (grant 14-07-00185_a "Development of the physical principles and technology of creating the electro-optical despeckler for laser information systems" for the support of this work. The authors also thank the Presidium of the Russian Academy of Sciences for the support of this work on the Program of Basic Research.

5. References

[1] A. L. Andreev, Y. P. Bobylev, N. A. Gubasaryan, I. N. Kompanets, E. P. Pozhidaev, T. B. Fedosenkova, V. M. Shoshin, Ju. P. Shumkina, "Electrically controlled light scattering in ferroelectric liquid crystals", J. Opt. Technol., Vol. **72**, pp. 702–707, 2005.

[2] A. L. Andreev, T. B. Andreeva, I. N. Kompanets, Y. P. Bobylev, V. M. Shoshin, M. V. Minchenko, "Electrically controlled light scattering in helix ferroelectric liquid crystals", J. Opt. Technol., Vol. **77**, pp. 776–783, 2010.

[3] A. L. Andreev, T. B. Andreeva, E.P. Pozhidaev, I.N. Kompanets, Y. P. Bobylev, V. M. Shoshin, "Electrooptics and dynamics of light-scattering FLC structures", Proceedings of the XXVII IDRC (EuroDisplay-2007), pp. 252–254, 2007.

Paper No S5.2: Polymer Stabilized Blue Phase Liquid Crystal Dispersions

Emine Kemiklioglu and Liang-Chy Chien

Liquid Crystal Institute and Chemical Physics Interdisciplinary Program, Kent State University, Kent, Ohio 44242, USA, E-mail: ekemikli@kent.edu

Abstract

A polymer-stabilized and polymer-dispersed blue phase (PS-PDBP) device operating at room temperature is demonstrated. The encapsulated blue phase liquid crystal droplets were formed in a polymer solution. With polymer stabilization, the blue phase temperature range of the blue phase dispersion was remarkably increased more than 53°C. In this presentation, we also describe the electro-optical properties of the PS-PDBP films made from different compositions.

1. Introduction

Recently, blue phase liquid crystal (BPLC) materials have generated great interest due to their outstanding optical and electro-optical properties[1] potential for applications in displays and photonic devices. One of the greatest advantages of BPLCs is their wide and symmetric viewing angle due to the fact that their "voltage off" state is optically isotropic and the "voltage on" state forms multidomain structures. Polymer dispersed liquid crystals (PDLCs), i.e., dispersions of micron-sized LC droplets inside a polymer matrix, have formed a class of important electro-optical (E-O) materials since their discovery by Fergason [2]. The operation principle of the PDLC films is to be electrically switchable between light scattering and transparent states due to index matching between guest and host materials. BPLC can be a substantial candidate for polymer-dispersed blue phase films due to their fast switching properties [3]. This article represents studies of a method for the stabilization of encapsulated blue phase droplets via encapsulation process. We have investigated for the first time polymer encapsulated and polymer-stabilized BPLC s and devices.

2. Experimental Part

Using the emulsification method, a mixture of blue phase and monomer was encapsulated in the polymer (Polyvinyl alcohol; PVA) wall (Figure1a). A BPLC comprising of a positive dielectric anisotropy nematic mixture and a chiral dopant (HTP~30 μm^{-1}) was mixed at the weight ratio of 88.5% and11.5%, respectively. The mixture was sonicated for 1.5 h at room temperature. After adding of a reactive monomer mixture of RM257 and HDDA and a small amount of the photoinitiator (Irgacure651, 0.5 wt%) in BPLC the mixture was sonicated for an additional 1.5 h at room temperature. After PVA solution was added, the resultant mixtures were stirred at 1500 rpm for 20 min at room temperature to form an emulsion. A small drop of the emulsion was coated on a glass substrate using another glass substrate. The top-down E-O cells were assembled by placing the second ITO-coated substrate on top of the first substrate and the cell gap was controlled by 15 μm spacers. The cell was placed in the vacuum oven for 2 h. The cells were irradiated with a UV light of 365 nm and intensity of 10 mW/cm^2 at blue phase temperature.

3. Results

The polymer-stabilized BPLC dispersions were examined with a polarizing optical microscope. Figure 1 shows the POM images of polymer-stabilized and polymer-dispersed blue phase (PS-PDBP) samples. The blue phase temperatures of these samples were found between 40°C and 32°C before the polymerization. After the polymerization, the temperature range of sample 1 was increased to 55°C and the droplets size of blue phase state at the room temperature was between 20 and 100 μm.

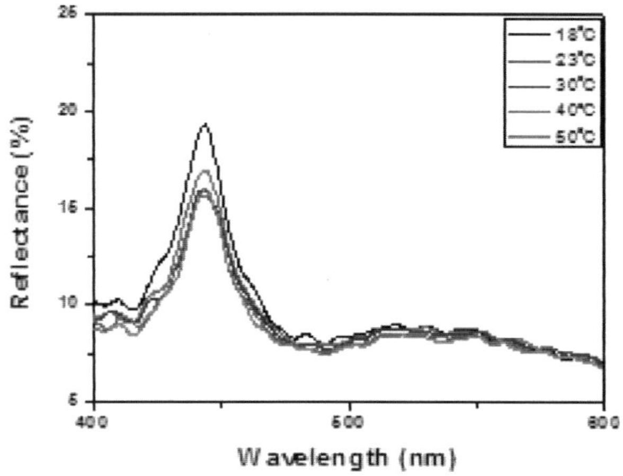

Figure 2. The reflection spectra of sample as a function of temperature.

The Bragg reflection peak of the PS-PDBP was temperature independent after the polymer stabilization. The reflected wavelength of sample appeared at 447 nm for BPII and 444 nm for BPI as a result of stabilization of disclination lines by polymer network in the encapsulated droplets (Figure 2).

Furthermore, the effect of the PVA concentration on the droplet shape was investigated. We also demonstrated the significant reduction in switching voltage of field-induced birefringence of the PS-PDBP with the addition of gelatin. This finding will be useful for further development of the PS-PDBP composites for Kerr or electrostriction mode devices able to operate at room temperature or subambient environment.

4. References

[1] H. Kikuchi, M. Yokota, Y. Hisakado, H. Yang, T. Kajiyama, "Polymer-stabilized liquid crystal blue phases", Nat. Mater., Vol. **1**, pp. 64–68, 2002.

[2] J. L. Fergason, "Polymer encapsulated nematic liquid crystals for display and light control applications", SID (Society for Information Display) Int. Symp. Dig. Tech. Pap., Vol. **16**, 68, 1985.

[3] E. Kemiklioglu, L. C. Chien, "Polymer encapsulated blue phase liquid crystal droplets", Appl. Phys. Exp. Vol. **7**, p. 091701, 2014.

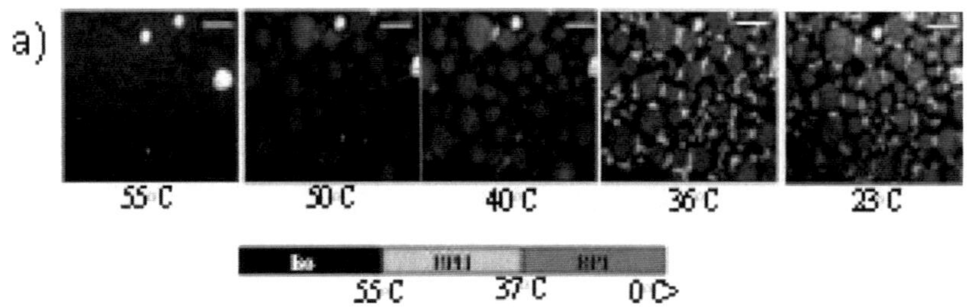

Figure 1. The POM images and phase sequences of PS-PDBP sample (white scalar bar re presents 100 μm).

Paper No S5.3: Importance of Alignment Layers in Blue Phase Liquid Crystal Devices

Pankaj Joshi,[1] Xiaobing Shang,[1] Jelle De Smet,[1] Dieter Cuypers,[1] Geert Van Steenberge,[1] Sandra Van Vlierberghe,[2] Peter Dubruel,[2] and Herbert De Smet[2]

[1]Centre for Microsystems Technology (CMST), IMEC and Ghent University, Gent 9000, Belgium; [2]Polymer Chemistry and Biomaterials Group, Ghent University, Gent 9000, Belgium

Abstract

In this article, we present how alignment layers affect blue phase liquid crystals and how we can use this effect to our advantage.

1. Introduction

Blue phases (BPs) are helical phases existing between isotropic and chiral nematic phases, in highly chiral liquid crystals. There are three types of BPs, BPI, BPII, and BPII, in the order of increasing temperatures of their existence. The building blocks of BPs are double twisted cylinders (DTCs) and the disclination lines. In BPI and BPII, DTCs are arranged in such a way that cubic arrangement of defects in the director fields is formed, making BPI body-centered cubic (bcc) and BPII simple cubic (sc) [1]. In BPII, DCTs are randomly distributed resulting in amorphous phase. Owing to the fundamental difference in their internal structures, BPI and BPII differ significantly in various aspects [2].

In recent years, blue phase liquid crystals (BPLCs) have emerged as the candidate material of future display and other advanced photonic components. Fast switching speeds [3], optically isotropic off state, insensitivity toward cell gap, and considerable ease of fabrication resulting from the nonrequirement of alignment layers are some of the outstanding features of this phase.

It was recently reported by Kikuchi et al. that the Kerr constant is not a scalar, but a tensor quantity as is true for various other physical properties in cubic crystals. By carefully controlling the orientation of domains, 20% increment in Kerr constant was demonstrated [4], which directly implies lowering of the operating voltage.

2. Results

The LC mixture used in this study has the following composition: nematic liquid crystals JC1041-xx (48.18%) and 5CB (38.08%), chiral dopant (3.2%), monomer EHA (3.43%), crosslinker RM257 (6.66%), and photoinitiator DMPAP (0.52%, from Merck). The polarization optical micrographs of BP in LC cells with and without alignment layers are shown in Figure 1. Both the samples are at 44.6°C. Considerable difference can clearly be seen. BP in the cell without alignment layers (Figure 1(b)) has randomly oriented domains reflecting in the deep blue wavelength range, whereas in the cell with alignment layers (Figure 1(a)), a uniform texture is present.

Further investigation by means of tracking changes in the peak Bragg reflection wavelength at various temperatures, it was found that the alignment layers have tremendous influence on the orientation of domains of BPLCs. Also, the magnitude of influence differs in the two types of cubic BPs. In BPII, smaller domains with assistance from the alignment layers merge forming larger domains and also experience reorientation which leads to shift in peak Bragg reflection wavelength. A shift form 338.5 to 486.3 nm was recorded.

Samples were also successfully polymer stabilized in various states of orientation.

3. Conclusions

Contrary to the prevailing perception, alignment layers can be of crucial importance in exercising control over the orientation of cubic domains of BPLCs and hence improving electro-optical properties of the same.

4. Acknowledgements

This work is partly supported by the Research Foundation-Flanders through the project 3GA04711 ("Study of liquid crystals dispersed in micro-structured elastic host materials") and partly by the IWT through the SBO project SECONDOS, IWT-nr 120019, 2013-2016.

5. References

[1] D. C. Wright, N. D. Mermin, "Crystalline liquids: The blue phases", Rev. Mod. Phys., Vol. **61**, p. 385, 1989.

[2] H. Choi, H. Higuchi, H. Kikuchi, "Fast electro-optic switching in liquid crystal blue phase II", Appl. Phys. Lett., Vol. **98**, p. 131905, 2011.

[3] Y. Chen, D. Xu, S.-T. Wu, S.-I. Yamamoto, Y. Haseba, "A low voltage and submillisecond-response polymer-stabilized blue phase liquid crystal", Appl. Phys. Lett., Vol. **102**, p. 141116, 2013.

[4] Y. Kawata, H. Yoshida, S. Tanaka, A. Konkanok, M. Ozaki, H. Kikuchi, "Anisotropy of the electro-optic Kerr effect in polymer-stabilized blue phases", Phys. Rev. E, Vol. **91**, p. 022503, 2015.

(a) (b)

Figure 1. POM of BPLC (a) with and (b) without alignment layers at 44.6°C.

Paper No S5.4: Polymer Stabilized Electrically Suppressed Helix Ferroelectric Liquid Crystal

Liangyu Shi, Ying Ma, Abhishek Kumar Srivastava, V. G. Chigrinov, and Hoi Sing Kwok

Department of Electronic and Computer Engineering, Hong Kong University of Science and Technology, Clear Water Bay, Hong Kong, E-mail: lshiac@ust.hk

Abstract

In this article, a polymer stabilized ferroelectric liquid crystal (FLC) is introduced. With the expose of UV light, the doped monomer formed a polymer network and thus stabilize the FLC working in electrically suppressed helix electric-optical mode. Therefore, we are able to achieve a high contrast ratio, fast response and low driving voltage display.

1. Introduction

Nowadays ferroelectric liquid crystal (FLC) is quite popular because of its unique characteristics such as the spontaneous polarization and fast switching speed Recently we proposed a new electrical-optical mode named electrically suppressd helix (ESH) ferroelectric liquid crystal [1] under the strict conditions that its helix pitch is comparable or less than the ferroelectric liquid crystal layer and elastic energy of the helix obligatory larger than the normalized anchoring energy of the alignment layer. Thus, FLC becomes a promising candidate for modern display and photonics [2] technology as it has fast response (usually 20 μs), low driving voltage and high contrast ratio over the traditional liquid crystal display. These qualities enable this mode to be used in field sequential color display (FSC) and high resolution displays such as Pico-projector, 3-D display. Anyway, it still has some intrinsic issues. The FLC parameters, like tilt angle has a strong dependence on varying temperature which made it not suitable for industrial. In this article, we propose a polymer stabilized FLC display cell. With the exposure of UV light at a certain temperature, the doped monomer in the FLC formed a stable polymer net so as to constrain the dynamics of FLC molecular at the necessary working conditions.

2. Experimental Details

Thus, in this experiment, we have chosen the monomer RMM257 from Merck, photo-initiator. A dimethacrylate as a guest and the pure FLC FD4004N from Dianippon Ink and Chemical Ltd.as a host to make

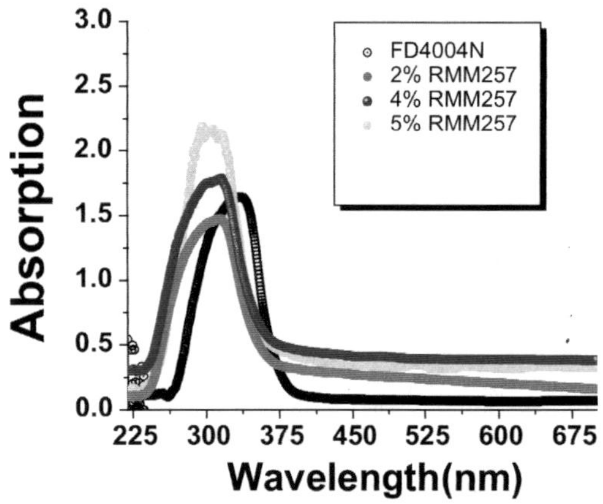

Figure 1. The absorption spectrum for different mixtures of pure FLC material and monomer.

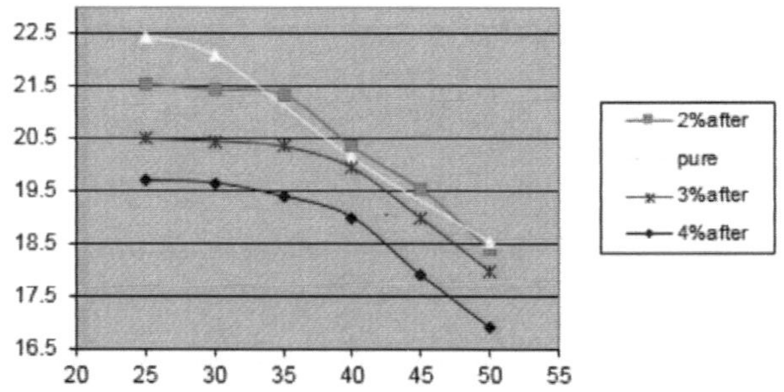

Figure 2. The temperature dependence of the tilt angle for the pure FLC and the monomer FLC mixture.

mixtures of different concentrations of 2%, 3%, 4%, 5% and 10%. Two glass substrate glasses coated with transparent and conductive ITO layers are used as electrodes. Both ITO glass substrates are then coated with photo-alignment material SD1 of 0.5% concentration and exposed under the polarized blue light to achieve a planar alignment perpendicular to the polarization direction of the exposed light. Then, the cell is assembled with two substrates and the cell gap is maintained at 1.5μm to meet the necessary conditions of ESH mode.

Therefore, the cell is composed of pure FLC material, RMM 257 and photo-initiator. We use the UV light (355nm) to expose it at the room temperature. When the polymer net is formed, the FLC host is stabilized in a certain region. The schematic diagram of polymerized ESH FLC cell is showed in the Figure 1.

3. Results and Discussions

For the mixtures of different concentrations, Figure 1 shows the absorption peak of different concentration mixtures and the peak wavelength of blue light shift due to the mixture composite from 200 to 800 nm. The absorption increases for highly doped FLC mixtures because of scattering. The concentrations within 5% wt/wt of the RMM257 in FD4004N are more suitable candidates.

The tilt angle for polymer stabilized ESHFLC (in Figure 2) shows that with adding polymer to FLC, the tilt angle decreased which will affect transmittance. But the stability of tilt angle is much better when comparing 3% polymer FLC system with pure FLC. When the polymer concentration increased to 4%, the tilt angle decreased a lot as well as the contrast decreased a lot which is not good for display applications.

4. References

[1] E. P. Pozhidaev, M. Minchenko, V. Molkin, S. Torgova, V. G. Chigrinov, A. K. Srivastava, H. S. Kwok, V. Vashenko, and A. Krivoshey, "High Frequency Low Voltage Shock-Free Ferroelectric Liquid Crystal: A New Electro-Optical Mode with Electrically Suppressed Helix", SID Conference Record of the International Display Research Conference, pp. 7–10, 2011.

[2] Y. Ma, Q. Guo, A. Srivastava, V. G. Chigrinov, H. S. Kwok, "Fast switchable 2-D structure ferroelectric liquid crystal grating, oral presentation", LCT2-4, IDW, 2012.

Paper No S6.1: Stable Color Gamut for High-End Professional Displays

S.P.W. Carton, F. van der Schans, and A.R. de Wit

NDF Special Light Products, The Netherlands, E-mail: stefan.carton@ndf.eu

Abstract

Displays for the medical and avionics market demand for operational lifetimes of up to 100.000 hours and typically 500 h at 85°C/85%RH. Recent developments with blue pumped backlight solutions employing color conversion foils are sensitive to differential aging leading to a shift toward blue over lifetime. It is argued that the proprietary ARPHOS® technology based on inorganic phosphors solves these problems with minor performance loss.

1. Introduction

NDF Special Light Products BV is known for their high-end customized cold cathode fluorescent lamps (CCFL).

Recently it has developed and matured a solid state backlight technology based on remote phosphor (ARPHOS®). NDF is focusing on high-end display markets like avionics, air traffic control, and medical displays.

Suppliers in these markets typically customize existing displays. NDF Backlight solutions allow these suppliers to meet the high customer requirement.

2. Professional Display Requirements

The improvements of the display characteristics can vary depending on the application. Frequent adaptions are: increasing brightness to sun light readable; increasing the uniformity; ruggedizing the construction; extending lifetime; reducing the influence of aging, for example, color shift and brightness drop; adapting the white point; and improving color gamut.

A typical customer request for NDF is to modify an existing display with CCFL or white LEDs to remote phosphor because of the possibility to adapt the white point to the customers' demand and the luminance and color point stability over life. In some cases, an improved color gamut is requested. Theoretically, this can be realized by using materials with narrow emission peaks, like silicates, nitrates, or quantum dots. However, the improvement is limited by the LC color filter.

3. Differential Aging

Typically a 450 nm blue LED is used as a light source for the excitation of the light conversion film. A first material in the active film converts a fraction of the blue light into green light, while a second material converts a fraction of the green and a fraction of the blue light into red light. The total amount of emitted photons depends on the amount of blue light and on the quantum efficiency of the materials.

Assuming the absorption is constant over lifetime and independent of the blue LED intensity, then the ratio between the blue, green and red backlight emission only depends on the quantum efficiency of the materials in the active film, that is, changes in the intensity of the blue LED over time only effect the amount of emitted light and not the spectral distribution.

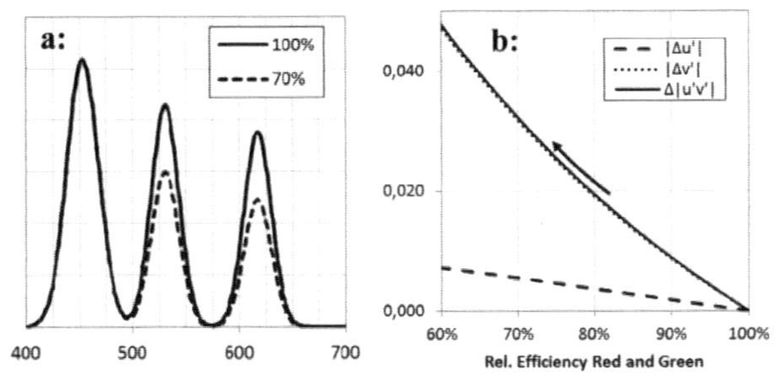

Figure 1. (a) Simulated change of backlight emission over time; (b) display white point shift.

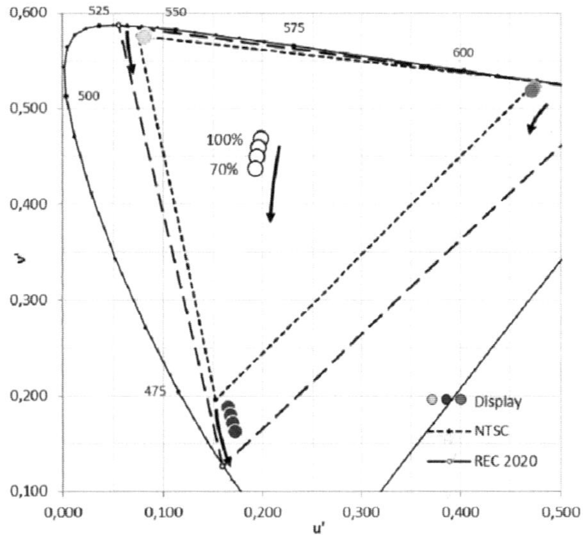

Figure 2. Simulated shift of gamut and white point.

The dominant degradation mechanism for color conversion materials like traditional phosphors and quantum dot materials is a reduction of the quantum efficiency. The impact of a relative reduction down to 70% of the initial quantum yield was calculated for a professional display. Figure 1(a) shows the initial backlight emission together with the emission at 70% of the initial green and red quantum yield. This results in a significant shift of the displays white point as depicted in Figure 1(b). Already at 10% reduction of red and green the white point is shifted over 0.01 for the combined |u′v′|.

Figure 2 shows how the color gamut and white point would shift over time.

4. Remote Phosphor in Practice

Backlight units were prepared with royal blue leds and ARPHOS® foils based on LuAG ($Lu_3Al_5O_{12}$:Ce) for green and BSSN (($(Ba,Sr)_2Si_5N_8$:Eu) for red emission.

These units were tested in real time under application conditions and show that the color point shift for the combined |u'v'| is limited to less than 0.004 after more than 2 years of continuous operation. A 500 h stress test of the ARPHOS® foils at 85°C/85%RH proves the robustness of the remote phosphor solution with an emission decrease of only 1.5% and a white point shift for |u′v′| of less than 0.010. The broadband emission of the phosphors does reduce the color gamut from 87% overlap with NTSC [for the backlight emission shown in Figure 1(a)] to 76%.

5. Conclusion

The high-end professional display market demands extreme lifetime requirement for light output and color stability. Currently, only more traditional phosphor materials can fulfill these requirements at the cost of a reduced color gamut.

Paper No S6.2: An Advanced Optical Thin Film Structure for Fabricating Multidomain Display

C. X. Zhao, F. Fan, T. Du, V. G. Chigrinov, and H. S. Kwok

Partner State Key Laboratory on Advanced Displays and Optoelectronics Technologies, Hong Kong University of Science and Technology, Clear Water Bay, Kowloon, Hong Kong, E-mail: czhaoaf@ust.hk

Abstract

*In this paper, an advanced optical thin film structure, which can be used for fabricating multidomain display is introduced. It is composed of multilayer patterned birefringent thin films, of which each thin film is formed by a liquid crystal **(LC)** polymer layer with spatially varying optical axes controlled by a patterned photoalignment layer so that it can spatially modulate light propagation directions and polarizations. The overall thickness of the multilayer films, excluding the substrate, can be less than 1 μm, which offers the flexibility to generate high resolution light wavefront structure and the light diffraction within the film is also suppressed. As a result, the optical thin film can be ideally working as a photomask for exposure on a LC photoalignment layer to generate multidomain alignment structures in a single exposure, which can be applied for the manufacturing of LC multidomain displays. To verify the effectiveness of the proposed photomask, a periodic two-domain thin film structure has been designed and fabricated and a liquid crystal cell with two-domain alignment structure has been successfully fabricated in a single exposure with the photomask.*

1. Introduction

The interaction of light with optical sensitive materials has provided huge benefit to the manufacturing of modern displays [1]. In the past decades, photosensitive materials are widely used in the liquid crystal display (LCD) industry. With the fast development of material science, another group of photo-sensitive material which is named the photoalignment material has been developed and used in the LCD industry in recent years. The photoalignment materials are mainly used to define the orientation of LC molecules, which is showing increasing popularity in LCD manufacture. In many applications where photoalignment materials are used, patterned alignment structures are required, for instance, the multidomain twist nematic LCD [2], multidomain vertical alignment LCD [3]. Thus, similar to the photomask for controlling the light intensity for photoresist, a new type of photomask that could spatially modulate light propagation directions and polarizations are in great demand. In this paper, such photomask is proposed and has been verified by experiments.

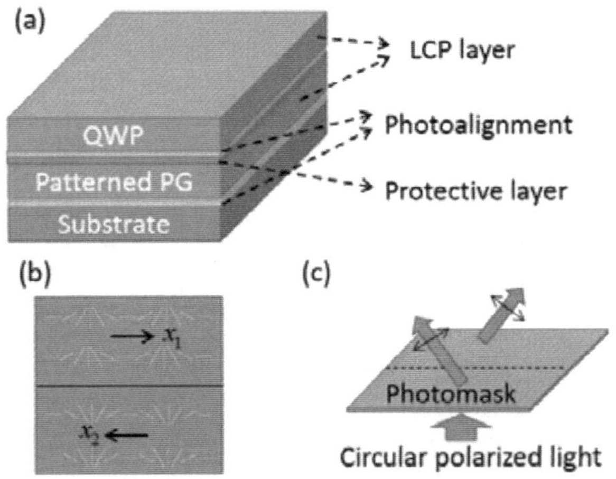

Figure 1. (a) Multilayer structure of the designed photomask; (b) the alignment structure of the patterned PG; (c) light property after passing through the photomask.

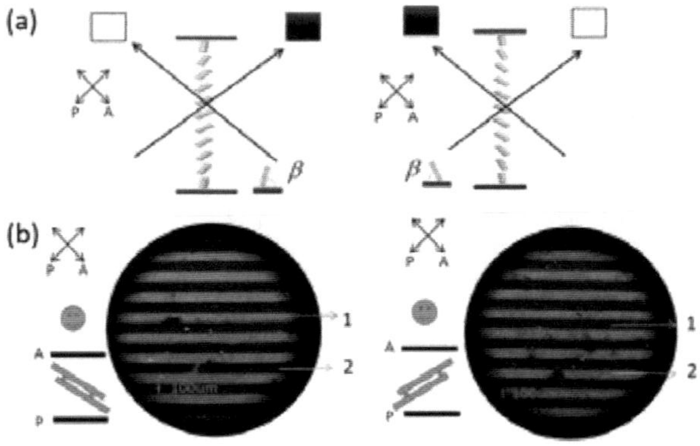

Figure 2. (a) Simulation result of the LC director distribution using Mouse-LCD and also show different transmittance for oblique observation in different directions; (b) micrographs of the obliquely observed LC cell under crossed polarizers.

2. Method

The photomask, as shown in Figure 1(a), has two functional LCP layers, of which the molecules follow the alignment directions of the pretreated photoalignment layer. The first layer is designed as patterned polarization grating (PG) with spatially varying grating vectors to spatially steer light propagation directions, and the second layer is a patterned retardation film (quarter wave plate) for controlling the output light polarizations. Figure 1(b) shows the alignment structure of a two-domain PG and (c) shows the light modulating property of this photomask. As one can see, after passing through the photomask, circular polarized light is transformed into linearly polarized light with two opposite steering angles.

3. Result

To verify the two-domain alignment structure in the LC cell, the LC cell is put under a microscopy with crossed polarizers for observation. A 1 kHz AC voltage with square wave peak-to-peak 2.4 V is applied on the LC cell to generate different LC director distribution of the two domains in the bulk. Figure 2 shows the simulation and experimental results.

4. Acknowledgements

This work is supported by the Partner State Key Lab on Advanced Displays and Optoelectronics Technologies, HKUST.

5. References

[1] V. G. Chigrinov, V. M. Kozenkov, H. S. Kwok, *Photoalignment of Liquid Crystalline Materials*, Wiley, New York, 2008.

[2] M. Schadt, H. Seiberle, A. Schuster, "Optical patterning of multidomain liquid-crystal [J]," Nature, Vol. **381**, p. 16, 1996.

[3] K. Miyachi, K. Kobayashi, Y. Yamada, S. Mizushima, "41.1: Distinguished Paper: The World's First Photo Alignment LCD Technology Applied to Generation Ten Factory." SID Symposium Digest of Technical Papers, Vol. **41**. pp. 579–582, 2010.

Paper No S6.3: Photoaligned Diffractive Thin Film Polymer Polarizer to Double the Efficiency of Conventional Polarizers

Tao Du, Fan Fan, Alwin Ming Wai Tam, Chenxiang Zhao, V. G Chigrinov, and H. S. Kwok

Partners State Key Laboratory on Advanced Displays and Optoelectronics Technologies, The Hong Kong University of Science & Technology, Clear Water Bay, Kowloon, Hong Kong, E-mail: ddtao@connect.ust.hk

Abstract

In this paper, we disclose a novel nano-scale photoaligned liquid crystals polymer thin film polarizer that converts ordinary nonpolarized light to polarized light with efficiency close to 100%, which aims to double the polarization efficiency of conventional polarizers. Different from the mechanisms of conventional film polarizers, which lie in either absorption or reflection and the loss is normally more than 50%, the proposed thin film polarizer is a diffractive polarizer that makes use majority of the incident light and convert it into linear or circular polarized light with minimum loss.

1. Introduction

The polarized light is an extremely important element for photonic and optoelectronic phenomena in particular for the liquid crystal displays (LCDs). However, ordinary light source is generally non-polarized and a polarizer is needed to make it polarized. There are several types of thin film polarizers that can be classified in two groups based on the polarizing mechanisms i.e. absorptive polarizers and reflective polarizers. In general, the efficiency of the conventional polarizers are limited to ~40 to 45% [1]. As a result, the overall efficiency of a device with available polarizers are seriously compromised, for example, for the modern LCDs it is limited to 5–7%. To increase polarization efficiency of the existing polarizers, one of the most common approaches these days is recycling of the light with a reflective polarizer and a reflector; however, only a small fraction of the reflected light could be recycled [2]. Overall, a polarizer out of the conventional polarizing mechanisms that is capable of breaking fundamental limit of 50% efficiency is highly desirable. On the other hand, a novel approach, disclosed in this article, to increase the efficiency of the polarizer and break the fundamental limit of the conventional film polarizers is based on the nanoscopic optical and material engineering for which a microscopic light manipulation based on nanoscopic redistribution of the EM waves is required and thus a nanoscopically defined orientational control is critically important.

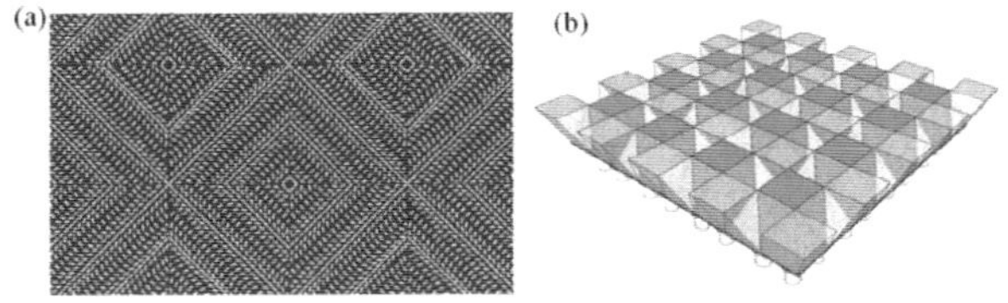

Figure 1. Structure and diffraction pattern of the proposed smart grating.

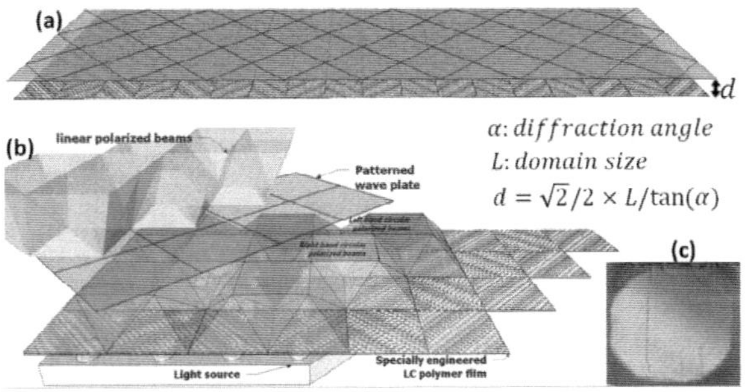

Figure 2. Structure and function of the thin film polarizer with ~100% polarizing efficiency.

2. Structure and Function

The concept to fabricate the diffractive thin film polarizer with optical efficiency close to 100% is based on the nanoscopic manipulations of the LCP director to form a smart diffraction grating with complex two dimensional alignment patterns as shown in Figure 1(a). The smart grating is smart because of its unique diffraction properties, wherein the short range diffraction pattern shows periodically spaced left hand and right hand circular polarized light domains, as shown in Figure 1(b).

The proposed thin film polarizer is an assembly of the nanoscopically engineered smart grating films and a patterned retardation film with a certain small space in between. Non-polarized incident light after passing through the smart grating gets diffracted into left hand circular and right hand circular polarized beams corresponding to the −1st and +1st diffraction orders with diffraction efficiency ~100%. At the same time, the left hand circular and right hand circular polarized beams each concentrates in periodically spaced domains so that they are completely separated. The circular polarized light domains then get collected by certain areas of the patterned quarter wave retarder to provide linear polarized output light, as shown in Figure 2.

3. References

[1] E. Hecht, *Optics, 4th*, International edition, Addison-Wesley, San Francisco, 2002.

[2] M. F. Weber, O. Benson, S. Cobb, J. Jonza, A. Ouderkirk, D. Wortman, C. Stover, "Brightness enhancing reflective polarizer", US Patent Application 10/369,014, 2006.

Paper No S6.4: $K_2SiF_6:Mn^{4+}$ as a Red Phosphor for Remote Phosphor LEDs

Heleen F. Sijbom,[1,2] Koen Van den Eeckhout,[1,2] Dirk Poelman,[1,2] and Philippe F. Smet[1,2]

[1]LumiLab, Department of Solid State Sciences, Ghent University, Krijgslaan 281-S1, 9000 Ghent, Belgium, E-mail: Heleen.Sijbom@UGent.be; [2]Center for Nano- and Biophotonics (NB-Photonics), Ghent University, Ghent, Belgium

Abstract

$K_2SiF_6:Mn^{4+}$ is a promising red phosphor for the use in LEDs for general lighting and displays. Its narrow red emission and excellent thermal stability make it suitable for improved color rendering. The long millisecond-range decay and saturation at high excitation power can be overcome by using a remote phosphor light emitting diode (LED) setup.

1. Introduction

In display backlighting, there is need for saturated primary colors, generated by blue LEDs and saturated green and red phosphors or quantum dots. Although several phosphors are available, there is still a need for efficient, stable materials with a narrow emission spectrum to improve the color rendering of the LEDs and the luminous efficacy [1]. $K_2SiF_6:Mn^{4+}$ is a promising red phosphor for the use in LEDs for general lighting and displays [2]. Its red line emission at 630 nm is comfortably within the eye sensitivity limit and the excitation band around 455 nm is ideally suited for blue LED excitation [3]. Simulations show high CRI and LER values for $K_2SiF_6:Mn^{4+}$ combined with a green or yellow phosphor and a blue LED, for a wide range of color temperatures. To maximize the application opportunities for this phosphor, we need to know more about the luminescence behavior at high excitation intensities and on single particle scale. This research presents a study of the saturation behavior and thermal properties of $K_2SiF_6:Mn^{4+}$, complemented by a combined investigation of structural and luminescence properties in cathodoluminescence in a scanning electron microscope (SEM-CL) mappings.

2. Saturation Behavior and Thermal Properties

The integrated emission intensity of $K_2SiF_6:Mn^{4+}$ in Figure 1 shows sublinear response at high excitation power due to the relatively long lifetime of the excited state of 8.1 ms at room temperature.

Thermal quenching is limited since the emission intensity stays at a high level until 400 K, which is above the normal working temperature of most LEDs. Nevertheless, upon high incident laser intensity, the phosphor is irreversibly damaged, as can be monitored by SEM-CL. A remote phosphor setup, where the phosphor is physically separated from the pumping LED, can overcome saturation issues at high excitation power by lowering the blue photon flux at the phosphor level.

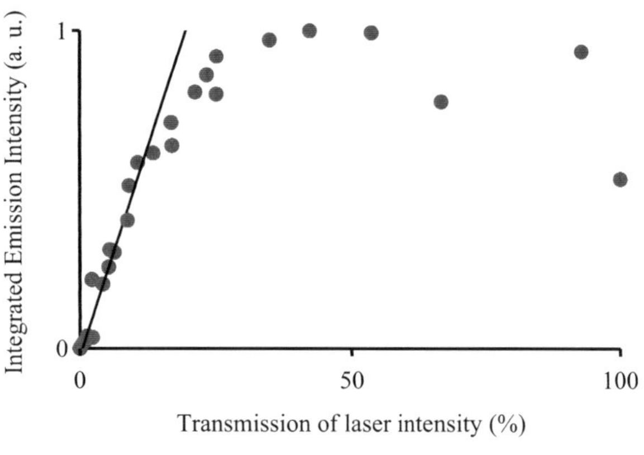

Figure 1. Sublinear response of $K_2SiF_6:Mn^{4+}$ emission with increasing excitation power.

Figure 2. SEM picture (top) and SEM-CL mapping of $K_2SiF_6:Mn^{4+}$ particles.

3. Cathodoluminescence Mappings

EDX-mappings show a homogeneous elemental distribution, proving a homogeneous incorporation of the Mn dopant. However, the SEM-CL mappings in Figure 2 show higher emission intensities at the edges of the well-crystallized, cubic particles, which indicates particular optical outcoupling paths. Smaller particles, surface roughening, or embedding could increase the emission intensity through improved outcoupling of the light.

4. Acknowledgements

This research is funded by the IWT SBO project LumiCoR.

5. References

[1] P. F. Smet, A. B. Parmentier, D. Poelman, "Selecting conversion phosphors for white light-emitting diodes", J. Electrochem. Soc., Vol. **158**, pp. R37–R54, 2011.

[2] T. Takahashi, S. Adachi, "Mn^{4+}-activated red photoluminescence in K_2SiF_6 phosphor", J. Electrochem. Soc., Vol. **155**, pp. E183–E188, 2008.

[3] M. G. Brik, A. M. Srivastava, "On the optical properties of the Mn^{4+} ion in solids", J. Lumin., Vol. **133**, pp. 69–72, 2013.

Paper No S7.1: Two-Layer Moiré Display

V. Saveljev[1,2] *and S.-K. Kim*[2]

[1]Hanyang University, Seoul, Korea; [2]KIST, Seoul, Korea, E-mail: saveljev.vv@gmail.com

Abstract

In this paper, we present a moiré display based on the finite distance effect, which has two non-coplanar layers installed at a non-zero gap.

1. Introduction

The moiré patterns basically appear as repeated light and dark stripes (bands) [1]. This gave rise to the moiré magnifier [2]. Also, it is possible to arrange the patterns so that they will comprise a useful image. The displays based on the moiré effect were demonstrated, including the flat 2D display [3] and the stereoscopic 3D display [4]. The currently proposed display is based on the finite distance effect [5] with a non-zero gap between the layers.

2. Principle

The display consists of two parallel opaque layers with regularly distributed transparent holes. The result of superposition of these layers can be represented as the convolution of the transparency functions of the layers. The locations of the holes in both plates are geometrically similar, but their size and shape are different. For example, if one layer contains small circular holes and another the holes shaped as letters, then the visible result is the magnified image of the letters.

When an observer moves laterally, the image of the moiré patterns follows his movement like in the moiré mirror [5]. When the observer approaches or moves away, the size of images changes in accordance to the wavelength of the moiré patterns, which depends on the distance as follows:

$$\lambda_m = \frac{\rho}{\left|1-\rho+\frac{d}{z}\right|} \qquad (1)$$

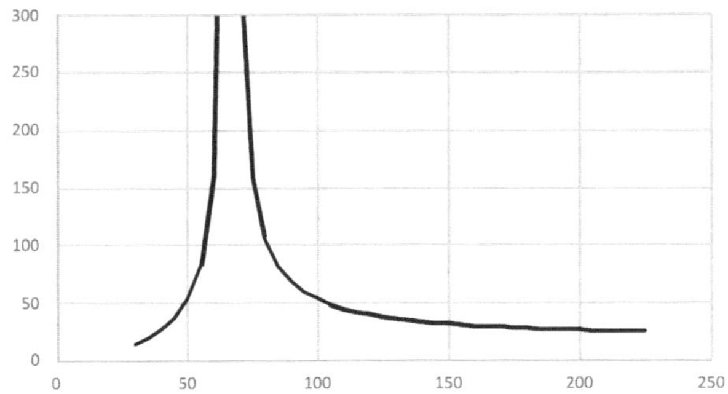

Figure 1. The wavelength of the moiré patterns λm versus the distance z.

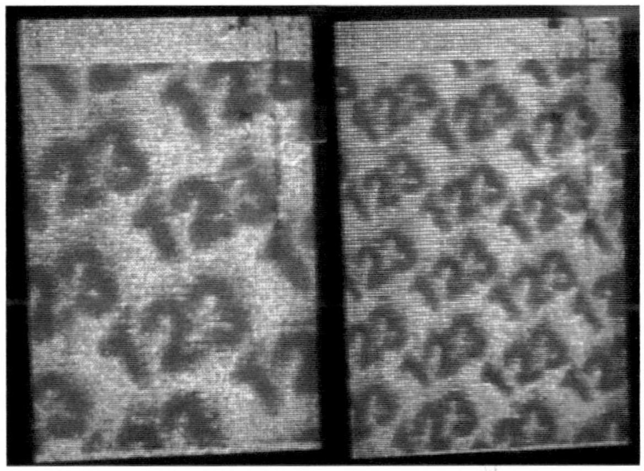

Figure 2. Images of letters observed from different distances (the visible area within the black frame = A4).

Equation (1) is adapted from [5]; it represents a linear rational function, which is degenerated into a linear proportionality for $\rho = 1$. The general case of Eq. (1) is illustrated in Figure 1.

3. Experiments

Examples of displayed images of digits are shown in Figure 2. These images are taken from distances 75 cm and 60 cm in a static A4 display with the gap between layers being 4 cm. The size and the angle of the observed images correspond to Eq. (1).

4. Conclusion

The displayed image does not look static; it changes while the observer moves away or laterally. This may make it attractive for advertisements.

5. References

[1] I. Amidror, The Theory of Moiré Phenomenon, Vol.**1**, Springer, Dordrecht, The Netherlands, 2009.

[2] M. C. Hutley, R. Hunt, R. F. Stevens, P. Savander, "The moiré magnifier", Pure Appl. Opt., Vol. **3**, pp. 133–142, 1994.

[3] V. Saveljev, S.-K. Kim, "A moiré display", Proc. 19th International Display Workshops (IDW/AD'12), Vol. **19**, pp. 1875–1877, 2012.

[4] V. Saveljev, S.-K. Kim, "A 3D moiré display", Proc. 33rd International Display Research Conference (EuroDisplay), London, UK, pp. 54–56, 2013.

[5] V. Saveljev, S.-K. Kim, "Simulation and measurement of moiré patterns at finite distance", Opt. Exp., Vol. **20**, pp. 2163–2177, 2012.

Paper No S7.2: Spatial Light Modulator on Glass for High Display Quality of Digital Holography

Chun-Won Byun, Jae-Eun Pi, Chi-Sun Hwang, Yong-Hae Kim, GiHeon Kim, Ji-Hun Choi, Jong-Heon Yang, Himchan Oh, and Myung-Lae Lee

Smart I/O Platform Research Department, ETRI, Daejeon, Korea, E-mail: cwbyun@etri.re.kr

Abstract

We successfully demonstrate a 1.89-inch SLMoG (spatial light modulator on glass) driven by oxide BCE (back channel etch) TFTs (thin-film transistor). It is necessary for SLM to have very fine pixel pitch and large panel size for realizing high display quality of digital holography. To confirm such technical demands, we fabricate 1.89-inch SLMoG with 20-µm pixel pitch, and apply ECB (electrically controlled birefringence) LC (liquid crystal) mode for light phase modulation. In this article, we report the results of demonstration and discuss technical issues of SLMoG technology.

1. Introduction

In digital holography techniques, the viewing angle and image size are decided by specification of SLM. Generally, the pixel pitch and the panel size of SLM decide viewing angle and the image size, respectively. But commercial SLMs have very small image size due to using Si wafer for fine pixel pitch and driving circuitry [1,2]. And in the case of glass substrate, it is very difficult to implement fine pixel pitch on account of limitation of photolithographic process and device performance. To overcome these hurdle, we try to fabricate SLM on glass substrate driven by oxide back channel etch (BCE) TFTs [3] and develop new driving method.

2. Experiments

Specification of spatial light modulator on glass (SLMoG) panel is described at Table 1. Our panel modulate the light phase, so we apply the electrically controlled birefringence (ECB) mode liquid crystal (LC) with 2.5-μm cell-gap to obtain sufficient phase shift value(more than 2π).

To fabricate SLMoG, we apply four metal process as shown in Figure 1. And to overcome the driver IC attachment problem on fine pixel pitch panel, we develop new demux driving method with low switching error. And the panel design is shown in Figure 1.

3. Results and Discussion

We successfully fabricate and demonstrate the SLMoG panel. Figures 2 and 3 show the fabricated panel and driving system and diffraction image, respectively.

Table 1. Specification of SLMoG panel.

Resolution	1,920 × 480	LC mode	ECB mode
Diagonal	1.89 inch	**Back plane**	OxTFT (BCE)
Pixel Pitch	60 μm × 20 μm	**Pixel**	1TFT-1CAP

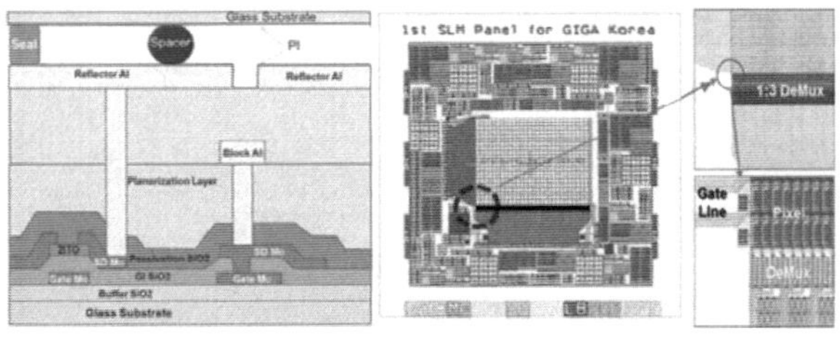

Figure 1. Vertial structure and panel design of SLMoG.

Figure 2. Fabricated 2-inch SLMoG panel.

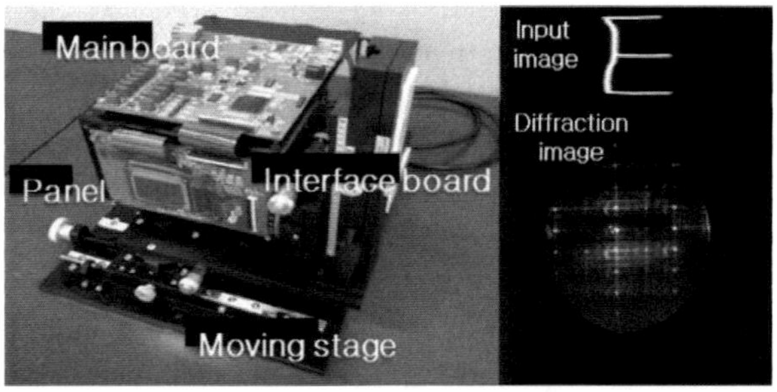

Figure 3. Driving system and diffraction image.

From the experimental results, we find out other technical issues for high display quality of digital holography. Strick cell-gap control, LC-inversion method, and diffraction uniformity of adjacent pixel are also very important. To resolve these issues, we are trying to optimize the vertical structure and develop the new driving method.

4. Acknowledgements

This research has been supported by Giga Korea Development of Telecommunications Terminal with Digital Holographic Table-top Display [GK13D0100].

5. References

[1] W. P. Bleha, L. A. Lei, "Advances in liquid crystal on silicon (LCoS) spatial light modulator technology," Proc. SPIE, Vol. **8736**, p. 87360A, 2013.

[2] D. E. Smalley, Q. Y. Smithwick, V. M. Bove Jr., J. Barabas, S. Jolly, "Anisotropic leaky-mode modulator for holographic video displays," Nature, Vol. **498**, pp. 313–318, 2013.

[3] L. JeaWon, Y. -H. Kim, C. -W. Byun, J.- E. Pi, H. Oh, G. Kim, M.-L. Lee, H. -Y. Chu, C.-S. Hwang , "High resolution TFT-LCD for spatial light modulator," Proc. SPIE Vol. **9117** 911719–1(2014

Paper No S7.3: Holographic Direct View System With 4K2K LCOS SLM and LED Reconstruction Light Source

Po-Sheng Chiu,[1] Cheng-Huan Chen,[2] Wilbur Wei-Chen Chiang[3]

[1]Department of Power Mechanical Engineering, National Tsing Hua University, East District, Taiwan; [2]Department of Photonics, National Chiao Tung University, Hsinchu City, Taiwan; [3]Jasper Display Corporation, Hsinchu City, Taiwan, E-mail: wilbur.chiang@jasperdisplay.com

Abstract

Instead of using laser as light source to generate hologram, light-emitting diode (LED) was used together with 4K2K liquid crystal on silicon (LCOS) panel to reconstruct LED light and enter computer generated hologram to LCOS panel, to generate interface pattern. Near eye holographic display is produced with off axis optical structure. 4K2K panel diffraction efficiency comparison between LED and laser is also measured.

1. Introduction

With the 4K2K liquid crystal on silicon (LCOS) spatial light modulator (SLM), it enhances holographic 3D effect. Its small pixel size, 3.74 μm; it provides a wider angle of diffraction. Inside this test, SLM panel's LC response time is still slow, ~30 ms. So, it can only build monochrome holographic image. With the upcoming SLM, we can expect more than 120 Hz or higher frame rate performance. Single panel full color holographic display will have a reasonable performance. Use of laser light source can have better image contract ratio. However, it is not safe to be used for direct view system. So, in this test, we use green LED as light source together with 0.3 mm pinhole size. It can simulate the same effect using laser light source. Our prototype shows promising result. Holography can produce image with multiple depth view which showing 3D effect. However, the way when the image is formed on a flat display panel, the image floating effect is normally limited.

The proposed architecture combines two elements, including holography and geometrical imaging optics, so that the system will possess the merit of both technologies. Figure 1(a) shows the overall light path. The virtual holographic image, two arrows with different depth, is generated with a phase type LCOS SLM, as shown in Figure 1(b). The inverted real image of the two arrows is formed by a concave mirror at the distance of 71 and 84 cm, respectively, away from the mirror, as shown in Figure 1(c). The reconstruction source is a green LED with a pinhole in the front.

2. 532 nm LED as Light Source

Systems have the green LED light going through pinhole, expand incoherent and polarized, parallel incident into 4K2K LCOS panel (pixel pitch is 3.74 μm), after panel reflection and going through the focus lens, all phase level of energy and diffraction efficiency are measured.

In total, five test grating designs were used to measure the diffraction efficiency (Figure 2).

Conclusion: The diffraction efficiency does not exceed 30%. There is an obvious difference from our theoretical estimation. LED as light source is still showing incoherence problem. The use of a small pinhole for the LED light source can improve the spatial coherence, but it seems there exists a large percentage of incoherence. Besides, during light transfer and focus, there is intensity loss. These can both contribute to low diffraction efficiency.

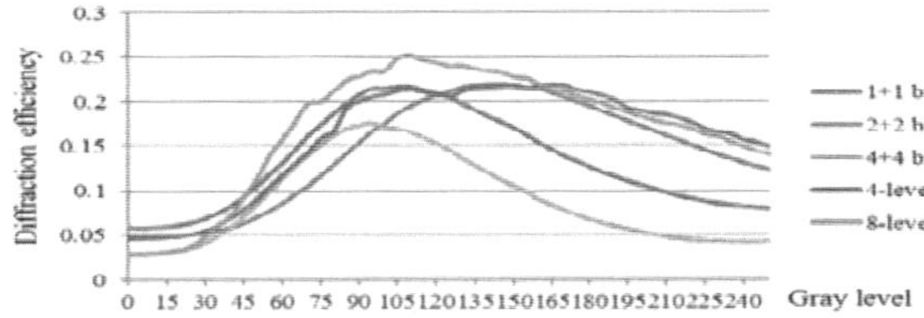

Figure 2. Diffraction efficiency vs. gray level for LED.

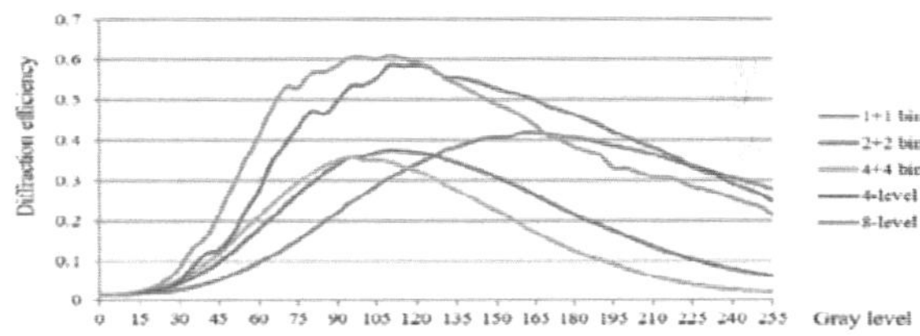

Figure 3. Diffraction efficiency vs. gray level for laser.

3. 532 nm Laser Light Source

Since diffraction efficiency with LED light source is lower than 30%, light source can be the major reason. So, 532 nm laser light source is used to verify this assumption (Figure 3).

Conclusion: With 532 nm laser as light source, even binary grating can reach over 30% efficiency. Four-phase-level grating is about 50%. Eight-phase-level grating can even achieve 60% or higher.

4. References

[1] Z. Zhang, Z. You, D. Chu, "Fundamentals of phase-only liquid crystal on silicon (LCOS) devices", Light Sci. Appl., Vol. **3**, p. e213, 2014.

[2] T. Ito, T. Shimobaba, H. Godo, M. Horiuchi, "Holographic reconstruction with a 10-μm pixel-pitch reflective liquid-crystal display by use of a light-emitting diode reference light", Opt. Lett., Vol. **27**, pp. 1406–1408, 2002.

[3] L.-Y. Liao, C.-H. Chen, F.-H. Chen, C.-H. Tsai, E. Liao, S. Hong, "Phase-modulation LCoS display system with off-axis LED reconstruction Light", Dig. Tech. Pap., Vol. **44**, pp. 905–908, 2013.

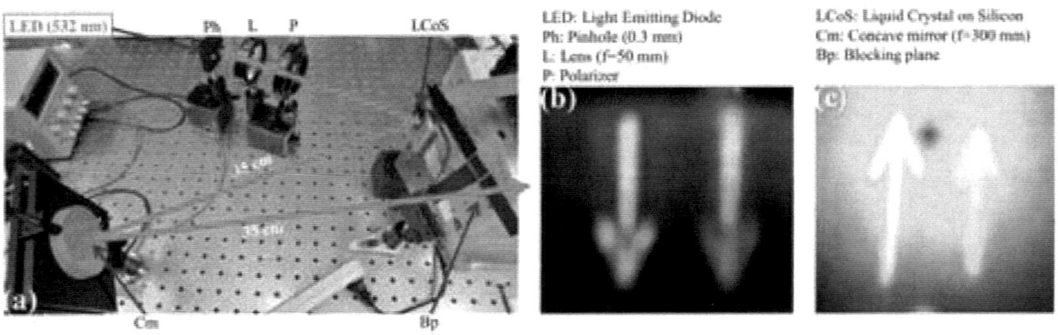

Figure 1. (a) System light path, (b) holographic image from LCOS, and (c) floating image formed by the concave mirror.

Paper No S7.4: Two Sides of the Moiré Effect in 3D Displays

V. Saveljev[1,2]

[1]Hanyang University, Seoul, Korea; [2]KIST, Seoul, Korea, E-mail: saveljev.vv@gmail.com

Abstract

We present the 3D moiré techniques. Practically most important of them are the minimization of the moiré effect in the autostereoscopic 3D displays and the 3D moiré displays. Other related issues are also discussed.

1. Introduction

The moiré effect is a physical effect originally known from optics when it produced vivid waves in a fabric making a dress more attractive. The moiré effect is a result of the optical interaction between several semitransparent layers [1]. The layers are typically periodic, although this is not a requirement. The combinational frequencies produce the patterns with a new spatial frequency which does not exist in either layer. The moiré effect is observed not only in visible light but also in ultrasound, infrared, electron beam, and in X-rays.

As any other physical effect, the effect under consideration has closely related manifestations which might seem opposite. For researchers involved in 3D displays, these "sides" are the minimal and the maximal appearance of the moiré patterns.

2. Minimization

The autostereoscopic 3D displays are typically designed from two parallel periodic layers with an integer ratio of periods. These factors provoke the moiré effect and make its elimination necessary. Known approaches to the minimization are the direct analytical minimization [2] and the spectral minimization [1]. The direct minimization works well, although its applications are limited because it is based on the sinusoidal approximation of the profile of the layers (gratings). The spectral approach works with any profile, being therefore a more general and maybe sort of a universal solution, for illustration refer to Figure 1. The close investigation of the moiré waves [3] resulted in a method of graphical minimization in the spectral domain without calculating spectra [4]. Other relates issues (finite distance, moiré mirror, irregular polygons, etc.) were also investigated.

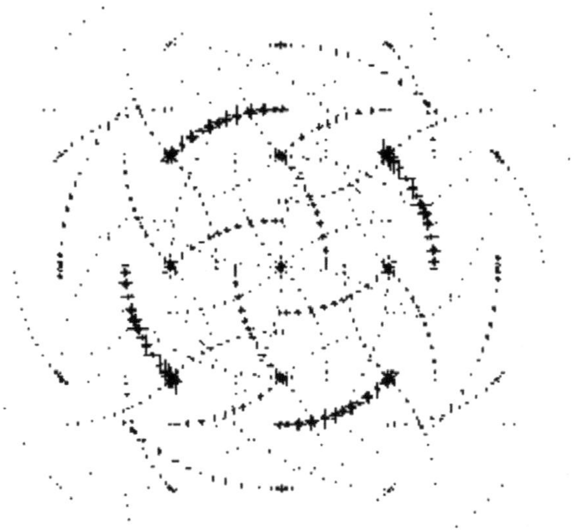

Figure 1. Spectral trajectories of the moire waves in the complex plane obtained in experiment.

Figure 2. Left and right images of the first 3D moire display.

3. Displays

On the other hand, the moiré measurements are well-known [5] providing the highly precise linear readings and the determination of the shape of surfaces. The measurements, however, have no direct connection to displays.

Nevertheless, it appeared possible to display arbitrary images using the moiré effect as the main physical principle of a displaying method. The 2D binary moiré displays were proposed, as well as the autostereoscopic 3D display [6], see Figure 2. The next step should yield gray-level and color moiré displays, both 2D and 3D.

4. Conclusions

A further complex research of the moiré effect in 3D case (like, e.g., a particular issue [7]) could bring some more useful practical applications, for example, nonplanar displays.

5. References

[1] I. Amidror, The Theory of Moiré Phenomenon, Vol. **1**, Springer, London, 2009.

[2] V. Saveljev, J.-Y. Son, J.-H. Chun, K.-D. Kwack, K.-H. Cha, "About a moiré-less condition for non-square grids", J. Disp. Technol., Vol. **4**, pp. 332–339, 2008.

[3] V. Saveljev, "Orientations and branches of moiré waves in three-dimensional displays," J. Korean Phys. Soc., Vol. **57**, pp. 1392–1396, 2010.

[4] V. Saveljev, S.-K. Kim, "Theoretical estimation of moiré effect using spectral trajectories," Opt. Exp., Vol. **21**, pp. 1693–1712, 2013.

[5] K. Patorski, M. Kujawinska, Handbook of the Moiré Fringe Technique, Elsevier Science Publishers B.V., Amsterdam, 1993.

[6] V. Saveljev, S.-K. Kim, "Three-dimensional moiré display", J. Soc. Inform. Disp., Vol. **22**, pp. 482–486, 2015.

[7] V. Saveljev, S.-K. Kim, B. Lee, "Experimental estimation of visibility of moiré patterns for 3D displays", Proceedings on Winter Meeting of the Optical Society of Korea, p. 64, 2015.

Paper No S8.1: Color Volume-Based Wide Color Gamut Mapping for Rec. 2020 Contents in Digital Television

Byungseok Min, Hocheon Wey, and Youngsu Moon

DMC R&D Center, Samsung Electronics, Suwon, South Korea, E-mail: byungseok.min@samsung.com

Abstract

In this article, we propose a wide color gamut mapping system for Rec. 2020 contents in digital television, based on the color volume information of the mastering display. By this methodology, the original color graded in the mastering display could be faithfully reproduced in the customer's display preserving director's intention.

1. Introduction

From a real scene captured by camera to be finally displayed on the screen in the customer's side, the captured image goes through several stages like video mastering at the studio, compression to be delivered within limited bandwidth, and image processing after decoding the contents at the television. Due to the hardware limitation of the camera and display as well as the bandwidth limitation, however, the displayed image on the screen happen to bring about poor user experiences not only lacking of realistic color representation with highly detailed expression but also producing spatial and temporal artifacts. To this end, the Rec. 2020 has been proposed to provide more realistic user experience than Rec. 709 by allowing more image resolution up to 7680 × 4320 (8K), higher temporal resolution up to 120 fps, wider gamut close to human visual system, and bit-depth resolution up to 12 bit [1]. The Rec. 2020 is also supported by H.264 and high-efficiency video coding for improved video quality in the limited bandwidth condition. The recent breakthrough of the flat panel display has been motivating content providers to produce premium contents by grading the content in Rec. 2020 with the mastering display which has peak luminance brighter than 1000 nit, wider gamut close to DCI-P3, and more than 10 bit panel resolution. To make better representation of the high dynamic range imaging, Rec. 2020 also supports other electro-optical transfer function (EOTF) like Perceptual Quantizer to allocate more bit-depth in the dark region and to provide color volume information of the mastering display in CIE-xy chromaticity coordinate of RGB primary color and white point [2,3]. The difficult part of the gamut mapping is in where the out-of-panel gamut color should be mapped to, otherwise those colors are distorted. Fortunately, with the color volume information of the mastering display, the color gamut mapping problem is narrowed down to the mapping between target and mastering display gamut, from the mapping between target display and Rec. 2020 gamut. But in case no color volume information is provided, it is necessary to estimate the actual gamut of the mastering display. In this article, we propose a wide color gamut mapping system based on color volume information, along with a color volume estimation methodology.

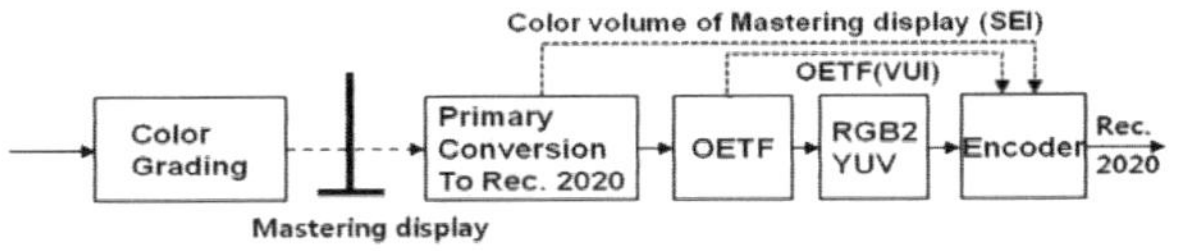

Figure 1. Typical color grading pipeline.

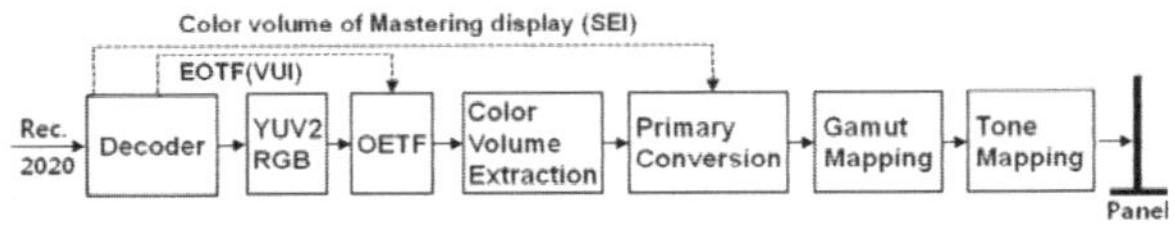

Figure 2. Proposed color gamut mapping pipeline.

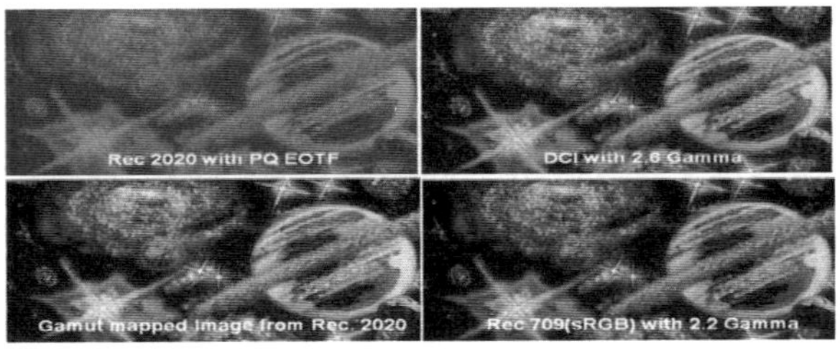

Figure 3. Images displayed on DCI-P3 monitor with 2.2γ.

2. Studio Color Grading Process

In typical color grading process, captured camera images are color graded by colorist in the reference environment, which are digital cinema projector, sRGB monitor for Rec. 709, or wide gamut monitor for Rec. 2020. To convert mastering display gamut to Rec. 2020 gamut, the RGB values is transformed by primary conversion matrix in linearized RGB space, then gamma encoded to be converted YUV for compression [4].

3. Color Gamut Mapping Process

When color volume information is provided by SEI message, the first gamut mapping is performed to change Rec. 2020 to mastering display gamut. Then, the next gamut mapping is followed to map the mastering display gamut to target display gamut. In case where no color volume information is provided, color volume estimation is performed by analyzing color distribution of the contents to examine the maximum CIE-xy coordinate. Thereafter, a color volume close to target display is chosen as mastering display gamut, to minimize the gamut mapping between mastering and target display gamut.

4. Results and Conclusion

The result of gamut mapped image for Rec. 2020 contents in DCI-P3 panel is shown in Figures 1–3, faithfully reproducing the color close to original content, compared with three different types of contents, premium video in Rec. 2020, DCI for digital cinema, and home video in Rec. 709.

5. References

[1] Rec. ITU-R BT.2020: Parameter Values for Ultra-High Definition Television Systems for Production and International Programme Exchange, 2014.

[2] SMPTE 2084, Dynamic Range Electro-Optical Transfer Function of Mastering Reference Displays, 2014.

[3] SMPTE 2086, Mastering Display Color Volume Metadata Supporting High Luminance and Wide Color Gamut Images, 2014.

[4] Rec. ITU-R BT.2250: Delivery of Wide Color Gamut Image Content Through SDTV and HDTV Delivery Systems, 2012.

Paper No S8.2: Quantifying the Ability of Individuals With Macular Disease to See and Read Content on Virtual and Augmented Reality Devices

Howard Moshtael,[1] Lanxing Fu,[2] Ian Underwood,[3] and Baljean Dhillon[3]

[1]Heriot-Watt University, Edinburgh, United Kingdom, E-mail: hfm30@hw.ac.uk; [2]Princess Alexandra Eye Pavilion, Edinburgh, United Kingdom; [3]University of Edinburgh, Edinburgh, United Kingdom

Abstract

A pilot study has been conducted to measure the ability of subjects with macular disease to read content on smart glasses and a smartphone headset. Compared to reading text on paper, participants could read text an average size of 30% smaller on the smart glasses and approximately the same size on the smartphone.

1. Introduction

Recent work has investigated the use of head-mounted displays (HMDs) as a platform for image enhancement techniques for the visually impaired [1–3]. Low vision aids have incorporated HMDs [4] but augmented reality devices, particularly smart glasses, are now available that offer a headset closer in appearance and feel to spectacles. In addition, smartphones, with appropriate optics and housing, are now capable of being used as simple virtual reality devices. A pilot study for a clinical trial was conducted to measure, through vision tests and self-rating, the visibility of these two display types to those with macular disease.

2. Methodology

Two devices were trialed: The Epson Moverio BT-200, smart glasses with a centrally positioned, partially transparent display with a 23° field of view; and an LG G3 smartphone mounted into a Homido headset which magnifies the screen to have a field of view of approximately 100°. The Radner reading test was adapted for both displays, maintaining the letter sizes at the same visual angle as the print version. Reading acuity—the minimum text size legible—and reading speed were measured for paper and the two displays. A visual field test and a contrast test were developed for the displays. The former aims to measure which parts of the screen are visible to the user and the latter measures the minimum contrast visible. A questionnaire was also written and administered to gain feedback on the use of HMDs. Ten individuals with macular degeneration participated.

3. Results and Discussion

Seventy percent of participants self-rated it easier or just as easy to read from the smart glasses compared to large print; and that percentage was 89% for the smartphone headset. When comparing their preference between paper and the display, in the case of the smart glasses an equal number preferred each, whereas for the smartphone two thirds selected paper. Figure 1(a) is a sample result from the field test, showing which points were and were not visible to one participant. In this case, the results suggest that the left half of the screen is more visible to this user. Figure 1(b) is the average reading acuity and shows that participants could read text as small on the smartphone headset as print, and 30% smaller on the smart glasses. Reading speed was, on average, about 20% faster when reading on paper compared to either display.

Given this study aimed to measure the reading ability when reading print-like text (static, black on white, and uniformly distributed across the screen), it is unsurprising that reading speed was faster for print. When using paper, participants retain control over the page, but the nature of the HMD is that its position remains fixed. Our intention is to use this property, which in this study may have slowed down the user, to develop a novel, user-tailored reading aid that presents text based on results from the measurement methods described here.

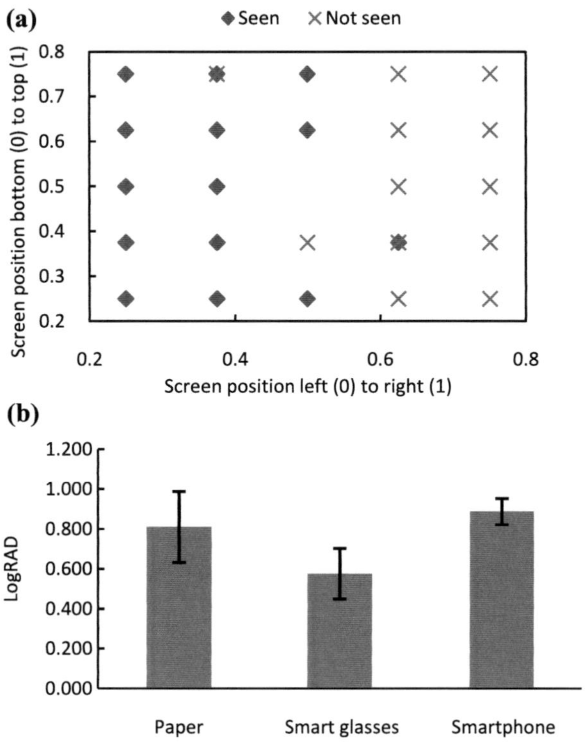

Figure 1. (a) Field test results from one participant using the smartphone; (b) average (±standard error) reading acuity using the three platforms.

4. Acknowledgements

The authors thank the following for their valuable assistance: Chi Can, Javid Khan, Ellie Brown, Ian Murray, Tariq Aslam, Peter Aspinall, Stephen Hicks, the Macular Society, Douglas Young, and Alex Bailey.

5. References

[1] A. Hwang, E. Peli, "An augmented-reality edge enhancement application for Google Glass", Optom. Vis. Sci., Vol. **91**, pp. 1021–1030, 2014.

[2] S. L. Hicks, I. Wilson, L. Muhammed, J. Worsfold, S. M. Downes, C. Kennard, "A depth-based head-mounted visual display to aid navigation in partially sighted individuals", PLoS One, Vol. **8**, p. e67695, 2013.

[3] P. Martínez Cañada, C. Morillas, R. Ureña, J. M. Gómez López, F. J. Pelayo, "Embedded system for contrast enhancement in low-vision", J. Syst. Arch., Vol. **59**, pp. 30–38, 2013.

[4] L. E. Culham, A. Chabra, G. S. Rubin, "Clinical performance of electronic, head-mounted, low-vision devices", Ophthalmic Physiol. Opt., Vol. **24**, pp. 281–290, 2004.

Paper No S8.3: Content Capture and View Interpolation Algorithm for Multiview Autostereoscopic Displays

Ljubomir Jovanov, Hiep Luong, and Wilfried Philips

Department of Telecommunications and Information Processing (IPI-TELIN-iMinds), Ghent University, Gent, Belgium, E-mail: ljj@telin.ugent.be

Abstract

Highly realistic visualization becomes crucial in numerous applications such as: medical imaging, simulation and entertainment systems. In this article, we describe the image/video capture system aimed for autostereoscopic multiview displays, as well as view interpolation and image restoration algorithms used to enhance the image quality. We evaluate the proposed algorithms on a head tracking based stereoscopic multiview display.

1. Introduction

Visual communication devices have undergone through a rapid development in the last few decades. This evolution has brought us improved visual user experience, like color, increased resolution, stereoscopic vision, etc. Next logical step in this evolution are certainly multiview autostereoscopic displays, capable of providing multiple distinct views at the scene for multiple spectators or for one moving viewer. In order to reach a high degree of realism, the number of views should be as large as possible. Besides this, transition between views should be unperceivable; geometry of the scene should not be distorted, while compression and other artefacts should not be visible. Despite the existence of high quality multiview autostereoscopic displays, their application remains limited due to the lack of realistic video content. While it is possible to achieve a sufficient quality when computer generated content is used, visual quality of the video content captured using multicamera systems is still not at the desired quality level.

2. System Overview

Current multi-view displays are capable for simultaneous display of hundreds of views. At the other side, multicamera capture systems are not capable of providing sufficient number of video streams. In practice it is not possible to position cameras close enough to provide seamless view transition. Due to the physical limitations, cameras are positioned at a larger baseline distance then needed to achieve seamless view transition.

One possible solution for generating sufficient number of views of a static scene is the light-field approach. However, such approaches are not applicable for video sequences of dynamic scenes. Required number of views of a dynamic scene can be obtained by means of view interpolation, where existing views, generated by cameras are used as input. Interpolated views are typically generated using depth image based rendering approaches [1] or by relying on view synthesis techniques based on warping [2]. However the visual quality of the interpolated views is highly dependent on disparity estimation method used, which is still not at the acceptable level. Moreover, disparity estimation techniques are highly computationally expensive, which often prohibits (near) real-time operation.

In this article, we present a hybrid system consisting of a combination of depth and color cameras for the capture of multi-view video content. By introducing 3-D depth sensors into the system we eliminate the need for high quality disparity estimation and reduce computational complexity.

The resolution of current 3-D depth sensors currently available on the market is lower than the resolution of the corresponding color images. In our setup the resolution of depth images is 320×240 pixels, while the resolution of corresponding color images is 1280×720. In order to perform view interpolation the resolution of depth and color video streams should be the same.

In order to achieve this, we first perform calibration of the cameras in the system in order to obtain parameters for mutual registration between pairs of color and depth cameras. The next step is sparse registration of depth pixels to the color image. Such registered depth image has large number of missing values, due to the lower resolution and larger viewing angle of the depth image. In order to interpolate the missing depth values, we rely on the information contained in the color images, e.g. contours of the objects in the scene. To prevent the mapping of details contained in the color image we propose the use of learning based filters, which rely only on high frequency content from the color image, collocated in both depth and color to perform the upsampling of the depth image. In order to avoid temporal flickering and deformations of contours in interpolated views, we perform temporal regularization of the interpolated depth maps. Moreover, we perform local enhancement of the depth maps in regions with unreliable depth measurements using local stereo matching.

Using the parameters obtained in the calibration step we convert upsampled depth values into disparities, which are used subsequently to generate interpolated views using depth image based rendering approach. Occluded regions are interpolated using the color images of the alternative view and the corresponding upsampled depth maps.

Finally, we evaluate the visual quality using the single viewer stereoscopic multiview display, which will be demonstrated at the conference.

3. References

[1] P. Ndjiki-Nya, M. Koppel, D. Doshkov, H. Lakshman, P. Merkle, K. Muller, T. Wiegand, "Depth image-based rendering with advanced texture synthesis for 3-d video", IEEE Trans. Multimedia, Vol. **13**, pp. 453–465, 2011.

[2] S. Rogmans, J. Lu, P. Bekaert, G. Lafruit "Real-time stereo-based view synthesis algorithms: A unified framework and evaluation on commodity GPUs", Signal Process. Image Commun., Vol. **24**, pp. 49–64, 2009.

Paper No S8.4: Viewpoint Image Generation for Head Tracking 3D Display Using Multicamera and Approximate Depth Information

Munekazu Date, Hideaki Takada, and Akira Kojima

NTT Media Intelligence Labs, Nippon Telegraph and Telephone Corp., Japan, E-mail: date.munekazu@lab.ntt.co.jp

Read the full article at DOI: 10.1002/jsid.315

Abstract

A simple and high image quality method for viewpoint image synthesis is proposed. Smooth motion parallax of wide depth range objects induced by viewpoint movement for left-and-right and front-and-back directions are achieved using multicamera images and approximate depth information. It is suitable for real-time 3D display applications.

1. Introduction

Viewpoint image synthesis from multicamera images is important for head tracking 3D displays, because observer requires continuous change of motion parallax. However, it is usually difficult to generate intermediate viewpoint images without precise depth information. We have demonstrated a viewpoint image generation method [1,2] using linear blending when depth range of objects is within the visual effect of depth fused 3D (DFD) [3]. The depth range was narrow and not enough to display multiple objects. In this article, we expanded depth range by multilayer calculation using approximate depth information.

2. Experiments and Results

We took picture of two toy-stuffed animals in front of a green background using five cameras. The distance of turtle, catfish, and wall from the cameras are 3, 4, and 5 m, respectively. The separations between cameras were 0.2 m. First, we made layer images from each camera using approximate depth information (Figure 1). Holes in the images, which are produced by occlusion of front objects, are filled by other camera images from closest one aligned on target depth.

Figure 2 shows image generation process for a single layer. Each layer image is aligned at target depth. Strips of images are generated to be close to observer's gaze line. They are aligned and blend linearly [2]. Since the depth range of each layered image is within the range, in which visual effect of DFD occurs, the synthesized image is natural for human eye and no doubled image can be observed. The final images are generated by stacking the images at target depths, the final viewpoint image is generated.

Figure 3 shows the generated images. In conventional method, target depth was that of turtle only. As shown in Figure 3(a) and (b), doubled image was generated at around catfish and black pole. Conversely, proposed method produces exact image (c). Moreover, motion parallax for near and far movement of viewpoint could be reproduced. As shown in Figure 3(d), catfish became smaller when view point is near the objects.

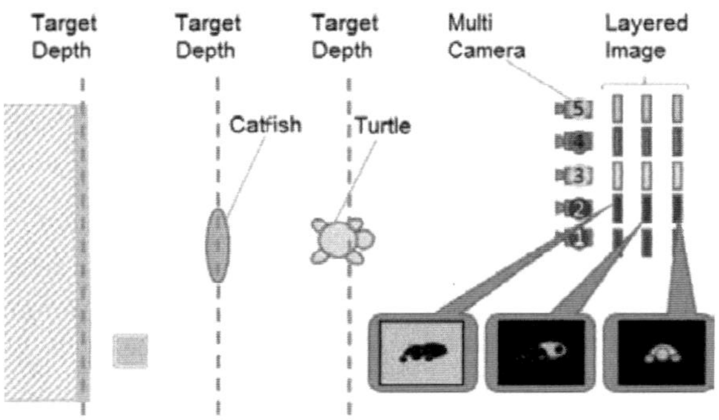

Figure 1. Experimental setup.

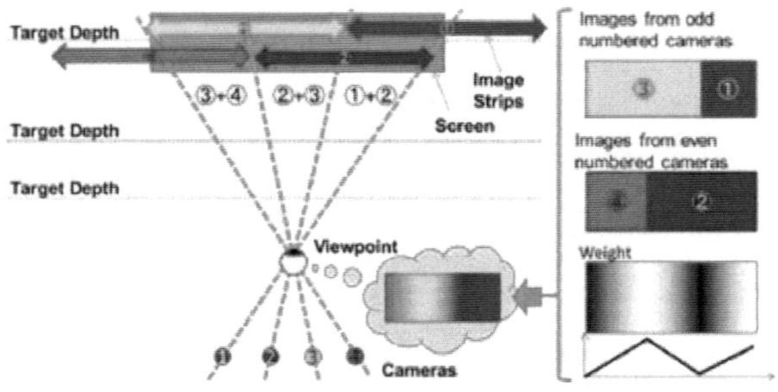

Figure 2. Viewpoint image generation for a single layer.

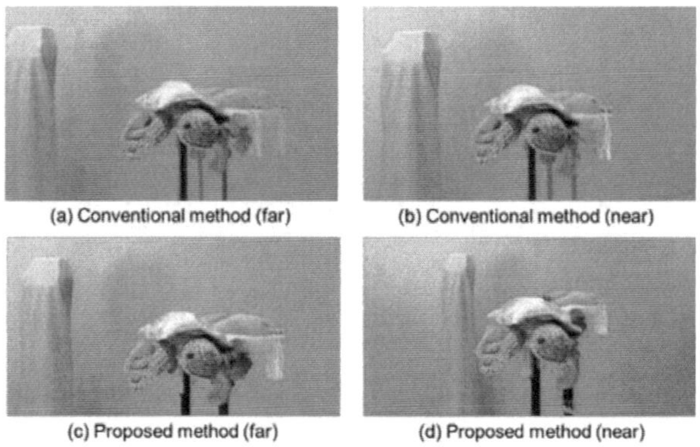

Figure 3. Synthesized images.

3. Conclusions

We have developed a new method of viewpoint image generation from discrete camera images. Smooth motion parallax for viewpoint movement of left-and-right and front-and-back directions was reproduced merely using approximate depth information. Since the proposed method is simple, it is suitable for real-time and high image quality applications. Our method also contributes to reduce number of image sources for autostereoscopic 3D display.

4. References

[1] M. Date, H. Takada, S. Ozawa, S. Mieda, A. Kojima, "Highly realistic 3D display system for space composition telecommunication", IEEE J. Disp. Technol., Vol. **11**, pp. 121–128, 2015.

[2] M. Date, H. Takada, A. Kojima, "Real-time viewpoint image synthesis using strips of multi-camera images", IS&T SPIE Electronic Imaging Stereoscopic Displays and Applications XXVI, San Francisco, 2015, 9391–7.

[3] S. Suyama, S. Ohtsuka, H. Takada, K. Uehira, S. Sakai, "Apparent 3-D image perceived from luminance-modulated two 2-D images displayed at different depths", Vision Res., Vol. **44**, pp. 785–793, 2004.

Thin Film Polarized Liquid Crystal Backlight

Mohammad Mohammadimasoudi,[1,2] Jeroen Beeckman,[1,2] and Kristiaan Neyts[1,2]

[1]ELIS Department, Ghent University, Gent, Belgium, E-mail: Mohammad.MohammadiMasoudi@elis.ugent.be; [2]Center for Nano- and Bio-photonics, Ghent University, Ghent, Belgium

Abstract

A thin polarized-light emitting film is fabricated by aligning nanorods in an electric field and subsequent polymerization. A polarization ratio of 0.60 is obtained with this method. The thickness of the film is in the order of a few micrometer, and the method is compatible with large-scale processing on cheap, flexible, and transparent substrates. The process can be realized in a roll-to-roll process as in a printing process, when one substrate is flexible and passes over a roll with electrodes.

Liquid crystal displays have a limited transmission, on the order of 10%. This is mainly due to the absorbing polarizers and color filters. In a conventional backlight, the emitted light is unpolarized because it originates for LEDs or phosphor materials. Because an LCD is designed to work with polarized light [1], the polarizer typically absorbs half of the light.

Light emission is usually the result of a dipole transition in an atom, molecule, or quantum dot. Recently, the development of red and green quantum dots has improved the color saturation of LCDs [2]. Anisotropic emitters can have characteristics that are close to that of a dipole antenna. If the emitters are aligned parallel to the electric field of the light that is transmitted by the polarizer, most of the light that is emitted will pass the polarizer and contribute to the emission of the LCD display as shown in Figure 1.

We propose a method for the fabrication of a thin polarized-light emitting film in which an electric field aligns 50-nm long semiconductor nanorods (NRs) in a preferred direction in a polymerized film. Figure 2 shows a photograph of the resulting film with 10 μm thickness.

NRs can emit saturated colors and the absorption and emission from these CdSe/CdS nanorods are highly polarized [3]. We have recently shown that NRs can be aligned effectively by applying an electric field [4].

Fluorescence microscopy images of thin polarized-light emitting NR film show the emission for the orientation of the polarizer parallel (Figure 3a) or perpendicular (Figure 3b) to the applied electric field. The ITO electrodes have a width of 6 μm and a spacing of 20 μm. The strongest photoluminescence is observed when the polarizer is parallel to the electric field, indicating that the NRs are aligned along the electric field lines. This is in agreement with earlier polarization measurements on individual NRs and aligned NR arrays [5]. The polarization ratio is defined as: $\Pi_r = (I_{\parallel} - I_{\perp})/(I_{\parallel} + I_{\perp})$[5] in which $I_{\square}$ and $I_{\perp}$ are the average photoluminescent intensity over the gap area between two electrodes, when the polarizer is oriented, respectively, parallel and perpendicular to the line electrodes. The polarization ratio for regions with NRs aligned according to the above procedure is about 0.6.

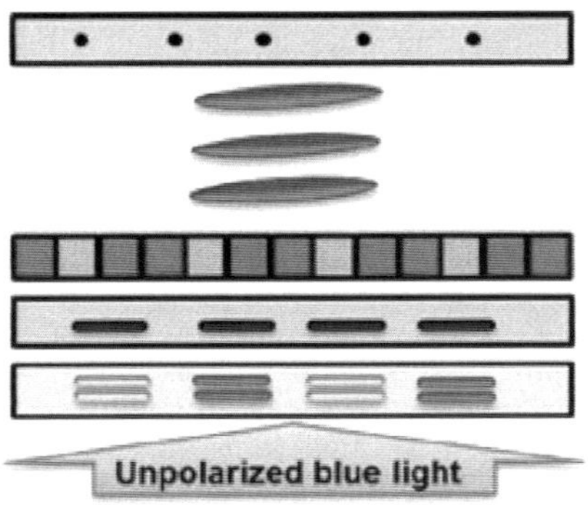

Figure 1. Scheme of polarized LC backlight.

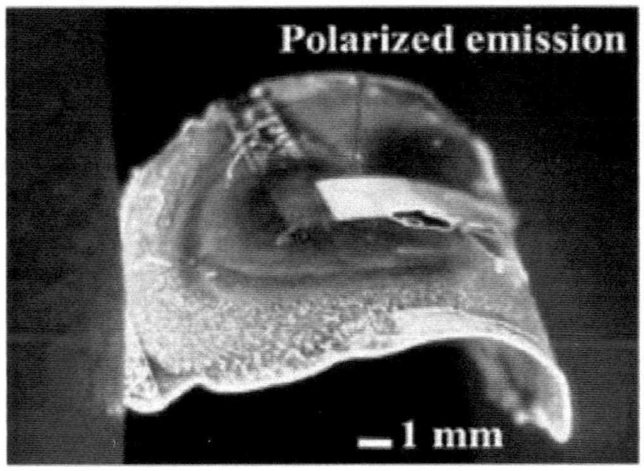

Figure 2. A photograph of thin film polarized emitter which is illuminated by a UV lamp.

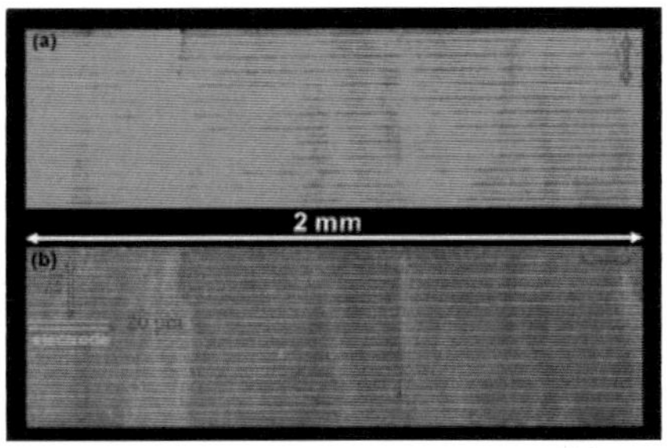

Figure 3. Fluorescence microscopy images of a thin film of NRs in a polymer with the polarizer oriented (a) parallel and (b) perpendicular to the applied electric field.

1. References

[1] Z. Luo, Y.-W. Cheng, S.-T. Wu, "Polarization-preserving light guide plate for a linearly polarized backlight", J. Disp. Technol., Vol. **10**, pp. 208–214, 2014.

[2] E. Jang, S. Jun, H. Jang, J. Llim, B. Kim, Y. Kim, "White-light-emitting diodes with quantum dot color converters for display backlights", Adv. Mater., Vol. **22**, pp. 3076–3080, 2010.

[3] M. Mohammadimasoudi, Z. Hens, K. Neyts, Full alignment of colloidal nanorods in solution using alternating electric fields, ACS Photon. Opt. Dev. Vol. **XI**, p. 917013, 2014.

[4] M. Mohammadimasoudi, L. Penninck, T. Aubert, R. Gomes, Z. Hens, F. Strubbe, K. Neyts, "Fast and versatile deposition of aligned semiconductor nanorods by dip-coating on a substrate with interdigitated electrodes", Opt. Mater. Exp., Vol. **3**, pp. 2045–2054, 2013.

[5] A. Persano, M. De Giorgi, A. Fiore, R. Cingolani, L. Manna, A. Cola, R. Krahne, "Photoconduction properties in aligned assemblies of colloidal CdSe/CdS nanorods", ACS Nano, Vol. **4**, pp. 1646–1652, 2010.

Paper No S9.1: Progress in Bridged-Grain TFT

H. S. Kwok, M. Wong, W. Zhou, and R. S. Chen

State Key Lab on Advanced Displays and Optoelectronics, Hong Kong University of Science and Technology, Clear Water Bay, Hong Kong, China, E-mail: eekwok@ust.hk

Abstract

There has been an explosive growth of low-temperature polycrystalline silicon (LTPS) thin-film transistor (TFT) fabrication lines recently. Several Gen 6 and Gen 5 LTPS lines are under construction in China. They all choose the excimer laser annealing (ELA) approach. For high ppi mobile displays, LTPS is essential. It is the technology of choice over metal oxide TFT because of the higher mobility and stability it offers. Circuits on substrate is also possible with LTPS. However, ELA technology is quite expensive in capital as well as operating costs. We have been working on alternatives to ELA for LTPS [1,2] for many years. In our approach, metal-induced crystallization (MIC) as well as solid-phase crystallization (SPC) LTPS are used. The crystallization of amorphous silicon is performed simply by heat treatment. But conventional MIC and SPC devices have poor performance. To improve the electrical properties of these devices, we add "bridged" structures to bridge the grains in the active channel of the TFT. With these BG lines, the threshold voltage is reduced, the on–off ratio and the mobility are increased significantly. Some of the improvement is due to short channel effects in the TFT. BG-MIC is indeed a viable alternative to ELA. We shall discuss some recent results on BG technique in this talk.

1. References

[1] S. Zhao, Z. Meng, W. Zhou, J. Ho, M. Wong, H.-S. Kwok, "Bridged-grain polycrystalline silicon thin-film transistors", IEEE Trans. Electron Devices, Vol. **60**, pp. 1965–1970, 2013.

[2] M. Zhang, W. Zhou, R. Chen, M. Wong, H.-S. Kwok, "Characterization of DC-stress-induced degradation in bridged-grain polycrystalline silicon thin-film transistors", IEEE Trans. Electron Devices, Vol. **61**, pp. 3205–3212, 2014.

Paper No S9.2: Segmented Electrochromic Display Demonstrator Showing Long-Term Switching Stability

Julian Remmele,[1] D. Eric Shen,[2] Tero Mustonen,[2] and Norbert Fruehauf[1]

[1]Institute for Large Area Microelectronics, University of Stuttgart, 70569 Stuttgart, Germany, E-mail: igm@igm.uni-stuttgart.de; [2]BASF SE, 67056 Ludwigshafen, Germany

Abstract

This work describes the manufacture and performance of an electrochromic display with solution-based processing. The presented process yields devices with very high life times of more than 100,000 cycles even when switched asymmetrically (with respect to time).

1. Introduction

During the last few years, there have been many advances in the field of organic electrochromic polymers (ECPs). Most of the ECP-based displays constructed up to this point in the literature have been window-type devices. Segmented displays [1,2] have also been demonstrated for use in simple low-power information-type displays as well as active-matrix displays for use in applications such as electronic readers [3–5]. In this work, a high-performance segmented clock display was fabricated with a PProDOT-based ECP that is magenta in its neutral and transparent in its oxidized state. The presented display is an all-solid state device achieving lifetimes of greater than 100,000 switching cycles.

2. Process

Figure 1 illustrates the setup of the electrochromic display described in this work. Indium tin oxide (ITO) electrodes are sputtered onto glass substrates and structured by photolithography. Afterwards SU-8 wells are spin coated and structured. This layer later embeds the electrolyte and acts as a passivation for underlying ITO tracks. Then, a negative tone photo resist is used as a mask for the spray coated ECP layer. Regions other than the segments are removed by lifting off the photo resist. A front plane is then laminated onto the substrate thereby also depositing the electrolyte into the individual SU-8 wells. The front plane consists of a PES foil with a layer of ITO and a spray-coated layer of a minimally color changing polymer (MCCP) that acts as the charge storage layer in the electrochemical cell and is oxidized prior to the cell assembly.

3. Result and Discussion

3.1. Performance

The devices were evaluated based on their electrochemical, spectroelectrochemical, and kinetic switching speed performance. Cyclovoltammetric (CV), switching speed and spectral measurements were taken after 0, 25,000, 100,000, and 200,000 switching cycles of the display. While the performance of symmetrically switched displays (i.e. one cycle equals 3.3 s magenta, 3.3 s transparent) easily exceeded 200,000 cycles (see Figure 2), asymmetrically switched displays (i.e., remains longer in one state than in the other, e.g., 6 s magenta, 3 s transparent or vice versa), that

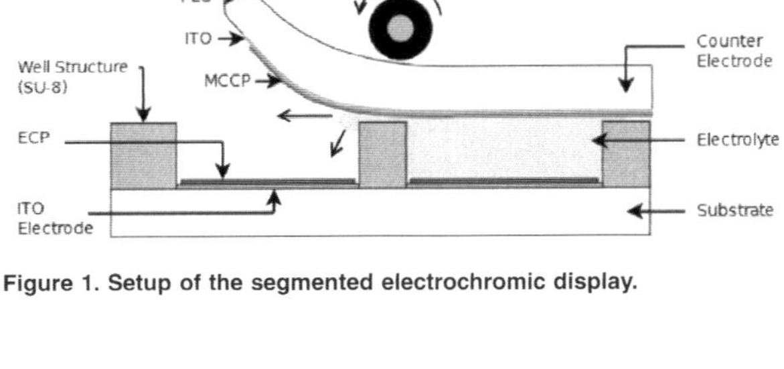

Figure 1. Setup of the segmented electrochromic display.

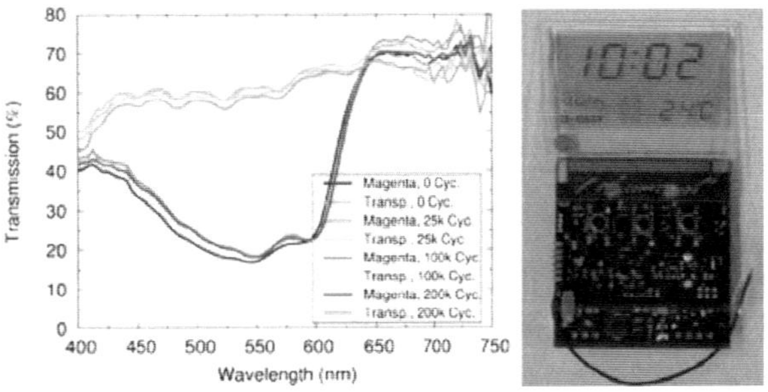

Figure 2. Spectra of symmetrically switched ECP device after 0, 25,000, 100,000, and 200,000 cycles (left) and picture of clock demonstrator (right).

are more similar to an actual application (e.g., for a clock), showed heavier degradation. Especially displays that were switched longer to their oxidized (transparent) state (i.e., one cycle is 3.3 magenta and 6.6 s transparent) degraded heavily. While lower driving voltages did resolve this issue and enabled more than 100,000 cycles, switching speeds decreased.

3.2. Clock Demonstrator

While testing was done in a laboratory environment, to demonstrate the display's capabilities a demonstrator PCB was fabricated that can run the display as a clock (see Figure 2).

4. Acknowledgements

The authors gratefully acknowledge financial support from the German Ministry of Education and Research (BMBF) within the project KOSADIS (FKZ 13N10766).

5. References

[1] N. Vlachopoulos N. Jarl, M. Martin, B. Alain, C. David, G. Christian, L. Nigel, M. Ralf, P. Francois, R. Michael, "Electrochemical aspects of display technology based on nanostructured titanium dioxide with attached viologen chromophores" Electrochim. Acta Vol. **53**, pp. 4065–4071, 2008.

[2] Berggren, M., G. G. Malliaras, R. M. Owens, in Organic Semiconductors in Sensor Applications, Chap. 9, edited by D. A. Bernards, R. Owens, G. Malliaras Springer: Berlin, Heidelberg, Germany, 2008, pp 263–280.

[3] Chung, D. S., J. W. Kim, Y. J. Yi, M. H. Jung, C. H. Noh, S. J. Jeon, R. R. Das, B. G. Song, J. Y. Wan, S. Y. Lee, "4.8" QVGA electrochromic displays driven by oxide TFTs", Dig. Tech. Pap.—Soc. Inf. Disp. Int. Symp. Vol. **41**, pp. 1640–1642, 2010.

[4] Yashiro, T., S. Hirano, Y. Naijoh, Y. Okada, K. Tsuji, M. Abe, A. Murakami, H. Takahashi, K. Fuijmura, H. Kondoh, "Novel design for color electrochromic display" Dig. Tech. Pap.—Soc. Inf. Disp. Int. Symp. Vol. **42**, pp. 42–45, 2011.

[5] Kawahara, J., P. A. Ersman, D. Nilsson, K. Katoh, Y. Nakata, M. Sandberg, M. Nilsson, G. Gustafsson, M. Berggren, "Flexible active matrix addressed displays manufactured by printing and coating techniques", J. Polym. Sci., Part B: Polym. Phys., Vol. **51**, 265–271, 2013.

Paper No S9.3: 3-D Grayscale Images Generation on Optically Rewritable Electronic Paper

W. Zhang, J. Sun, A. K. Srivastava, V. G. Chigrinov, and H. S. Kwok

Partner State Key Laboratory (PSKL) on Advanced Displays and Optoelectronics Technologies, Department of Electronic and Computer Engineering, Hong Kong University of Science & Technology, Clear Water Bay, Hong Kong, E-mail: Derek19890615@gmail.com

Abstract

Optically Rewritable Electronic Paper (ORW E-Paper) is based on the optically addressed bi-stable display which needn't any power to display the image after being uploaded. In this article, we disclose an easy and practical method to generate 3-D grayscale images on the ORW E-Paper by using a grating mask and printed transparent films and written by polarized blue LED light.

1. Introduction

Optically Rewritable (ORW) technology is a modified method of azo-dye photo-alignment that possesses traditional high azimuthal anchoring energy and has a unique feature of reversible in-plane aligning direction reorientation. It gives possibilities to deposit all electronic elements separately from plastic card and for changing information on display using 450 nm LED light direct writing on display by optical method. Written information on display can be saved for long time without any extra power supply [1].

Several methods to generate 3-D patterns on ORW E-Paper have already been proposed. In this letter, we show a method which has high potential to display 8 bits grayscale 3-D images on ORW E-Paper [2].

2. 3-D Grayscale Images Display

2.1. Grayscale Generation

Based on the working principle of inkjet printers, dots sizes are controlled to perform different gray levels: the larger dot size, the darker of the pixel is shown on the paper. Grayscale images can be printed by this kind of binary methods which could be good masks for writing patterns on ORW E-Paper by blue led light (shown in Figure 1).

2.2. 3-D Effect Generation

The concept is based on the generation of two opposite handedly circularly polarized light for the two different images for left and right eye of the observer. In this respect, two domains with twist angle +45° and −45°, with respect to the easy axis of the optically passive alignment layer, have been created. Thus the light passing through these domains followed by quarter-wave plate (QWP) becomes right-handed circularly polarized (RCPL) and left-handed circularly polarized light (LCPL) that can be discriminated by the polarizing glasses.

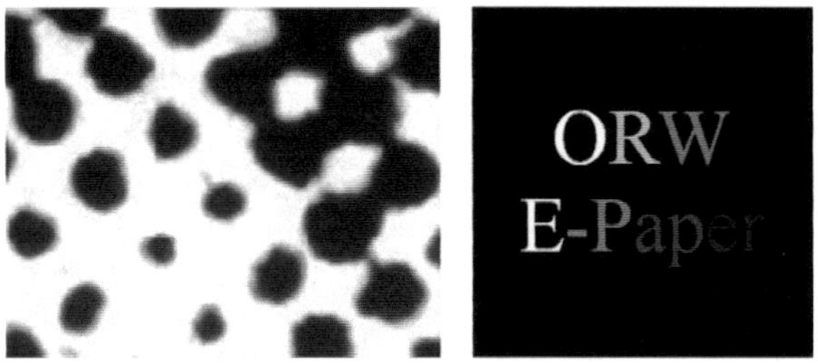

Figure 1. Dots on ORW E-Paper & grayscale image mask.

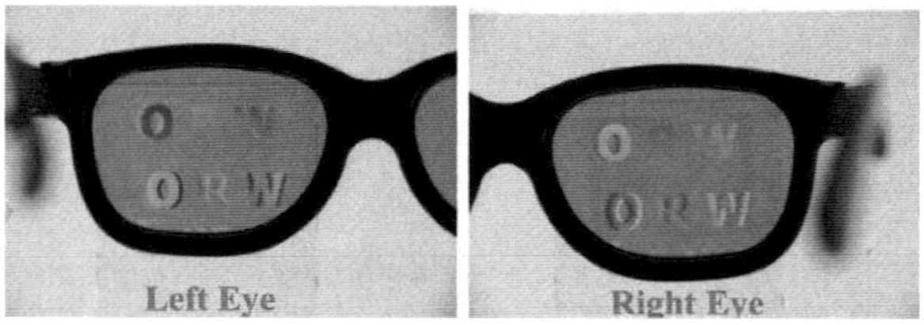

Figure 2. 3-D effect with polarizing glasses.

After passing through the QWP, the output light takes the form:

$$\vec{E_{out}} = \begin{pmatrix} 1 & 0 \\ 0 & \exp\left(-i\frac{\pi}{2}\right) \end{pmatrix} \begin{bmatrix} cos\theta \\ sin\theta \end{bmatrix} = \begin{bmatrix} cos\theta \\ -isin\theta \end{bmatrix}$$

When $\theta = \pi/4$, $-\pi/4$ and 0, the output light is $\frac{1}{\sqrt{2}}\begin{bmatrix} 1 \\ -i \end{bmatrix}$ (LCPL), $\frac{1}{\sqrt{2}}\begin{bmatrix} 1 \\ -i \end{bmatrix}$ (RCPL), $\begin{bmatrix} 1 \\ 0 \end{bmatrix}$ (linearly polarized light), respectively.

3. Methodology

We can start to write the 3-D image on the cell following steps below:

1. Expose the cell under the polarized LED light at +45° with the mask to write left eye image on the ORW E-Paper cell;
2. Erase the cell to 0° with 100 μm grating in order to write right eye image at odd columns. Now we keep left eye image at even columns.
3. Expose the cell to −45° with grating (period 100 μm) and image mask (with a little bit shifted to the even columns pattern) together to rewrite right eye image at odd columns on the ORW E-Paper cell.

Therefore, when we are wearing the polarizing glasses, right eye can only see the right circular polarization of light as the right glass only analyze right circular polarization and vice versa. As left and right eyes obtain similar but position shifted images simultaneously, our brain will generate the 3-D perception (shown in Figure 2).

4. Acknowledgements

This work is supported by HKUST grant ITP/039/12NP.

5. References

[1] A. Muravsky, A. Murauski, X. Li, V. Chigrinov, H. Kwok, "Optical rewritable liquid crystal alignment technology", J. Soc. Inf. Display, Vol. **15**, pp. 267–273, 2007.

[2] J. Sun, A. K. Srivastava, W. Zhang, L. Wang, V. G. Chigrinov, H. S. Kwok, "Optically rewritable 3D liquid crystal displays", Opt. Lett., Vol. **39**, pp. 6209–6212, 2014.

Paper No S9.4: ESHFLCS High-Resolution Display a Better Alternative for the IPS Displays Technology

A. K. Srivastava, V. G. Chigrinov, and H. S. Kwok

State Key Laboratory on Advanced Displays and Optoelectronics Technologies, The Hong Kong University of Science and Technology, Clear Water Bay, Kowloon, Hong Kong

Abstract

In this article, we disclose an ESHFLC display that is characterized by the outstanding optical quality with contrast 10k: 1, response time 10 μs, wide viewing angle, and low driving voltages. Thus, the proposed ESHFLC displays, with simpler fabrication procedure, have great potential and cloud offer better alternatives for the high-resolution displays technology.

1. Introduction

Recently the in-plane switching (IPS), advanced super-dimension switching (ADS), and fringe field switching (FFS) have been heavily exploited for the high-end LCDs because of its wide viewing angle, high-resolution, etc. [1,2] However, several limitation in terms of the image-sticking that arises because of the residual DC (RDC) of the alignment layer, nonuniformity, and loss of light transmittance that occurs at the edge of the pixels due to nonuniform liquid crystal alignment, which is a big problem for high-resolution displays. Additionally, the complex fabrication and manufacturing cost is another challenge for rapidly growing high-resolution smart phone market for which low power consumption is highly desirable.

In Figure 1, the bottom solid red circles represent the response time against the driving voltages. The blue solid circles show optical contrast against the applied frame frequency. The inset represents the electro-optical response of the ESHFLC's.

On the other hand, FLC because of their intrinsic IPS behavior could offer better solution with simpler and cheaper fabrication. The FLC, because of the fast switching speed and low power consumption, is considered to be one of the potential candidates to serve as the building block for the modern high-resolution display devices. However, due to several limitations i.e., geometrical, optical, and mechanical defects, these structures are less popular among the research and industrial regime. Recently, we have established that the nanoscale photoalignment technology could be used to improve characteristics of FLC systems.

In this article, by leveraging potentials of the Nanoscale photoalignment and ESHFLCs, a concept for the LCD has been developed that is characterized by fast electro-optical response, high contrast ratio, wide viewing angle, and less power consumption.

The ESHFLC demands balance between the anchoring energy and the elastic energy of the ESHFLC helix. The photoalignment technology has been used in the present case that offers tunable anchoring energy. [3,4] The contrast ratio dependence of the ESHFLC on the anchoring energy of the alignment layer is shown in Figure 2. For the optimum anchoring energy, we have achieved contrast ratio >10k: 1.

2. Conclusion

The ESHFLC display mode provides a better alternative with extreme optical quality and low power consumption. The driving voltage ~ 1 V/μm is enough to drive the ESHFLC with optimal quality and fast response time ~200 μs. Furthermore the ESHFLC show no sign of degradation in electro-optical performance even after 5 billion of cycles of operation that is roughly equal to the 20 k hours of stress test. Thus ESHFLC display cell (Figure 3) could be a perfect alternative for the high-resolution display.

3. Acknowledgment

The funding for the State Key Laboratory on Advanced Displays and Optoelectronics Technologies are gratefully acknowledged.

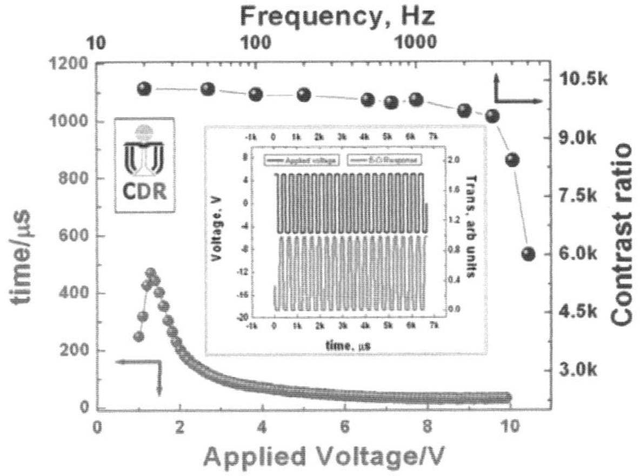

Figure 1. The electro-optical characteristics of the ESHFLC display cell.

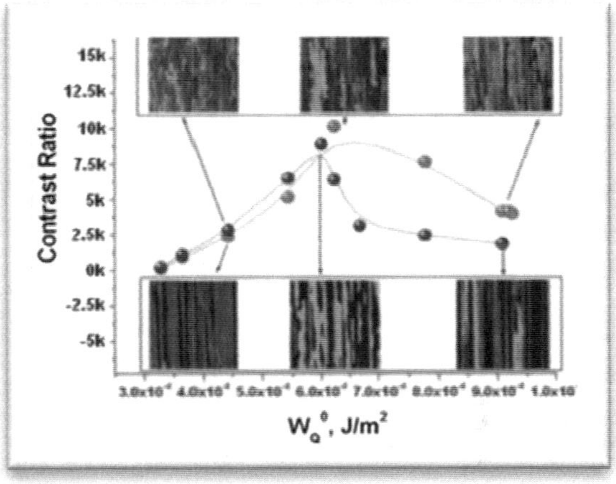

Figure 2. Contrast ratio and texture of FLC cells with different anchoring energies.

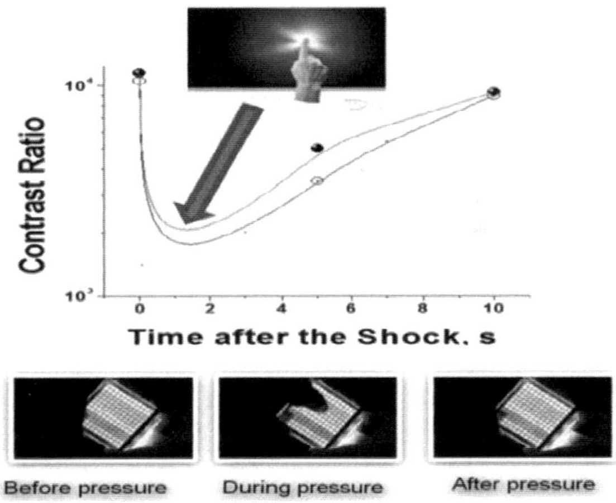

Figure 3. The shock stability of the ESHFLC display cell.

4. References

[1] M. Oh-e, K. Kondo, "Electro-optical characteristics and switching behavior of the in-plane switching mode", Appl. Phys. Lett., Vol. **67**, p. 3895, 1995.

[2] T. Jung, D. Park, J. Park, J. Lee, S. Kim, B. Kim, H. Kim, "Pixel Design Optimization of Fringe-Field Switching Mode for Applying Negative Liquid Crystals in High-Resolution Mobile Displays", J. Disp. Technol., Vol. **11**, No. 3, pp. 229–235, 2015. DOI: 10.1109/JDT.2014.2375823.

[3] V. G. Chigrinov, V. M. Kozenkov, H. S. Kwok, Photoalignment of Liquid Crystalline Materials, Wiley, New Jersey, 2008

[4] A. K. Srivastava, V. G. Chigrinov, H. S. Kwok, "Photo-aligned ferroelectric liquid crystals for modern photonics", SPIE news room Article, 2014. DOI: 10.1117/2.1201412.005595.

Paper No S10.1: Emerging Materials and Processes for Quantum Dots based Display Technology

Haizheng Zhong

Beijing Key Laboratory of Nanophotonics and Ultrafine Optoelectronic Systems, School of Materials Science & Engineering, Beijing Institute of Technology, Beijing 100081, P. R. China, E-mail: hzzhong@bit.edu.cn

Abstract

Quantum dots have size- and composition- tunable photoluminescence and can provide saturated colors for display technology. The use of QDs in display technology strongly relies on the materials science as well as process technique. Here I present some of emerging materials including pervoskite QDs, alloyed nanocrystals and their corresponding process techniques for display applications.

1. Introduction

The incorporation of quantum dots (QDs) into lighting and display technology provide better color quality. Current research work focus on two topics. One is using quantum dots to substitute rare earth phosphors for the fabrication of high color rendering and wide color gamut white lighting-emitting diodes. In the other topic, QDs are sandwiched between electron and hole transport layers for the fabrication of electroluminescence devices with saturated emissions through solution process. Although great success has been made in the past 20 years and there are commercialized products in the market. From the viewpoint of fundamental science and industrial requirements, we still need to develop new materials with low cost at large scale amount, also prefer to use less toxic elements, develop new processing to incorporate QDs into color conversion films or sandwiched devices, design and fabricate new devices with enhanced performance and improved stability. In this presentation, I will present our exploration on graded alloyed $Cd_xZn_{1-x}Te$ QDs, pervoskite QDs, alloyed CdSeS nanowires for display technology.

2. Progress

1. Organometal halide perovskites are inexpensive materials with desirable characteristics of color-tunable and narrow-band emissions for lighting and display technology, but suffering from low photoluminescence quantum yields at low excitation fluencies. Here we developed a ligand-assisted reprecipitation (LARP) strategy to fabricate brightly-luminescent and color-tunable colloidal $CH_3NH_3PbX_3$ (X = Br, I, Cl) quantum dots with absolute quantum yield up to 70% at room temperature and low excitation fluencies. We further demonstrated wide-color gamut white light-emitting diodes using green emissive $CH_3NH_3PbBr_3$ quantum dots and red emissive $K_2SiF_6:Mn^{4+}$ as color converters, providing enhanced color quality (~130% of NTSC 1931 standard with a matching rate of 96%) for display technology.
2. Holography is regarded as a real 3D display technique which can produce all the depth cues without using any special glasses. In holographic display systems, display mediums play a key role in determining the quality of reconstructed images and have been studied intensively in the past years. We describe the concept that employs luminescent hydrogels embedded with QDs as display medium for holographic 3D applications. The QDs and PVA hydrogel composites exhibit very attractive advantages including high transparency, highly saturated color fast response, low cost, simple processability as well as scalable and healable characteristics. PVA hydrogel embedded with QDs can display the computer-generated holograms efficiently (yields emission at a QY of ~40%) and reconstruct 3D visual effects almost instantaneous on laser irradiation.

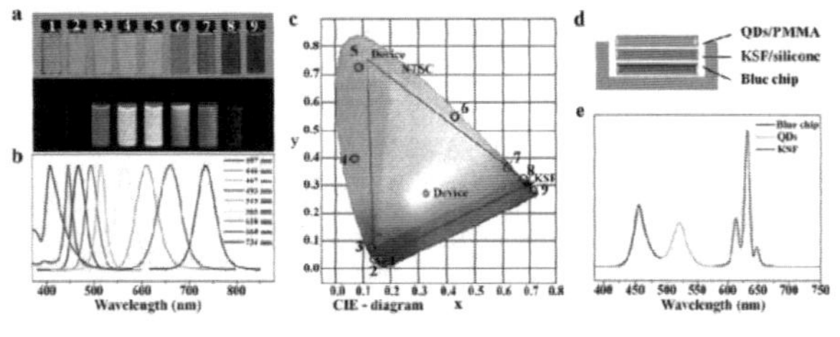

Figure 1. Colloidal $CH_3NH_3PbX_3$ QDs and their use in wide-color gamut pc-WLED devices.

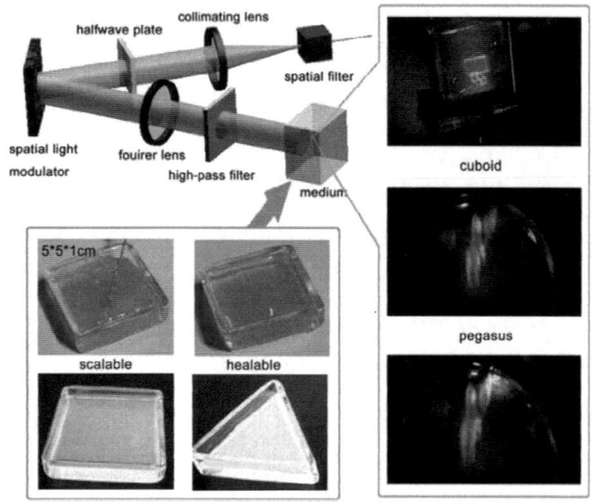

Figure 2. PVA hydrogel embedded with QDs for holographic 3D applications.

3. Acknowledgements

This study was supported by The National Basic Research Program of China (No. 2013CB328804 and 2011CB933600), National Natural Science Foundation of China Grant (No. 21343005), Beijing Nova program (No. xx2014B040).

4. References

[1] Y. Shirasaki, G. J. Supran, M. G. Bawendi, V. Bulovic, "Emergence of Colloidal Quantum-dot Light-emitting Technologies", Nat. Photonics, Vol. **7**, pp. 13–23, 2013.

[2] F. Zhang, H. Z. Zhong, C. Chen, X. G. Wu, X. M. Hu, H. L. Huang, J. B. Han, B. S. Zou, Y. P. Dong, "Brightly-luminescent and color-tunable colloidal CH3NH3PbX3 (X= Br, I, Cl) quantum dots: Potential alternatives for display technology", ACS Nano, Vol. **9**, pp. 4533–4542, 2015.

[3] M. Zhu, H. Z. Zhong, J. Jia, W. P. Fu, J. Liu, B. S. Zou, Y. T. Wang, "PVA Hydrogel Embedded with Quantum Dots: A Potential Scalable and Healable Display Medium for Holographic 3D Applications." Adv. Opt. Mater., Vol. **2**, pp. 338–342, 2014.

Paper No S10.2: Cathodoluminescence Imaging and EELS of Quantum Dot in Rods Excited in a Field Emission Transmission Electron Microscope

George R. Fern,[1] Jack Silver,[1] Terry G. Ireland,[1] Ashley Howkins,[1] Tobias Jochum,[2] Jan S. Niehaus,[2] Frank Schröder-Oeynhausen,[1] and Horst Weller[1]

[1]Centre for Phosphors and Display Materials, Wolfson Centre for Materials Processing, Brunel University London, Uxbridge, Middlesex, UB8 3PH, United Kingdom, E-mail: george.fern@brunel.ac.uk; [2]Centrum für Angewandte Nanotechnologie (CAN) GmbH, Grindelallee 117, 20146 Hamburg

Abstract

Red light filtered cathodoluminescent (CL) imaging and chemical spectroscopy are combined with STEM imaging to analyze CdSe/CdS core/shell quantum dot in rods. Shape and uniformity is shown in conjunction with the location of the selenide containing cores.

1. Introduction

CdSe quantum dots with an elongated shell of CdS, the so called quantum rods or dot-in-rod (DR) offer potential efficiency improvements in display backlighting [1]. DRs are able to emit directional and polarized light which means their use in backlighting for liquid crystal displays is an obvious candidate for investigation. Previously we have been unable to obtain electron energy loss data in support of our scanning transmission electron microscopy (STEM) and simultaneous CL data due to machine setup that was required but are now in a position to show that data.

The objective of this work was to:

Add to our portfolio of CL imaging data for luminescent materials with supplementary evidence supplied from EELS data and demonstrate how the DRs vary from particle to particle.

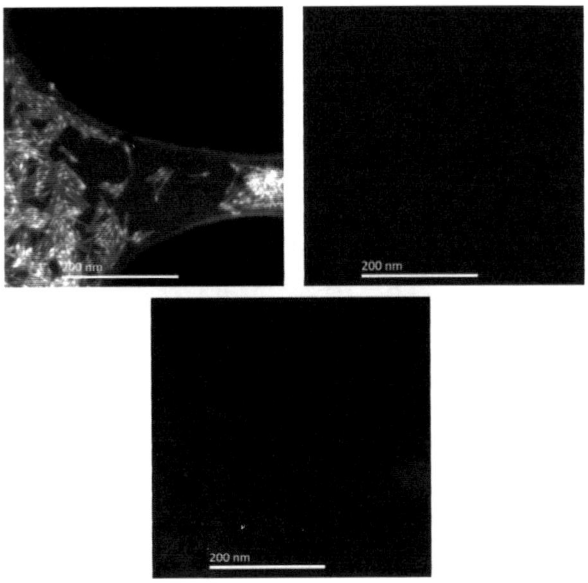

Figure 1. (Top left) Dark Field STEM image, (top right) 625(50) nm energy filtered CL image, (bottom) overlay of the above images.

2. Results and Discussion

The HAADF STEM image is shown in Figure 1 (top left) and the DRs are observed with a rod-like shape. In Figure 1 (top right), the cathodoluminescent image is shown that was collected simultaneously with 1 (top left) and a large number of the DRs are seen to be weakly CL emissive. CL emission is seen when the electron beam is near to the rod or if the beam contacts the dot before the rod (see Figure 1 bottom). Our prior work on DRs [2], quantum dots [3], and nano-phosphors [4], using this TEM-CL technique show perfect overlap of the DF STEM and CL images. As shown previously, the DRs show emission that perfectly aligns with the STEM image, however the particles are highly beam sensitive, even at temperatures near to 100K. Hence the CL emission is rapidly lost and therefore the emission is not always observed from the dot as observed for other materials that we have studied.

Thickness is taken into account and the DRs are analyzed using electron energy loss spectroscopy to identify the location of the selenide cores and to show the significance of these selenide containing regions in conjunction with the observable CL emission. Hence the previously postulated evidence based on STEM contrast is added to.

3. Conclusions

Cathodoluminescence light is observed from individual DRs and combined with chemical data to directly show the influence of the dot in rod significance.

4. Acknowledgements

We are grateful to the EPSRC and the TSB for funding the PURPOSE (TP11/MFE/6/I/AA129F; EPSRC TS/G000271/1) and CONVERTED (JeS no. TS/1003053/1) programs.

5. References

[1] "Merck on Quantum Rod-based Displays, Dertinger, S., Interview with N. Tanaka, Nikkei Electronics", May 8, 2014, Available at http://techon.nikkeibp.co.jp/english/NEWS_EN/20140508/350462/?P=1, accessed on June 25, 2014.

[2] G. R. Fern, J. Silver, T. Jochum, J. S. Niehaus, F. Schröder-Oeynhausen, H. Weller, "Red quantum rods under the electron microscope", Proc. IDW, MEET1-3, 2014.

[3] G. R. Fern, J. Silver, S. Coe-Sullivan, "Cathodoluminescence and electron microscopy of red quantum dots used for display applications", JSID, 2015. DOI: 10.1002/jsid.278.

[4] G.R. Fern, X. Yan, N. Wilkinson, J. Silver, "Cathodoluminescence spectra of single $Gd_2O_2S:Tb^{3+}$ nanometer sized phosphor crystals excited in a field emission scanning transmission electron microscope", Proc. IDW, pp. 820–822, 2013.

Paper No S10.3: Efficiency Enhancement of InP-Based Inverted QD-LEDs by Polyethylenimine-Modified Al:ZnO Layer

Yohan Kim, Christian Ippen, and Armin Wedel

Functional Materials and Devices, Fraunhofer Institute for Applied Polymer Research, Geiselbergstr. 69, 14476 Potsdam, Germany, E-mail: yohan.kim@iap.fraunhofer.de

Read the full article at DOI: 10.1002/jsid.322

Abstract

In this paper, we report efficiency enhancement of indium phosphide (InP) quantum dot-based light-emitting diodes (QD-LEDs) using polyethylenimine (PEI) surface modifier. Adapting solution processed PEI layer on top of the aluminum-doped zinc oxide (Al:ZnO) nanoparticle (NP) layer, the leakage current of inverted device was suppressed and electron injection into conduction band of InP/ZnSe/ZnS QDs also facilitated by interfacial dipoles of thin PEI layer. As a results, the current efficiency was dramatically increased from 0.07 cd/A to 2.84 cd/A.

1. Introduction

Over the past several years, colloidal quantum dots (QDs)-based light-emitting diodes (QD-LEDs) has been actively researched due to the potential impacts to the display and lighting industry base on the unique properties of QDs itself such as size-controllable color tunability by the quantum confinement effect, narrow bandwidth of emission, and low-cost solution-based processing. The performance of QD-LEDs has been increased enough to compete with phosphorescent OLEDs (PHOLEDs) by the combination of various device structure and the efficient emitting materials [1]. However, most of promising results used cadmium (Cd) contained II-VI semiconductor nanocrystals. Therefore, a prominent future task is the substitution of Cd-containing QDs with less toxic materials. InP-based QDs is a promising material among the III-V semiconductor nanocrystals [2]. Since organic-inorganic hybrid structure has better device performance, zinc oxide (ZnO) nanoparticle (NP) charge transport layer has a lot of attention due to the advantage of device stability and easy preparation process [1]. Here, we investigated the performance of inverted QD-LEDs fabricated with synthesized InP/ZnSe/ZnS QDs and commercially available aluminum doped ZnO (Al:ZnO) NP. The device efficiency was over 40 times increased by applying polyethylenimine (PEI) interfacial layer, widely used in organic electronics to modify interfacial condition mainly work function [3], between Al:ZnO and QD layer.

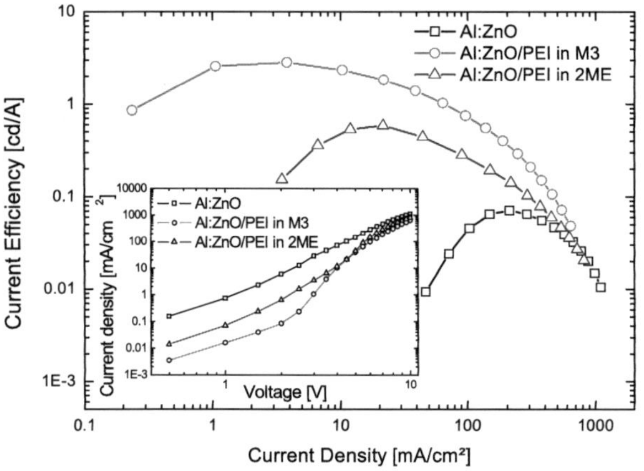

Figure 1. Current efficiency-current density characteristics of QD-LEDs (inset: current density-voltage characteristics).

2. Experimental

The InP/ZnSe/ZnS muitishell QDs were synthesized by heating-up method simple and reproducible compared to conventional hot-injection method [2]. The inverted devices were fabricated with the fallowing structure; ITO/Al:ZnO/QDs/TCTA/MoO_3/Ag. First, Al:ZnO NP (Nanograde N-10x, 2 wt % in IPA) was spin-coated on cleaned ITO substrate at 3000 rpm for 30 s fallowed by drying at 120°C for 10 min as electron transport layer. Then, dispersed QDs in nonane were spin-coated on the Al:ZnO layer at 3000 rpm for 20 s. TCTA as hole transport layer (HTL) and MoO_3/Ag as anode layer were thermally evaporated. PEI (Fluka analytical, 50% (W/V) in H_2O) diluted in in 2-methoxyethanol (2ME) or alcoholic mixture M3 (IPA, Ethanol) was spin-coated at 3000 rpm for 30 sec fallowed by drying at 120°C for 10 min before the QD deposition. A spectroradiometer (Minolta CS-2000) and source meter (Keithley SMU 236) were used to detect EL spectrum as well as current density-voltage-luminance (J-V-L) characteristic. Surface roughness was investigated by atomic force microscope (AFM, Nanosurf Easyscan-2)

3. Results and Discussion

Applying thin PEI layer from different solvent, maximum current efficiency was increased from 0.07 cd/A to 2.84 cd/A. The leakage current was also suppressed and turn-on voltage also reduced from 3 V to 2.5 V (inset of Figure 1). The leakage current was decreased due to the surface roughness of Al:ZnO layer (R_q = 7.41 nm/R_{pv} = 57.35) was modified by PEI layer (R_q = 6.34 nm/R_{pv} = 51.63 and R_q = 5.70 nm/R_{pv}=46.39, 2ME and M3 solvent, respectively). As a result, the current efficiency was dramatically enhanced because thin PEI interfacial layer modified the surface roughness of Al:ZnO layer and reduced energy barrier from the conduction band of Al:ZnO to that of QDs by lowing work function of Al:ZnO layer through interfacial dipole effects. With further investigation, the performance of InP-based QD-LEDs would be more improved by optimizing the surface roughness of each layer and charge balance in multi-layered system.

4. Acknowledgements

The authors thank the "Deutsche Forschungsgemeinschaft" SPP 1708 for financial support and Mr. Christopher Pries for helps in synthesis.

5. References

[1] B. S. Mashford, M. Stevenson, Z. Popovic, C. Hamilton, Z. Zhou, C. Breen, J. Steckel, V. Bulovic, M. Bawendi, S. Coe-Sullivan, P. T. Kazlas, "High-efficiency quantum-dot light-emitting devices with enhanced charge injection", Nat. Photonics, Vol. **7**, pp. 407–142, 2013.

[2] C. Ippen, T. Greco and A. Wedel, "InP/ZnSe/ZnS: A novel multishell system for InP quantum dots for improved luminescence efficiency and its application in a light-emitting device", J. Inf. Display, Vol. **13**, pp. 91–95, 2012.

[3] Y. Zhou, C. Fuentes-Hernandez, J. Shim, J. Meyer, A. J. Giordano, H. Li, P. Winget, T. Papadopoulos, H. Cheun, J. Kim, M. Fenoll, A. Dindar, W. Haske, E. Najafabadi,T. M. Khan, H. Sojoudi, S. Barlow, S. Graham, J. L. Brédas, S. R. Marder, A. Kahn, B. Kippelen, "A universal method to produce low–work function electrodes for organic electronics", Science, Vol. **336**. pp. 327–332, 2012.

Paper No S10.4: Transmission Electron Microscope Study of Symmetry-related Transitions in Cubic $Y_2O_3:Tb^{3+}$

Daniel den Engelsen, George R. Fern, Terry G. Ireland, Paul G. Harris, and Jack Silver

Centre for Phosphor and Display Materials, Wolfson Centre for Materials Processing, Brunel University London, Uxbridge, Middlesex, UB8 3PH, United Kingdom, E-mail: jack.silver@brunel.ac.uk

Abstract

In this paper, we describe measurements of the cathodoluminescence of nanosized cubic $Y_2O_3:Tb^{3+}$ with a transmission electron microscope. From the CL-spectra we determined the energy flow from excited Tb^{3+} in a S_6 lattice site to Tb^{3+} in a C_2 site.

1. Introduction

The industrial applications of yttrium oxide doped with europium or terbium have stimulated scientists to investigate the energy flow in these materials upon excitation by electrons or UV-radiation. For cubic $Y_2O_3:Eu^{3+}$ a symmetry-related energy flow scheme was proposed in the 1980s [1,2], while we have recently proposed such a scheme for $Y_2O_3:Tb^{3+}$ [3]. The complicated nature of the spectrum of $Y_2O_3:Tb^{3+}$ impedes the assignment of the transitions in the $^4D_5 \rightarrow {}^7F_J$ (where J = 2, 3, 4, 5, and 6) clusters. Y_2O_3 doped with various concentrations of Tb^{3+} and annealed at temperatures above 950°C has the cubic structure of the mineral bixbyite. This cubic structure has two different Y^{3+} lattice sites, which possess the point symmetries C_2 and S_6: 24 lattice sites have C_2 symmetry, while the other 8 have S_6 symmetry [1–3]. From the concentration dependency of a few spectral lines of $Y_2O_3:Tb^{3+}$ we could assign these as being S_6; the majority of the spectral lines has C_2 symmetry [3]. The strongest S_6 line in the $Y_2O_3:Tb^{3+}$ spectrum is located in the $^4D_5 \rightarrow {}^7F_5$ cluster at 544.4 nm. This line and the strong C_2 line at 542.8 nm were the main targets for an in-depth investigation with the transmission electron microscope (TEM) of Brunel University, which is equipped with a cathodoluminescent attachment [4].

2. Experiments and results

The nanometre sized $Y_2O_3:Tb^{3+}$ phosphor particles were synthesized by the urea method described in our earlier work [3]. The TEM, model 2100F, JEOL, Japan, was equipped with a Vulcan™ CL detector, Gatan, USA, for imaging and spectroscopic purposes. By collecting the visible light with the Vulcan system simultaneously with the JEOL high angle annular dark field detector it was possible to study the visible light that was emitted from the particles. A small cryostat connected to the sample holder enabled cooling of the samples in the TEM down to 103 K (−170°C); adjustment of the sample temperature anywhere between 102 and 303 K could be made.

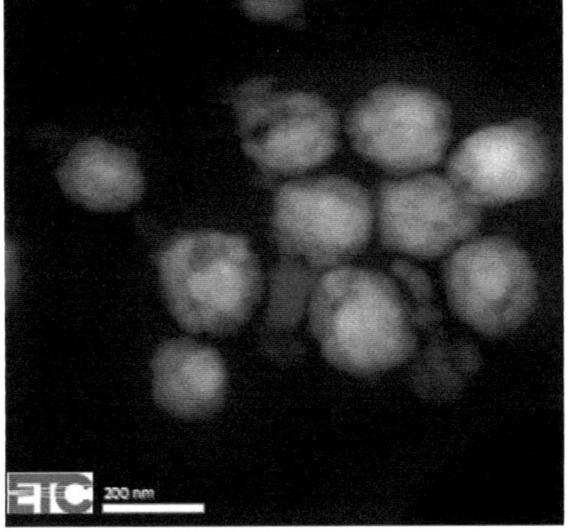

Figure 1. Panchromatic image of 0.1%$Y_2O_3:Tb^{3+}$.

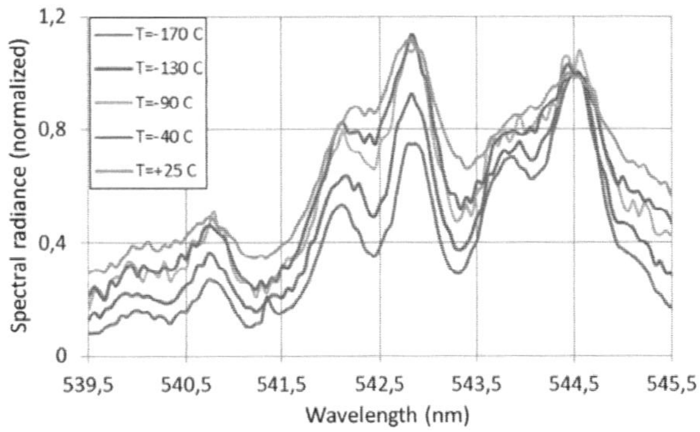

Figure 2. CL spectra (TEM) of 1% $Y_2O_3:Tb^{3+}$ at various temperatures.

Figure 1 shows a panchromatic image of the CL emitted by 0.1% $Y_2O_3:Tb^{3+}$ at −171.3°C and beam energy of 200 keV. The particle size varied from 130 to 200 nm. It can be seen that the particles consist of smaller crystallites, which have dimensions of about 40 nm. Figure 2 shows CL spectra of 1% $Y_2O_3:Tb^{3+}$ ($^5D_4 \rightarrow {}^7F_5$) at various temperatures. The lines at 542.8 and 544.4 nm are split at low temperatures: at low temperature the vibronic broadening of the lines becomes less pronounced. In the paper, we shall discuss the effects of temperature and concentration on the spectral properties and we shall present a model for the energy flow from excited Tb^{3+} ions at S_6 sites to Tb^{3+} at C_2 sites.

3. Conclusions

Detailed analyses of the concentration and temperature dependence of the CL spectra of $Y_2O_3:Tb^{3+}$ has enabled the assignment of a few S6 lines in the spectrum. It also enabled the determination of the energy flow from excited Tb^{3+} ions at S_6 sites to Tb^{3+} at C_2 sites.

4. References

[1] M. Buijs, A. Meyerink, G. Blasse, "Energy Transfer between Eu^{3+} Ions in a Lattice with two Different Crystallographic Sites: $Y_2O_3:Eu^{3+}$, $Gd_2O_3:Eu^{3+}$ and Eu_2O_3", J. Lumin., Vol. **37**, pp. 9–20, 1987.

[2] D. B. M. Klaassen, R. A. M. van Ham, T. G. M. van Rijn, "Energy transfer processes in yttrium oxide activated with europium", J. Lumin., Vol. **43**, pp. 261–274, 1989.

[3] D. den Engelsen, P. G. Harris, T. G. Ireland, G. Fern, J. Silver, "Symmetry-related transitions in the spectrum of nanosized cubic $Y_2O_3:Tb^{3+}$", ECS J. Solid State Sci. Technol., Vol. **4**, pp. R105–R113, 2015.

[4] J. Silver, D. den Engelsen, G. R. Fern, P.G. Harris, A. Lipman, T. G. Ireland, "Cathodoluminescence images and spectra of single nanometre sized phosphor crystals excited in a field emission transmission electron microscope", Eurodisplay, Ghent, 2015.

Paper No S11.1: Display-Metrology: A Historical Review

Michael E. Becker

Display-Messtechnik&Systeme, Rottenburg am Neckar, Germany, E-mail: mB@display-messtechnik.de

Abstract

This article sketches the winding path of the art of measurement of LC-display contrast and other visual properties versus viewing direction from the beginnings of LCD-manufacturing in the 1970s until today. It describes two methods of directional scanning: conoscopy—an optical approach without moving parts—and gonioscopy, the motorized scanning of the range of directions of interest, and introduces their features and limitations and a range of instrumental implementations.

1. The Early Stage: Foundations

When the French crystallographer Charles-Victor Mauguin, during his research on the liquid crystals of Lehmann ("sur les cristaux liquides de Lehmann" [1]) carried out observations on twisted structures ("... des lames à structure hélicoïdale de propriétés vraiment fort curieuses.") in convergent light ("... en lumiere convergente") this was an important moment for both liquid crystal display technology and for display metrology. During his meticulous experiments, he discovered that the rotation of polarization of light is following the twist of the LC-director through the layer which later on became the basis for the twisted-nematic cell (TN-cell, aka. Schadt-Helfrich cell) and he used an optical technique for determination of the orientation of the optical axes ("observation en lumiere convergente") that six decades later became the basis for a range of instruments for measurement of directional effects related to display devices.

The microscopic technique used by Mauguin for determination of the orientation of the optical axes of his liquid crystal samples (*conoscopy*) has been described earlier by Mallard, then improved by Becke and Wright. It later turned out that "the dark areas in the conoscopic image of an LCD directly show the angular field of view where good contrast is obtained" [2] as Kmetz states in his contribution to the SID Conference in 1978.

2. The Second Stage: LCD Manufacturing

In the later 1970s when the first TN LCDs have been researched and manufactured in Europe by companies such as BBC, Philips, AEG, Siemens, and others, the need for detailed characterization and evaluation of the annoying variations of contrast of TN-LCDs with viewing direction became obvious.

In a first step, arrangements with movable light sources and/or receivers have been improvised in several laboratories to provide some results, and later, the polarization microscope in the conoscopic mode of observation (despite its limitations concerning the angular range of measurement) became the most widespread instrument used for analysis of the variation of transmittance and contrast versus viewing direction. Conoscopy made direct visual observation of the directions image possible ("conoscopic observation allows the whole field of view to be seen at once"[2]), but quantitative measurements vs. direction required special modifications of the microscope [2]. A more straight-forward and analytical way to analyze the viewing-direction-dependent optical properties of TN-cells, those days mostly operated in the reflective mode, as a function of the direction of observation was proposed by Barna in 1976 [3] in form of a simple mechanical device comprising two rotational stages for alignment of a microscope with respect to the display to be measured.

In the year 1977, the German physicist Kurt Fahrenschon [4] felt the urgent need for an instrument to support his optimization of the TN-effect and so he motivated a group of engineers at the University of Karlsruhe to realize a motorized scanning system for his laboratory work. The resulting apparatus together with the first contrast-contour plots in the polar coordinate system of the conoscopic directions image was featured in the first issue of the Displays Journal in 1979 [5]. That device for automated motorized scanning of the viewing cone up to 60° inclination under diffuse illumination turned out to be the starting point for a family of instruments used for R&D as well as CQ purposes all around the globe since then. These devices display measurement system (DMS) finally comprised a range of features for measurement of all electro-optical and colorimetric characteristics of light emitting, transmitting, and reflecting displays as a function of electrical driving, viewing direction, and temperature.

While motorized scanning remained unrivaled state-of-the art for a couple of years, the availability of affordable CCD-cameras in the late 1980s stimulated considerations at the University of Karlsruhe on advanced conoscopic methods with evaluation of the recorded directions images [6]. Another big step forward in the same direction was made by introduction of a conoscopic lens with an acceptance angle of 120° and a measurement field of 2 mm diameter by Leroux during the Eurodisplay Conference 1993 in Strasbourg [7]. Even though the initial exaltation on this achievement provoked claims, that instruments based on mechanical scanning would all soon be replaced by conoscopic devices, instruments of both types co-exist on the market since then, each having specific advantages and limitations as will be described in this contribution.

3. The Third Stage: Commercialization of Display Metrology

Complex instruments for measurement of the variations of optical properties of electronic display screens (e.g., TV and portable devices) vs. viewing direction and temperature are being assembled by specialized companies all around the globe as will be detailed in this article. The inglorious role of standards in commercial competition in the LCD field will be explained.

4. References

[1] Ch. Mauguin, "Sur les cristaux liquides de Lehman", Bull. Soc. Fr. Miner., Vol. **34**, pp. 71–117, 1911.

[2] A. R. Kmetz, "Characterization and optimization of twisted nematic displays for multiplexing", SID Digest, Vol. **9**, pp. 70–71, 1978.

[3] G. G. Barna, "Apparatus for optical characterization of displays", Rev. Sci. Instrum., Vol. **47**, pp. 1250–1260, 1976.

[4] K. Fahrenschon, H. Gruler, F. Schiekel, "Deformation of a pretilted nematic liquid crystal layer in an electric field", Appl. Phys. B, Vol. **11**, pp. 67–74, 1976.

[5] R. Cremers, P. M. Knoll, D. A. Mlynski, K. Fahrenschon, "A new method for the characterization and evaluation of the optical appearance of reflective TN-LCD's", Displays, Vol. **1**, pp. 12–16, 1979.

[6] M. Fritsch, G. Haas, H. Wöhler, D. A. Mlynski, "Faster contrast measurement of LCDs with improved conoscopic methods", The 9th International Display Research Conference,, Kyoto, Japan, pp. 372–375, 1989.

[7] T. Leroux, "Fast contrast vs. viewing angle measurements for LCDs", Conference on IDRC 1993 Digest, pp. 447–450.

Paper No S11.2: Spectral BRDF and BTDF of Display Optical Components

Pierre Boher, Thierry Leroux, Véronique Collomb-Patton, and Thibault Bignon

ELDIM, 1185 rue d'Epron, Hérouville, France, E-mail: pboher@eldim.fr

Abstract

Liquid-crystal display (LCD) have seen their emissive properties much improved these last years due to many efforts at all the levels of the manufacturing. In this respect, the improvement of the films used inside the LCD structure can be noticed. To go further and answer to new needs like autostereoscopic 3D, the future structures will become more and more complex and realistic computer simulations will become mandatory. In this respect, simulations using theoretical reflective and transmission properties do not lead to realistic results. It becomes mandatory to measure the optical properties of all the optical components as accurately as possible and versus all the parameters (angles but also wavelength).

Measurement of simple optical component can be made using standard spectrophotometers or reflectometers. The introduction of complex films with diffusion or diffraction properties requires measurement of the transmittance and the reflectance at many angles to obtain realistic results in the simulations. The standard method using goniospectrophotometer can be extremely time consuming if medium angular resolution is required.

In 2008, ELDIM has introduced EZContrastMS a Fourier optics viewing angle multispectral system to measure the emissive properties of displays [1]. The system measure the full viewing angle up to 88° versus wavelength thanks to 31 band-pass filters regularly distributed in the visible range every 10 nm. This system also capable to measure the polarization state was used to characterize polarization 3D displays [2].

For reflective measurements, it is necessary to illuminate the sample. In the EZContrastMS system, this possibility is offered using a beam splitter and an additional optics that allows illumination at all the angles easily and accurately [3]. This capacity has been used to measure different types of surfaces and e-papers [3] and to evaluate the outdoor properties of displays [4]. It is in particular possible to illuminate and to measure at the same angle in this system allowing backscattering investigation of cosmetic foundations for example [5].

In this article, we want to show how to obtain full characterization of different display components using this multispectral reflective option and also a new multispectral transmissive option using an additional illumination goniometer. Using these two options, it is possible to measure the spectral BRDF and spectral BTDF of the component at all incidence angles with an excellent angular resolution in reasonable measurement times.

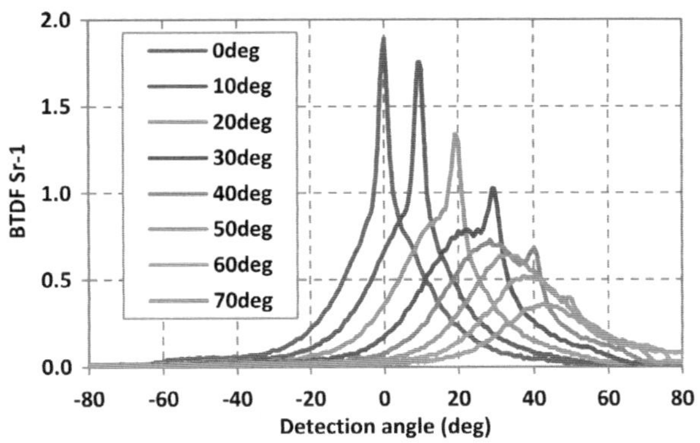

Figure 1. BTDF of a diffusor film measured at 549 nm in the incidence plane for different incidence angles.

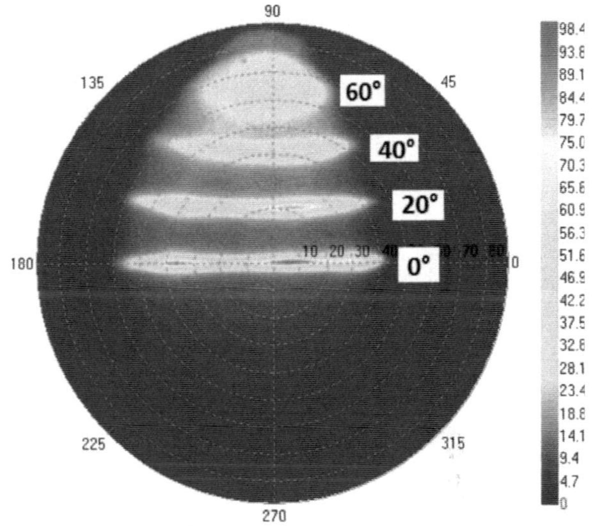

Figure 2. BTDF of a prismatic film at 609 nm with four incidence beams along −90° azimuth.

The BTDF of a simple diffusor film can be for example quite complex as shown in Figure 1. This type of measurement is needed at all the wavelengths in the visible range since the diffusion process is highly wavelength dependent. The capacity to measure outside the incidence plane is also mandatory in this case.

In the case of a prismatic film used classically to enhance the contrast near normal incidence (BEF or brightness enhancement film), the situation is much complex. The overall impact of the film can be measured easily using a full diffused illumination. The spectral BTDF can be also studied to get a better understanding of the internal reflections and the impact of the diffusion for this type of film (cf. Figure 2).

1. References

[1] P. Boher, T. Leroux, T. Bignon, D. Glinel, "New multispectral Fourier optics viewing angle instrument for full characterization of LCDs and their components", SID, Los Angeles, USA, May 18–23, 2008, P89.

[2] P. Boher, T. Leroux, T. Bignon, V. Collomb-Patton, "Multispectral polarization viewing angle analysis of circular polarized stereoscopic 3D displays", Electronic Imaging, SPIE, San Jose, USA, January 18–21, 2010.

[3] P. Boher, T. Leroux, T. Bignon, "Spectral BRDF of color shifting paints and e-papers using multispectral Fourier optics instrument", Eurodisplay, 2011, 7.4.

[4] P. Boher, T. Leroux, T. Bignon, V. Leroux, "Optical measurements for comparison of displays under ambient illumination and simulation of physico-realistic rendering", SID Vehicle Displays And Interfaces, Dearborn, Michigan, October 20–21, 2011.

[5] P. Boher, T. Leroux, L. Cavé, L. Blain, V. Boulier, "Fast spectral reflectance & BRDF measurements of cosmetic foundations and their components", Pigment & Color Science Forum, Montreal, Canada, October 2014.

Paper No S11.3: On the Value and Impact of a Display Measurement Standard

Joe Miseli
JVM Research, San Francisco Area, CA, USA, E-mail: joe.miseli@jvmresearch.com

Abstract

"Standards play an important role in everyday life. ... They can specify performance of products.... They also can define terms so that there is no misunderstanding among those using the standard." [1]

When one wants to buy a display, they have many choices of displays. When they wish to use stated performance characteristics (specification or technical details listing) for the display, they are often filled with omissions, confusing, and sometimes misleading. The correct display measurement standard used properly could help overcome this problem. This paper presents the need for the adoption and adherence to display metrology standards, and uses inconsistencies of the specified characteristics of displays.

1. Specifications in Product Literature

Numerous examples of published display performance items exist that may be misleading and assesses for consistency, proper presentation, and accuracy. Some examples often stated inadequately are contrast, viewing angle, luminance, and response time.

We address response time as one of these examples to demonstrate the lack of clarity and accuracy of advertised display performance characteristics expressed in inconsistent and misleading ways.

Response time, also called total response time or temporal response time, is the time it takes a pixel to change from one luminance level to another. It is usually measured from 10% to 90% luminance levels. It is the sum of the rise and fall times of the level changes. In addition, there exists gray-level (gray-to-gray or g-g) response time. While response time is the sum of the black-white and white-black luminance level changes, gray-to-gray is the time of a single change in level between any two gray levels. The g-g can have up to 256 levels measured for eight-bit/color systems.

Erroneously, g-g and response time are often used interchangeably in specifications making much confusion and inconsistency on their meaning. Table 1 shows an example. It is the summary of response time publications for 20 arbitrary displays exactly as published. It shows inconsistencies and variations with naming conventions, how the values are stated, and terminology for each. Gray-gray response time and regular response time are intermingled. This demonstrates some of the uncertainties about what is published, such as how the items were measured, if they are stated properly what metrics were applied to derive the numeric values, or if they are accurate. Advertisers can state whatever they want for performance values and there is no easy way to know if they are correct. A good standard is needed as a reference to verify their accuracy and legitimacy.

Table 1. Twenty examples of "response time" in product literature

Response time specifications listings		
Naming conventions	Values & description given for each name	Times used
Response Time (Gray to Gray)	7ms	1/20
Response Time	6 ms (gray to gray, avg)	1/20
" "	5 ms (back to white)	1/20
" "	Various: 3.5ms to 16ms	8/20
" "	12 ms ⇐ alt spelling	1/20
" "	5 ms (gray-to-gray)	1/20
Response rate	<20 ms	1/20
Pixel response time (gray to gray)	1 millisecond	1/20

2. Display Standards Today

There are various display standards bodies like ISO, IEC, and CIE that publish standards for display evaluation. Generally they have individual documents for display assessment that must be purchased separately and can be expensive. For example, IEC 61747-30 series for LCD measuring methods cost an average of $316 apiece. The complete IEC 61747 series on LCDs consists of approximately 52 documents up to $359 in price. This makes it quite exclusive and limits its use to all but a select few in professional organizations who can obtain these standards.

The solution is from the ICDM. There is now is a single, comprehensive display measurement and metrology standard from the ICDM with over 140 measurements within a single document. The cost is free as a PDF download [2]. It is called the IDMS1 (Information Display Measurements Standard, version 1) and is the most comprehensive display measurement document yet written, and arguably the most widely-used display measurement standard in publication (Figure 1). Now everyone can have access to a high-end display measurement/metrology standard – from professionals to end users or consumers.

Figure 1. Information Display Measurements Standard, version 1 (IDMS1).

We now have a standard that can be used nonexclusively and can help to produce guidelines for all involved with displays to have a point of reference for their specification listings and measurement methods.

3. Conclusions

There is a lack of usable stated performance characteristics for displays. This is a problem in which the lack of suitable stated performance characteristics published for displays cannot attest to the validity of the values that are stated. A standard is needed against which to reference the specified items and served as a guideline to state both what performance items should be given and how they should be specified.

Most standards for display performance (IEC, ISO, CIE, etc.) are segmented into numerous standards based on specific technologies and measurement or evaluation categories, they are hard to find, are expensive, and are out the reach of most people.

The ICDM has worked to solve these issues and has produced a single display measurement and metrology standard that is comprehensive, complete, well founded, and is free (as a PDF download). This is the IDMS display measurement and metrology standard and can help address the problem of inconsistent, widely varying, and potentially incorrect stated display performance of displays.

All that is missing is a guideline. The ICDM is addressing that.

When the day comes when there is a proper and well-accepted guideline for display advertised performance, saying what to measure, how to measure it, and how to specify it, and we know it is used (e.g. by a logo or statement), one can finally have confidence in published display specifications as reliable tools to help select displays.

4. References

[1] ANSI, Frequently Asked Questions.
[2] ICDM standard: www.icdm-sid.org

Paper No S11.4: High-Accuracy Imaging Colorimeter

Martin Wolf, Jürgen Neumeier, and Richard Young
Instrument Systems, Munich, Germany, E-mail: wolf@instrumentsystems.com

Abstract
We present a new approach to 2D-imaging colorimetry yielding significantly improved measurement accuracy for virtually all sample sources [1]. This approach essentially combines two important innovations. The first is to use a camera equipped with six optical filters instead of the commonly used three or four channels. This clearly improves the fitting to the human eye's color matching function (CMF). However, simply extending the number of filters, i.e. the number of data acquisition channels will not necessarily improve the measurement accuracy. Here we present how the performance of a six filter CCD-camera can be enhanced by the use of an advanced matrix optimization employing a set of 20 training sources. This combination guarantees a clearly better overall performance, which is especially advantageous when it comes to measuring typical LEDs.

1. Introduction

Imaging colorimetry is becoming the routine tool of choice due to its ease of use and potential for making sophisticated automated analysis. Unlike spot colorimeters, exact alignment is often not required and multiple regions may be compared and processed.

Imaging colorimeters provide CIE X, Y, and Z tristimulus values as well as derivative color quantities such as CIE xyz, *u'v'*, *L*a*b**, CCT, etc. In order to match the response to the CIE CMF ($\bar{x}$, $\bar{y}$, $\bar{z}$), colorimeters employ different filters. The $\bar{x}$-CMF has two peaks and thus is often split into two channels to improve the match, that is, four filters are used to represent the three CMFs. Spectral mismatch of the colorimeter responses relative to the CMFs means that the accuracy of measurement varies with the spectrum of the specific device under test (DUT) [2]. The closer the spectra resemble the calibration source the more accurate are the measurements. However, as calibrations are often performed using white incandescent sources, LEDs and colored sources often produce large errors in the measurement. An exception is the matrix correction method, which is used to correct display measurements. In this case, there are generally three primaries of the display that are mixed to give the test color, i.e. there is a limited variation in spectra. This matrix method [3] is frequently applied to such measurements but if the spectrum is completely unknown, still significant errors can occur for the different stimuli.

2. Method

One approach to improve results is the use of two additional filters compensating the errors in the regions where the spectral match of the four filters is worst. The CMF matching can then be enhanced by weighing the channels by the use of a 3 × 6 adaption matrix. However, there are limitations again as the spectral components lying between the wavelength range of the two additional filters still cannot be corrected, which may produce large errors for narrow-banded sources such as LEDs.

However, if the types of spectral sources are anticipated, a set of training sources can be used to determine a transformation that minimizes errors across this set. This means, the spectral responsitivities of the channels are no longer required but knowledge of the tristimulus values of the training sources. In principle, this optimization can be performed for any specific derivative color space or output parameter.

Figure 1 shows the effect of an *xyz* optimization, compared to the CMF optimization [1].

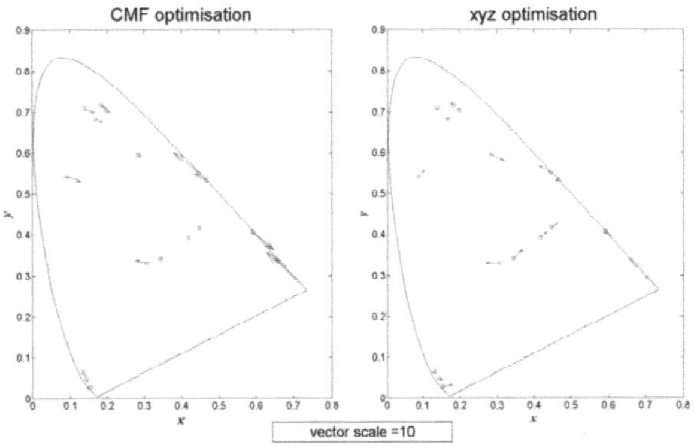

Figure 1. Color difference vector plot of training sources (represented by circles) [1]. For clarity, the vectors are scaled by a factor of 10.

The plot on the left shows the results derived from a least squares matching of the CMFs. Some sources among the training set show large errors (indicated by large vectors) whereas others are rather small. In contrast, the xyz optimization, shown on the right plot, reduces large errors at the expense of the smaller errors. Thus, a significantly better overall performance is obtained.

It has to be noted that this procedure may increase errors of sources that are located outside the training gamut. Therefore, it is important to use a representative set of training sources.

3. Impact

A new approach for imaging photometers and colorimeters is described. Combining an extension of optical filters and an advanced matrix optimization, which is based on a representative set of training sources, clearly improves the overall performance of colorimeters for two-dimensional color measurements of DUTs lying within the gamut of the training sources. Compared to today's standard devices, six-filter cameras optimized by the proposed procedure yield significantly increased accuracy especially for measurements of a variety of different LED colors, without the necessity of recalibrating to specific DUTs.

4. References

[1] R. Young, J. Neumeier, "High accuracy imaging colorimetry", SID Symposium Digest, Vol. **33**. pp. 538–541, 2014.

[2] G. P. Eppeldauer, "Spectral response based calibration method of tristimulus colorimeters", J. Res. Natl. Inst. Stand. Technol., Vol. **103**, p. 615, 1998.

[3] Y. Ohno, J. E. Hardis, "Four-color matrix method for correction of tristimulus colorimeters", Proc., IS&T Fifth Color Imaging Conference, pp. 301–305, 1997.

Paper No S11.5: Colorimetric Evaluation of Directional Variations

Jürgen Neumeier and Michael E. Becker
Instruments Systems GmbH, München, Germany, E-mail: Neumeier@instrumentsystems.com

Abstract
We introduce an approach for measurement of the directional distribution of light scattered during reflection and transmission (i.e. scattering distribution function, SDF) which is based on evaluation of photometric and colorimetric images rather than on mechanical scanning or conventional conoscopic imaging. Planar and cylindrical samples are illuminated by either point light sources or by linear lamps and the lateral distributions of luminance and chromaticity resulting from scattering are recorded by an advanced imaging colorimeter. The SDFs can be used for evaluation of a range of appearance characteristics (e.g. gloss, sheen, luster, clarity, haze, etc.), their chromaticity components can be applied for characterization of media that change color with direction of illumination and observation.

1. Introduction
The directional distribution of light scattered during transmission and reflection can be evaluated by sequential gonio-metric scanning, by conoscopic imaging, by projection on a screen and by catadioptric imaging [1]. These approaches are usually based on complex mechanical goniometer setups, or require arrangements with special optical components (e.g. spherical screens, spherical or elliptical mirrors, complex lens systems, etc.). Alternatively, directional scanning can be realized in the case of planar or cylindrical samples illuminated by point light sources or linear lamps by analysis of the lateral distribution of the scattered light (point-spread or line-spread function, PSF, LSF, respectively, depending on the light source geometry). Such approaches have been reported in 1998 for evaluation of the bidirectional reflectance distribution function (BRDF) of textile fabric (velvet) [2] and of paper [3] in a cylindrical geometry. At the same time display metrologists used to visually explore the reflectance of display screens with a point light source for distinguishing the three main reflection components specular, diffuse and haze [4]. Since the lateral distribution of light reflected from displays under point source illumination obviously contained all required information, the question arose, how such lateral intensity distributions could be transformed into the two-dimensional BRDF. A method for BDRF evaluation of planar display screens under point-source illumination had then been published in 2004 [5].

2. Realization
In this contribution we introduce realizations of a measurement approach for evaluation of the scattering distribution function of transmissive and reflective samples based on high-dynamic range (HDR) imaging colorimetry without mechanical scanning. The following source-sample geometries can be covered: planar samples with point or line-source illumination, cylindrical samples in combination with a linear lamp. The case of planar samples under point source illumination is also suited for rotationally anisotropic samples, the other combinations are limited to isotropic samples. Directional analysis of scattered light is possible with transmissive and reflective samples. A prerequisite for these image-based directional evaluations is the uniformity of the sample properties across the area included in the evaluation. A method for assigning a direction (a set of two spherical coordinates) to each element of the photometric or colorimetric image is described in more detail in [5].

3. Calibration
Since each area element on the sample surface is at a different distance from the light source, even with isotropic emission there is a variation of illuminance across the sample surface. This variation can be recorded with a diffuse white reflectance standard via the reflected luminance and the sample reflectance can be corrected accordingly. A nonscattering mirror can be used in order to calibrate the sample reflectance in terms of specular reflectance.

4. Impact
This paper introduces a framework for measurement of the scatter distribution function of planar and cylindrical samples in reflection and transmission without mechanical scanning or expensive and complex conoscopic optical systems. Advanced imaging colorimeters are used for evaluation of directional chromaticity variations in combination with linear lamps and point light sources. Selection of the geometry allows either high directional resolution in the vicinity of the specular direction or a large range of angles can be covered with cylindrical samples.

The method can be applied for characterization of electronic display screens and related components (AG-layers, diffusers), of paintwork, films and coatings with color-changing effects, for arbitrary scattering surfaces and films and for assessment of photometric appearance characteristics and chromaticity of e.g. textiles and fabric [2], coated paper [3] and strands of hair [6]. Colorimetric characterization of color changing media will be presented in the paper.

Advantages of the approach are: simple and compact setup and apparatus without moving parts, low sensitivity with respect to parameter variations (robustness), bi-spectral analysis possible (spectrally tunable source, monochromatic LED emission and colorimetric LMD), and, depending on sample geometry high angular resolution or extended angular range.

Limitations of the methods are: samples must be uniform over area included in the measurement, BRDF of the sample must be rather invariant to source inclination, only a limited range of directions can be measured centered about the specular ray.

5. References
[1] B. Karamata, M. Andersen, "A review and analysis of parallel goniophotometry", Proceedings of LuxEuropa, 2013.

[2] R. Lu, J. Koenderink, A. M. L. Kappers, "Optical properties (bidirectional reflection distribution functions) of velvet", Appl. Opt., Vol. **37**, pp. 5974–5984, 1998.

[3] J. S. Arney, "An Inexpensive Micro-Goniophotometry You Can Build", IS&T's 1998 PICS Conference, p. 179, 1998.

[4] E. F. Kelley, G. R. Jones, "Utilizing the BRDF to predict reflections from FPDs", SID'97 Digest, p. 831, 1997.

[5] M. E. Becker, "Measurement and Evaluation of Display Scattering", SID'04 Digest, p. 184, 2004.

[6] R. F. Stamm, M. L. Garcia, J. J. Fuchs, "The optical properties of human hair. I. Fundamental considerations and goniophotometer curves", J. Soc. Cosmet. Chem., Vol. **28**, p. 571, 1977.

Paper No S12.1: Architectures of Oxide TFT for High Resolution Display

S.-H. Ko Park,[1] C.-S. Hwang,[2] H. I. Yeom,[1] J. B. Ko,[1] and S. Cho[2]

[1]KAIST, Republic of Korea, E-mail: shkp@kaist.ac.kr; [2]ETRI, Republic of Korea

Abstract

In this paper, we present the architecture of oxide TFT selected from diverse TFT structures for the application to the high resolution mobile display. Due to the selection of proper materials and process, we can achieve highly stable BCE TFT and show the promise of vertical oxide TFT with the smallest TFT footprint.

1. Introduction

After longer than a decade of effort, oxide TFT has been adopted as the backplane of the high-resolution TFT-LCD and AMOLED TV. One of huge merits of oxide TFT would be that we can select the most suitable structure with keeping proper performance depending on the application. For example, back channel etch (BCE) oxide TFT is considered as the best candidate to drive LCD regardless of display size or resolution. In the case of FHD OLED TV, dual gated oxide TFT with etch stop structure is applied.

Recently high-resolution displays become one of the biggest concerns and even holography display seems to be in our hand sooner or later. The architecture of oxide TFT for high-resolution display should be carefully selected depending on the size and application of display.

Here we introduce architecture of oxide TFT suitable for the mobile UHD display and holography display.

2. Back Channel Etch TFT

Since the footprint of BCE TFT is smaller than ESL TFT and self-aligned TFT, it is best in realizing ultra-high resolution display of not only TFT-LCD but AMOLED. The electrical stability of high mobility BCE TFT, however, has not been verified yet. We developed chemically inert high mobility oxide semiconductor consisted of In, Sn, Zn, and Al. Furthermore, SiO_2 gate insulator deposited by plasma-enhanced atomic layer deposition (PEALD) showed high barrier property to the H diffusion from the underlying SiN_x as well as the good stoichiometry to result in high stability under gate bias stress. The mobility of TFT is 38.5 cm^2/V.s and ΔV_{th} under positive and negative bias stress for 10,000 s at 60°C were −0.6 and 0 V, respectively. Figure 1 shows the BCE structure and performance of BCE TFT. Optimization of gate insulator, passivation layer give highly stable high mobility BCE oxide TFT of which stability is enough to drive even OLED.

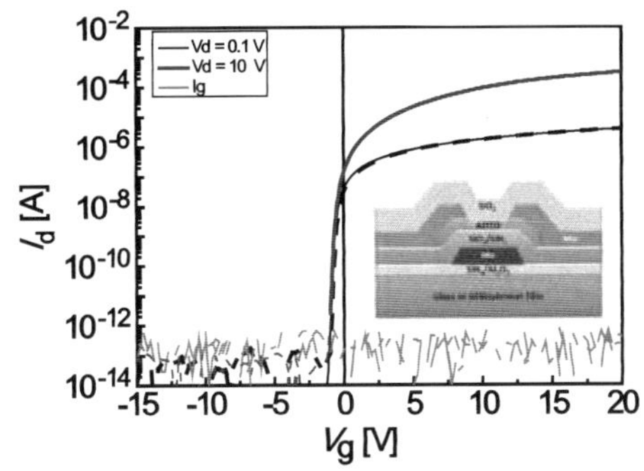

Figure 1. Transfer characteristics of BCE-structured Al:ITZO TFT.

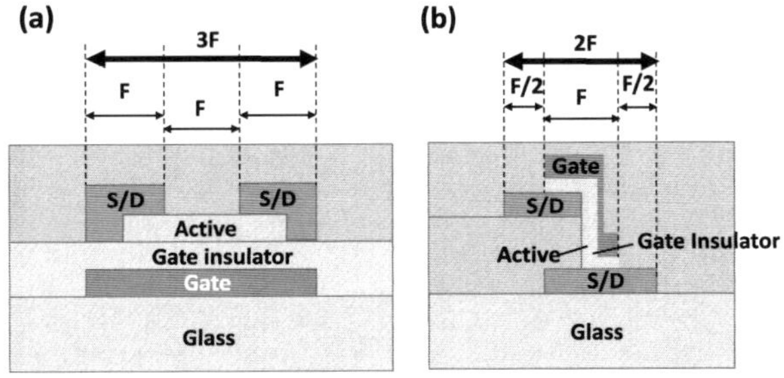

Figure 2. Comparison of pixel pitch and cross section of (a) BCE TFT and (b) vertical TFT.

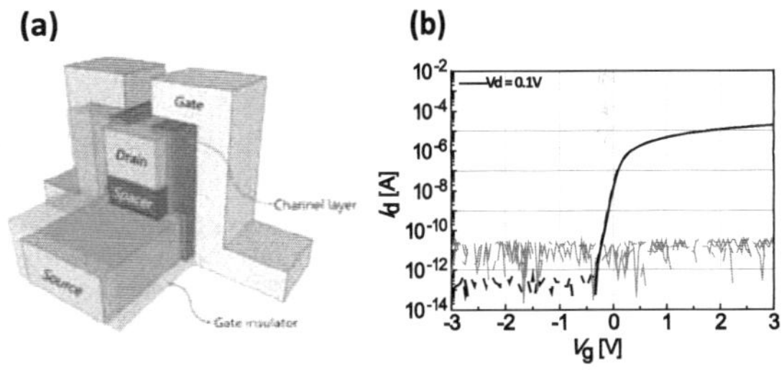

Figure 3. (a) Cross section and (b) transfer characteristics of vertical TFT.

3. Vertical TFT

We predict that vertical TFT is the most suitable TFT architecture since the footprint of vertical TFT is the smallest among the TFTs. Even though vertical TFT can have precisely controlled short channel length defined by not the lithography instrument but the thin film thickness of spacer, research on this architecture has not been stimulated so far. The contradictory advantage of vertical TFT is we can increase channel length, for example, length of 2 μm even in a sub-pixel area less than 3μm × 3μm. This would be the most important advantage of vertical TFT for the application to the high-resolution display since properly designed vertical TFT allows high current gain at proper driving voltage.

With the development of high mobility active layer of InO_x and high quality of gate insulator of SiO_2 and/or Al_2O_3, which have superior step coverage by means of PEALD method, we can fabricate vertical oxide TFT. Figure 3 shows the structure and performance of vertical TFT. Although TFT performance is not comparable to that of bottom gate bottom contact TFT, we are optimizing TFT performance by reducing contact resistance of SD and back channel damage. We will report the optimized vertical oxide TFT with short channel and long channel.

4. Acknowledgements

This research has been performed as a cooperation project of project No KK1502-H00 (Development of Organometallics and Device Fabrication for IT·ET Convergence) and supported by the Korea Research Institute of Chemical Technology (KRICT).

Paper No S12.2: High-Mobility Indium Oxide Thin-Film Transistors by Means of Plasma-Enhanced Atomic Layer Deposition

H. I. Yeom,[1] J. B. Ko,[1] C.-S. Hwang,[2] S. Cho,[2] and S.-H. K. Park[1]

[1]KAIST, Daejeon, Republic of Korea, E-mail: shkp@kaist.ac.kr; [2]ETRI, Daejeon, Republic of Korea

Abstract

Indium oxide film has been deposited by plasma-enhanced atomic layer deposition and adopted as channel materials for high-mobility thin-film transistors. The resultant device fabricated at temperature of 200°C showed a field-effect mobility of as high as 31 cm^2/V s in linear region.

1. Introduction

As the demands in high-resolution displays have been increased, the importance of high-mobility active materials has risen quickly. Indium oxide (InOx)-based semiconducting materials have been widely considered as a channel material of thin-film transistors (TFTs) in flat panel displays because its carriers show small effective mass from large s-orbital overlap [1]. However, active materials with high mobility have suffered from the susceptibility of threshold voltage shift due to high degree of intrinsic carrier in channel layer [2]. To overcome the weakness of high-mobility channel materials, high quality and thinner active layers are required to control the amount of carriers.

Plasma-enhanced atomic layer deposition (PEALD) is one of prospective tool that fabricate uniform and well-defined thin films over large area with precisely controlled thickness. In this study, InOx channel layers were prepared using oxygen plasma. There has already been an attempt to obtain ALD-InOx films with same indium source and water reactant [3]. However, this film was studied not as a semiconducting material but transparent conducting oxide for its low resistivity.

In this study, we examined the chemical and physical properties of InOx films by PEALD with atomic-force microscopy, X-ray diffraction (XRD), and X-ray photoelectron spectroscopy (XPS). On the basis of these results, InOx TFTs were fabricated and their characteristics were examined by various tools.

2. Methods and Results

2.1. Properties of Indium Oxide Film

The InOx films deposited on silicon oxide substrates at the plasma power of 100 W and the various temperatures were analyzed. The deposition rate of the films were 1.28, 1.25, and 1.20/cycle at the temperatures of 150, 200, and 250°C, respectively. According to XRD results, the crystallinities of (222) and (400) orientations were observed at deposition temperatures of both 150 and 200°C. The amorphous form of the film grown at 250°C could be verified by XPS data which presents the existence of noticeable amount of Si from the indium precursor. All of those films also showed considerably smooth surfaces with the root-mean-square value lower than 0.5 nm.

2.2. Characteristics of Indium Oxide TFTs

To estimate the InOx film by PEALD as a channel layer, the bottom-gate bottom-contact TFTs were prepared using ITO as a gate and source/drain electrodes, and alumina as a gate insulator. Then, the 10-nm-thick InOx layers were deposited and the devices were completed with the passivation layers of SiO_2 for stable operation. The transfer curve of the TFT with InOx channel layer fabricated at 200°C was shown in Figure 1. This device showed best performance with a proper value of subthreshold swing, threshold voltage, and a field-effect mobility of as high as 31 cm^2/V s in linear region while the TFTs with other deposition temperatures of active layers showing linear mobility less than 20 cm^2/V s.

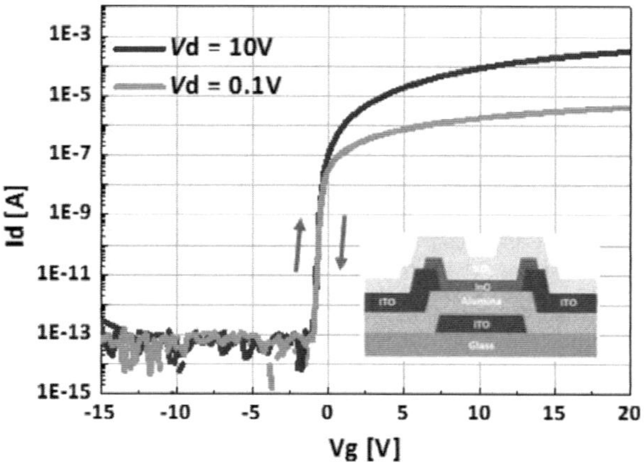

Figure 1. Cross-sectional structure, and transfer characteristics of indium oxide TFT fabricated by PEALD.

3. Conclusion

We optimized and examined the properties of InOx films with oxygen plasma by means of PEALD which enables us to get a stoichiometric and high quality film. As deposition temperature increased, the crystallinities of the films seemed decrease due to the Si incorporation from the precursor. Finally, poly-crystalline InOx TFT by PEALD at 200°C was successfully fabricated and showed good electrical characteristics comparable with high-mobility amorphous oxide TFTs fabricated by sputtering [1]. We will compare and discuss about the electrical stability of TFTs with amorphous and poly-crystalline InOx.

4. Acknowledgements

This research has been performed as a cooperation project of project no. KK1502-H00 (Development of Organometallics and Device Fabrication for IT·ET Convergence) and supported by the Korea Research Institute of Chemical Technology (KRICT).

5. References

[1] T. Kamiya, H. Hosono, "Material characteristics and applications of transparent amorphous oxide semiconductors", NPG Asia Mater., Vol. **2**, pp. 15–22, 2010.

[2] Y. KiKuchi, K. Nomura, H. Yanagi, T. Kamiya, M. Hirano, H. Hosono, "Device characteristics improvement of a-In-Ga-Zn-O TFTs by low-temperature annealing", Thin Solid Films, Vol. **518**, pp. 3018–3021, 2010.

[3] W. J. Maeng, D. Choi, K.-B. Chung, W. Koh, G.-Y. Kim, S.-Y. Choi, J.-S. Park, "Highly conducting, transparent, and flexible indium oxide thin-film prepared by atomic layer deposition using a new liquid precursor $Et_2InN(SiMe_3)_2$", Appl. Mater. Interfaces, Vol. **6**, pp. 17481–17488, 2014.

Paper No S12.3: Influence of Layer Thickness and Homogeneity on Contactless Deposited High-Performance Indium Oxide Thin-Film Transistors

S. Meyer,[1,2] S. Grenz,[2] A. Merkulov,[2] G. Renner,[2] R. Anselmann,[2] and R. Schmechel[1]

[1]Nanostructures & Technology and Center for NanoIntegration Duisburg-Essen (CENIDE), University of Duisburg-Essen, 47057 Duisburg, Germany, E-mail: sebastian.meyer@uni-due.de; [2]Evonik Industries AG, 45772 Marl, Germany

The advantages of vacuum deposited metal oxide semiconductors in thin-film transistor (TFT) backplanes are widely shown in commercial products recently introduced by leading display manufacturers in Asia [1]. These materials are ideally suited for the TFT driving in the next generation of flat panel display screens due to their ability to retain high charge carrier mobility over large-areas. In addition, a fully solution-based deposition of the semiconductor via functional precursor inks (soluble oxides) for example with slot-die coating equipment is possible and has many advantages in terms of equipment cost, stoichiometric homogeneity and flexibility of elemental film composition [2,3]. Nevertheless, the thin-film must be patterned by multiple, expensive masking and etching steps to avoid current superposition and cross-talking in the final backplane TFT matrix. Especially for thin indium containing metal oxide films, this patterning step is much more important due to the high overall lateral film conductivity [4].

A non-lithographic, selective and direct deposition of the functional material is still challenging and the goal of many research efforts today [5]. Despite all advantages of soluble oxide inks, a deep knowledge of the precursor chemistry is necessary and it is challenging to adapt the functional inks rheology to direct deposition methods without the loss of TFT device performance or stability.

A high performance indium-based formulation (iXsenic® S, an Evonik product) is fitted to the rheology requirements of an industrial ink-jet printhead by choice of precursor concentration and solvent mixture with respect to complex stability. The soluble oxide ink properties are controlled with contemplation to viscosity shear-stress behavior (6-8 mPas), surface tension (38 mN/m) and vapor pressure of the solvent composition. We show that the drying behavior of the semiconductor ink is mainly influenced by the choice of the solvent and substrate conditions. The layer thickness and homogeneity of rectangular, line and single ink droplet structures are investigated on silicon oxide surfaces with different thermal energy conditions. The coffee-stain effect in these printed structures can be reduced by substrate heating or proper solvent selection. TFT devices were fabricated with sputtered ITO electrodes in a bottom-contact coplanar device structure. Transfer curves were measured after precursor conversion at 350°C and discussed in terms of change in contact resistance, charge carrier concentration and its influence on onset-voltage and saturation mobility. A homogeneous TFT channel with low average surface roughness (< 580 pm) can be realized by single droplet deposition on ITO contacts which is associated with the highest possible pattern resolution (d = 40 μm) of the operational printhead with 10 pL droplet volume. After fine tuning of film thickness by variation of precursor concentration and substrate temperature the TFTs are showing saturation mobilities at around 2-3 cm^2/Vs.

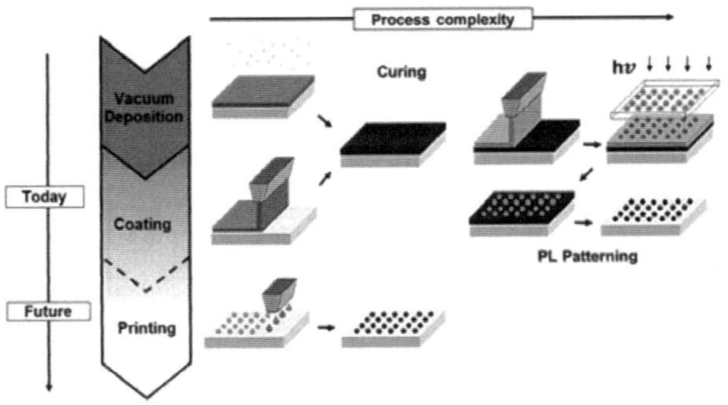

Figure 1. Possible semiconductor patterning routes for TFT backplane fabrication today and in the near future.

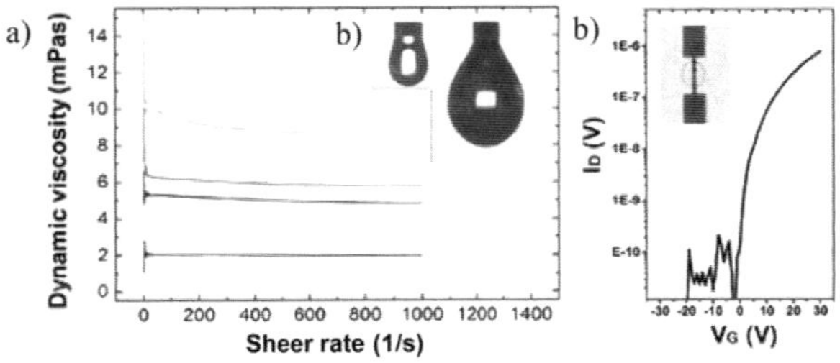

Figure 2. (a) Dynamic viscosity range, (b) drop contoure analysis of the soluble oxide ink, and (c) transfer curve of single droplet TFT with ITO source and drain electrodes.

1. References

[1] T. Kamiya, H. Hosono, "Material characteristics and applications of transparent amorphous oxide semiconductors", NPG Asia Mater, Vol. **2**, pp. 15–22, 2010.

[2] K. Myny, S. Smout, M. Rockelé, A. Bhoolokam, T. H. Ke, S. Steudel, B. Cobb, A. Gulati, F. G. Rodriguez, K. Obata, M. Marinkovic, D.-V. Pham, A. Hoppe, G. H. Gelinck, J. Genoe, W. Dehaene, P. Heremans, "A thin-film microprocessor with inkjet print-programmable memory", Sci. Rep., Vol. **4**, Article number 7398, 2014.

[3] F. Jaehnike, A. Hoppe, D. V. Pham, J. Steiger, "Illumination & Displays High performance, stable solution-processed thin-film transistors", SPIE Newsroom, 2012.

[4] M. Bender, N. Katsarakis, E. Gagaoudakis, E. Hourdakis, E. Douloufakis, V. Cimalla, G. Kiriakidis, "Dependence of the photoreduction and oxidation behavior of indium oxide films on substrate temperature and film thickness", J. Appl. Phys., Vol. **90**, pp. 5382–5387, 2001.

[5] D. S. Engstrom, B. Porter, M. Pacios, H. Bhaskaran, "Additive nanomanufacturing–A review", J. Mater. Res., Vol. **29**, pp. 1792–1816, 2014.

Paper No S12.4: Effect of Plasma Power of Plasma Enhanced Atomic Layer Deposition Process for Gate Insulator Deposition in Top-Gate Thin-Film Transistors

J. B. Ko,[1] H. I. Yeom,[1] C.-S. Hwang, S. Cho,[2] and S.-H. K. Park[1]

[1]KAIST, Daejeon, Republic of Korea, E-mail: shkp@kaist.ac.kr; [2]ETRI, Daejeon, Republic of Korea

Abstract

In this work, plasma enhanced atomic layer deposition process (PEALD) was used for the depositing SiO_2 as the insulating layer with various plasma power. We investigated the effect of plasma power on the TFT performance in top-gate structure.

1. Introduction

As demands for high resolution with large area display increase, driving devices with high performance attract much attention. Especially, amorphous oxide semiconductor (AOS) thin-film transistors (TFTs) become key technology due to the benefits of outstanding performance [1].

For the high frame rate display, self-aligned top-gate structured TFT with high mobility is actively researched due to both the reduced resistance-capacitance delay by less parasitic capacitance and the charging time.

To obtain the favorable characteristic of devices with high mobility channel, however, the gate insulator (GI) deposition process and their quality is important, especially in top-gate structure. During the GI-deposition process, the oxide channel can be degraded [2]. In addition, the plasma power during GI-deposition process is important parameter to obtain high stability of to the top-gate structured TFT.

In this work, we adopted plasma enhanced atomic layer deposition (PEALD) to deposit GI of SiO2 and investigated the effect of plasma power on the top-gate structured high mobility oxide TFT.

2. Method and Results

2.1. Fabrication and Measurement

Indium tin oxide was used as source and drain. For the active layer, sputtered indium zinc oxide (IZO) was used and following the process, 10nm of SiO_2 (protective layer, PL) was deposited to protect the active layer from the damage of patterning process. The PL was deposited at 300°C by PEALD with 60W, 80W and 100W of plasma power separately. To compare, the another device's PL was deposited by conventional PECVD process as reference. After depositing PL, the active layer and PL were patterned simultaneously. First layer of GI was deposited at 300°C by PEALD of which plasm power was same with PL deposition process. To reduce fabrication time, second GI was deposited by PECVD at 300°C. The reference device's GI was deposited by PECVD only. Finally, molybdenum was used for gate electrode. The inset of Figure 1 shows the schematic diagram of the fabricated device. The fabricated devices were thermally annealed at 350°C in vacuum environment. The electrical characteristics of fabricated devices were measured by semiconductor parameter analyzer at room temperature in dark condition.

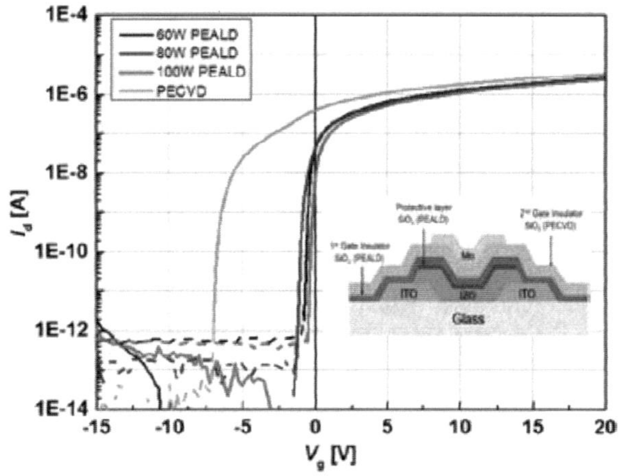

Figure 1. Transfer curve of fabricated oxide TFT with 60 W, 80 W, and 100 W of PEALD and PECVD processed GI.

Table 1. Parameters of fabricated oxide TFT with 60 W, 80 W, and 100 W of PEALD and PECVD processed GI.

	Mobility (cm^2/Vs)	S.S (V/dec)	V_{on} (V)
60W PEALD	39.3	0.09	−0.44
80W PEALD	39.1	0.10	−1.25
100W PEALD	39.8	0.10	−0.50
PECVD	43.1	0.13	−8.50

2.2. Transfer Characteristics

Figure 1 shows the transfer characteristics of PEALD and PECVD processed devices with 0.1 V of drain voltage. The devices with PEALD processed GI have favorable transfer characteristics even after annealing at higher temperature than process-temperature. However, the PECVD processed device shows negatively shifted turn-on voltage (V_{on}) than those by PEALD. Table 1 summarizes the calculated parameter of fabricated devices. Within our experimental condition, there is no correlation between the plasma power and the performance of the TFTs in terms of mobility, subthreshold-swing (S.S) value, and V_{on}.

3. Conclusion

The top-gate staggered TFTs were fabricated with changing the power of PEALD in the deposition of gate insulator. The PEALD processed devices show favorable characteristics rather than PECVD processed one. The plasma power splits of PEALD was not that effective to devices' transfer characteristic. The stability of high mobility IZO TFTs with various SiO_2 will also be investigated and presented.

4. Acknowledgements

This work was supported by Open Innovation Lab Project from National Nanofab Center (NNFC).

5. References

[1] J. S. Park, W. J. Maeng, H. S. Kim, J. S. Park, "Review of recent developments in amorphous oxide semiconductor thin-film transistor devices", Thin Solid Films, Vol. **520**. pp. 1679–1693, 2012.

[2] J. C. Park, H. N. Lee, S. Im, "Self-aligned top-gate amorphous indium zinc oxide thin-film transistors exceeding low-temperature poly-Si transistor performance", ACS Appl. Mater. Interfaces, Vol. **5**, pp. 6990–6995, 2013.

Paper No S12.5: Self-Aligned a-IGZO TFTs: Impact of S/D Contacts Formation on Their Negative-Bias-Illumination-Stress (NBIS) Instability

Manoj Nag,[1,2] Soeren Steudel,[1] Steve Smout,[1] Ajay Bhoolokam,[1,2] Jan Genoe,[1,2] Brian Cobb,[3] Abhishek Kumar,[3] Groeseneken Guido,[1,2] and Paul Heremans[1,2]

[1]IMEC, Kapeldreef 75, 3001 Leuven, Belgium, E-mail: manoj.nag@imec.be; [2]ESAT, Katholieke Universiteit Leuven, Kasteelpark Arenberg 10, 3001 Leuven, Belgium; [3]Holst Centre, High Tech Campus 31, 5656 AE Eindhoven, The Netherlands

Read the full article at DOI: 10.1002/jsid.351

Abstract

In this work, we present the impact of S/D contact formation, that is, by SiN plasma doping (hydrogen incorporation), metallic reduction (by calcium) and by argon plasma (compositional change) on NBIS instabilities of self-aligned a-IGZO TFTs.

1. Introduction

The increased resolution (4k2k pixel) and high frame-rate (120 Hz) of future display backplanes demands thin-film transistors (TFTs) having low parasitic capacitances and high switching speed. Amorphous oxide semiconductors (AOSs) TFTs with large gate-source/drain (S/D) overlap as in conventional etch-stop-layer (ESL) and back-channel-etch (BCE) configurations are less suitable, so the self-aligned (SA) TFT configuration is preferred. The S/D region conductivity enhancement is one of the challenges in this configuration. Various integration techniques have been reported to enhance the conductivity of the S/D regions such as implants (B and P), UV illumination, metal-reduction (Ti and Al) and plasma treatments (Ar and H_2). In this study, we compared the performance of SA a-IGZO TFTs whereby the S/D region's conductivity is enhanced by three different ways i.e. using a SiN plasma (hydrogen incorporation), using calcium (Ca) as reducing metal and using an argon plasma [1–6].

2. TFT Fabrication

In the first step, a-IGZO is deposited/patterned on glass substrate and then the gate stack (200 nm SiO_2/100 nm Mo) is formed. This is followed by a S/D treatment using the three aforementioned techniques. The reduction of exposed a-IGZO occurs during plasma (SiN and Ar) and annealing (Ca) steps. In case of the Ca-treated sample, a water rinse is added to get rid of unreacted calcium and CaO formed during the treatment. In the next step, an interlayer (SiN for the hydrogen plasma treated sample whereas ALD Al_2O_3 for Ca reduction and Ar plasma samples) was deposited. Post interlayer deposition, via and then S/D metal (100 nm Mo) were patterned, which followed by a final anneal at 250°C in N_2 ambient.

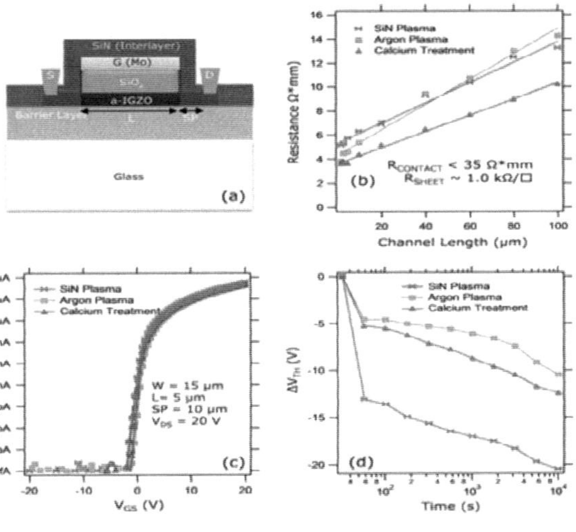

Figure 1. (a) Cross-sectional view, (b) S/D contact resistance comparison, (c) transfer characteristics, and (d) NBIS stability of SA a-IGZO TFTs.

3. Result and Discussion

A schematic cross-section of an integrated SA a-IGZO TFT is shown in Figure 1(a). For sheet conductivity of the IGZO spacing (SP) between gate and drain contact and between gate and source contact, a value of ~1 kΩ/ϒ would be the target in our TFT layout to avoid an increased contact resistance. All the three S/D treatments showed quite comparable sheet resistance as shown in Figure 1(b). Also the three types of TFTs showed comparable electrical characteristics, with field-effect mobility of 10.0 $cm^2/(V.s)$, sub-threshold slopes of 0.4 V/decade and off-currents of lower than 1.0 pA as shown in Figure 1(c). However, under NBIS (conditions of −1 MV/cm field for duration of 10^4 s under light source of 425 nm wavelength with photon flux of 10^{16} $cm^{-2}s^{-1}$), SiN plasma-treated TFTs showed extremely poor results, that is, a V_{TH} shift of more than −20.0 V, compared to less than −10.0 V shift in case of Ar plasma and Ca treated TFTs as shown in Figure 1(d). We associate the poor stability of the SiN plasma treated TFTs to the high hydrogen content present near the channel [7] compared to other two treatments.

4. Conclusion

We have investigated three different doping techniques for in SA a-IGZO TFT configuration and identified SiN (hydrogen incorporation) plasma-treated TFTs negatively impact the NBIS.

5. Acknowledgements

This work was performed in collaboration between IMEC and TNO in the frame of the Holst Centre.

6. References

[1] Z. Ye, L. Lu, M. Wong, "Zinc-oxide thin-film transistor with self-aligned source/drain regions doped with implanted boron for enhanced thermal stability", IEEE Trans. Electron. Dev., Vol. **59**, No. 2, pp. 393–397, 2012.

[2] A. D. Mourey, D. A. Zhao, T. N. Jackson, "Self-aligned-gate ZnO TFT circuits", IEEE Electr. Device Lett., Vol. **31**, No. 4, pp. 326–328, 2010.

[3] N. Morosawa, Y. Ohshima, M. Morooka, T. Arai, T. Sasaoka, "A novel self-aligned top-gate oxide TFT for AM-OLED displays", Sony Corporation, SID 2011 Digest, pp. 479–482, 2011.

[4] N. Morosawa, M. Nishiyama, Y. Ohshima, A. Sato, Y. Terai, K. Tokunaga, J. Iwasaki, K. Akamatsu, Y. Kanitani, S. Tanaka, T. Arai, K. Nomoto, "High mobility self-aligned top-gate oxide TFT for high-resolution AM-OLED", SID 2013 Digest, pp. 85–88, 2013.

[5] M. Nag, K. Obata, Y. Fukui, K. Myny, S. Schols, P. Vicca, T. Huei Ke, S. Smout, M. Willegems, M. Ameys, A. Bhoolokama, R. Muller, B. Cobb, A. Kumar, J.-L. van der Steen, T. Ellis, G. Gelinck, J. Genoe, P. Heremans, S. Steudel, "Flexible AMOLED display and gate-driver with self-aligned IGZO TFT on plastic foil", SID 2014 Digest, pp. 248–251, 2014.

[6] R. Muller, Patent no. WO2013167374 A1.

[7] M. Nag, A. Bhoolokam, S. Steudel, A. Chasin, J. Maas, J. Genoe, M. Murata, G. Groeseneken, P. Heremans, "Medium Frequency Physical Vapor Deposited Al2O3 and SiO2 as Etch-Stop-Layers for Amorphous Indium-Gallium-Zinc-Oxide Thin-Film-Transistors", ECS J. Solid State Sci. Technol., Vol. **4**, Q38–Q42, 2015.

Projection-Displays: New Technologies, Challenges, and Applications

Patrick Candry and Bart Maximus
Barco n.v. Belgium, E-mail:patrick.candry@barco.com

Read the full article at DOI: 10.1002/jsid.316

Abstract
Color, light-output, dynamic range, and 3D aspects of projection displays based on light-emitting diodes, lasers, and new micro-displays will be described, including the remarkable characteristics and the improving understanding of the human visual system.

1. Introduction
Important improvements of projection-display characteristics to achieve better image reproductions are possible thanks to the considerable advancements of light-emitting diodes LEDs, lasers, and micro-displays (MDs). However, for new projector developments, it is essential to take into account the progressing understanding of the human visual system (HVS).

2. Color and Light Output
Displays cannot reproduce all the colors occurring in nature. The BT.709 color gamut is still in use although its origins date back to the era of the available CRT phosphors. SMPTE RP 431-2:2011 describes a wider color gamut with three primary colors for Digital Cinema. A very wide color gamut is defined in BT.2020 with primaries for red, green, and blue corresponding with monochromatic light at the wavelengths 630, 532, and 467 nm, respectively. Because of the large LED étendue and the limited LED luminance, LED-based projectors can achieve a maximum light output of around 1000 lm with a BT.709 white point. Numerous phosphor-converted blue laser diode architectures have been developed in order to increase the light output up to ~12,000 lm. Projectors with a light output up to ~60,000 lm and high color saturation can be realized with multiple solid state RGB lasers because of their good efficacy, very small optical étendue and almost monochromatic light. With the introduction of LED- and laser-based illumination systems, more attention is required to the Hunt effect and the Helmholtz-Kohlrauch effect, and the use of RGB-lasers requires substantial attention to optical architectures with measures to reduce the speckle noise to acceptable levels [1].

3. Dynamic Range
The HVS can adapt to a luminance range from 10^{-6} to 10^{8} cd/m^2 through a variety of adaptation mechanisms. When viewing a single visual scene, the HVS can function in range of about 4 log units [2]. Conventional contemporary projection displays have a typical sequential contrast ratio of ~2000:1, but some types of LCoS projectors can realize a sequential contrast ratio of more than 20,000:1. The luminance range of projectors can be substantially increased with an incorporated iris and optical dimmer to more than 20 10^6:1, or with "sequential modulation"' to more than 10^6:1. However, in a projected image, the contrast ratio depends on the "white content" of the image, because multiple reflections and scattering in the optical system of the projector are reducing the contrast ratio significantly. When increasing the sequential contrast ratio, additional care has to be taken for these effects. The ANSI contrast ratio, measured on a checkerboard pattern with a white image content of 50%, is typically around 200:1. However in this case, the dark parts of the checkerboard will be perceived as deep black because of the simultaneous contrast and light adaptation phenomena of the retina. But in the case of images with low white content, the light scattering and luminance redistribution have a significant influence on the perceived image contrast. Also by increasing the display's dynamic range by increasing both the luminance of peak white and decreasing the luminance of the dark content, contouring artifacts can occur. For a given luminance range, the electro-optical transfer function (EOTF) and the bit-depth of the display system determine the minimum luminance modulation that can be realized. In order to make more efficient use of the available code values for a given bit depth, for these high dynamic range (HDR) displays, instead of the typical power functions, an EOTF that provides a better fit to the results of the perception model of Barten was proposed.

4. Three-Dimensional Displays
Several monocular and binocular depth information sources are contributing to the perception of depth. Many of these depth information sources vary in effectiveness at different viewing distances. There are several 3D display technologies including: stereoscopic, auto-stereoscopic, and holographic displays. Stereoscopic displays require special viewing glasses and are based on wavelength-, polarization-, or time-multiplexing of the images for the left and the right eye. One of the most recent and power efficient examples of wavelength-multiplexing stereoscopy realized with two sets of RGB-lasers in a single projector is the Barco DP4K-60L. Multiview auto-stereoscopic displays produce multiple different stereo-pairs, and each of these stereo-pairs is only visible in a particular viewing zone, as for example, the prototype described in [3] using 63 LED illuminated HD projectors (130 million pixels). Stereoscopic and auto-stereoscopic displays exhibit in general the accommodation–vergence conflict. A solution to this problem could be realized by increasing the amount of views further to that is, 256. Another solution to this problem is the electro-holographic display. However in this case, an extremely large number of very small pixels, exceeding the capabilities of the current MD technologies, are required to realize a useful display size and viewing zone.

5. Acknowledgements
The support of the Flemish Agency for Innovation by Science and Technology (IWT) and the EC (FP7) for part of the research at Barco on LED and laserprojectors, and HDR is gratefully acknowledged.

6. References
[1] S. Roelandt, Y. Meuret, G. Craggs, G. Verschaffelt, P. Janssens, H. Thienpont, "Standardized speckle measurement method matched to human speckle perception in laser projection systems", Opt. Express, Vol. **20**, pp. 8770–8773, 2012.
[2] J. H. Van Hateren, "Encoding of high dynamic range video with a model of human cones", ACM Trans. Graphics, Vol. **25**, pp. 1380–1399, 2006.
[3] S. Iwasawa, M. Kawakita, S. Yano, H. Ando, "Implementation of autostereoscopic HD projection display with dense horizontal parallax", Proc. SPIE, Vol. **7863**, p. 78630T, 2011.

Paper No S13.1: Visual Performance Characterization of Flexible Mobile Displays

Jyrki Kimmel
Nokia Technologies, Finland, E-mail: jyrki.kimmel@nokia.com

Read the full article at DOI: 10.1002/jsid.353

Abstract
The measurement of flexible displays is possible only with special measurement arrangements using common display characterization devices. A conoscope with a working distance of 15 mm was used to demonstrate the dependency of viewing properties of a flexible active-matrix organic light-emitting display.

1. Introduction

Flexible displays have been in the interest of mobile telecommunication device developers during the recent years [1]. The benefits for flexible technology first were seen as the opportunity to design light-weight and robust mobile terminals [1], and only at a later stage did the possibilities of nanotechnology to create new, flexible form factors for mobile devices present themselves as viable alternatives [2].

The visual effects of bending a mobile display are not straightforward, and some of these effects present themselves to the viewer only with sufficient bending. One of the visual effects shown is the tendency of the white point to shift with viewing angle [3,4].

This article presents the viewing geometry of curved mobile displays and discusses some aspects of the measurement methodology associated with flexible displays, deriving from the viewing geometry requirements. Results from measuring a sample active-matrix organic light-emitting display (AMOLED) are shown.

2. Viewing and Measurement Geometries

The usual assumption that the viewing angle equals the angle of the gaze of the viewer with respect to the normal of the surface of the display is incorrect for flexible displays. The actual viewing angle deviates for convex and concave displays for curved displays. The visual effects are especially pronounced when viewing a curved display away from the center, toward the bent edges [4]. Although the gaze deviates only a few degrees from the normal, for sharply bent displays, the viewing angle can actually be over 50° at the edge [4].

Figure 1 presents a close-up of the measurement geometry for conoscopic measurement [4]. In most conoscopes, the working distance is only a few millimeters, in effect preventing the measurement of concave displays due to the intrusion of the measurement head. Some conoscopes have a longer working distance, allowing the measurement of concave displays to for example, −100 mm bending radius [4].

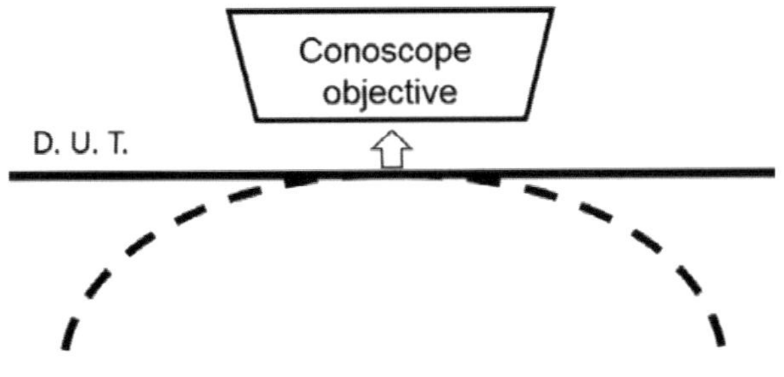

Figure 1. Conoscopic measurement of a flexible display. The dashed line shows a convex display under test (DUT).

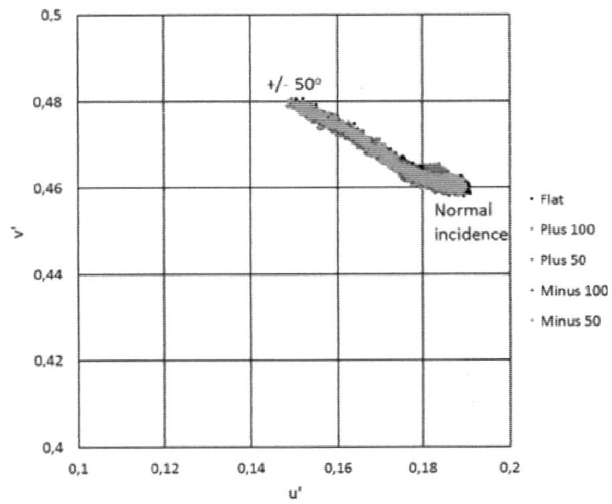

Figure 2. Shift of the white point in CIE 1976 coordinates with viewing angle.

3. Characterization Study

3.1. Display Properties

The display under test (DUT) was a 4.5 in. VWGA AMOLED with red, green, and blue subpixels arranged in a side-by-side fashion, each with their own emitter material.

3.2. Measurement Setup

A conoscope (Eldim VCMaster 3D Li) was used to characterize the primary color characteristics of the DUT. The measurement range was ±50° with respect to the normal of the display, and the display was arranged on jigs for the curvatures ranging from flat to bending radii of ±200, ±100, and ± 50 mm. The positive sign refers to convex curvature and negative to concave curvature. Since the working distance of the conoscope was 15 mm, only the −50 mm radius arrangement was out of focus for the measurement.

4. Results and Discussion

Figure 2 shows how the white point shifts with viewing angle for different curvatures.

It is evident that the effect of the viewing angle to the color performance of a curved display needs to be taken into account when designing a device with a flexible display.

5. References

[1] J. Kimmel, J. Hautanen, T. Levola, "Display technologies for portable communication devices", Proc. IEEE, Vol.**90**, pp. 581–590, 2002.
[2] T. Ryhänen, M. A. Uusitalo, O. Ikkala, A. Kärkkäinen, Nanotechnologies for Future Mobile Devices, Cambridge University Press, 2010.
[3] J. Kimmel, "Visual effects of curved AMOLEDs", International Display Workshops, Niigata, Japan, 2014.
[4] T. Mustonen, J. Kimmel, J. Hakala, J. Häkkinen, "Visual performance with small concave and convex displays", Hum. Factors, Vol. **57**, pp. 1029–1050, 2015.

Paper No S13.2: Quantification Model of Proper Curvature for Large-Sized Curved TVs

Yongmin Park, Dongwoo Kang, Sungjin Kim, and Jang Jin Yoo
LG Display, Paju, Republic of Korea, E-mail: nohungry@lgdisplay.com

Read the full article at DOI: 10.1002/jsid.348

Abstract
We present a feasible modeling method to estimate proper curvature for large-sized curved TVs. The proposed method was derived from subjective quality assessment and statistical analysis. This model can be used to design large-sized curved TVs that can offer higher preference and less perceived distortion.

1. Introduction
In order to maximize the advantages of curved TV, most TV manufacturers have developed curved TVs in consideration of ergonomics and viewing conditions. In this paper, we investigated methods to determine optimal curvature values of display using physical parameters such as size and viewing angle. We suggest a quantification model which derives from visual assessments and statistical analysis. This model can be used to estimate the proper curvature of large-sized curved TVs using physical parameters.

2. Results
We focused how both preference and perceived distortion can be explained by physical parameters. Our proposed method simply consists of two steps. First, a series of visual assessment was conducted to evaluate preference and perceived distortion of curved displays (Table 1). Next, we analyzed the relation between physical parameters and experimental results.

2.1. Visual Assessment of Curved Displays
A series of visual assessment using LCDs, curved screens and projectors was performed. Ten observers participated in the visual assessment. Both the viewing distance and the viewing angles were determined in consideration of average TV watching environment [1,2]. Two questions were asked to observers: preference and perceived distortion.

2.2. Quantification Model of Curvature
The results of preference and perceived distortion depending on size, curvature, and viewing angle from visual assessment were acquired as shown in Figure 1. A statistical model regarding the relation between the experimental results and conditions—size, curvature, and viewing angle was designed. Our proposed statistical model consists of two submodels,

Table 1. A series of visual assessment.

Experiment	Size (inch)	Viewing Angle (degree)	Curvature (mm)
#1 (LCD)	65"	0	4000R, 5000R, 6600R, Flat
	65"	22.5	4000R, 5000R, 6600R, Flat
	65"	45	4000R, 5000R, 6600R, Flat
#1 (Screen)	85"	0	3000R, 5000R, 5000R, Flat
	85"	22.5	3000R, 5000R, 5000R, Flat
	85"	45	3000R, 5000R, 5000R, Flat
#3 (Screen)	120"	0	4000R, 5000R, 7000R, Flat
	120"	22.5	4000R, 5000R, 7000R, Flat
	120"	45	4000R, 5000R, 7000R, Flat

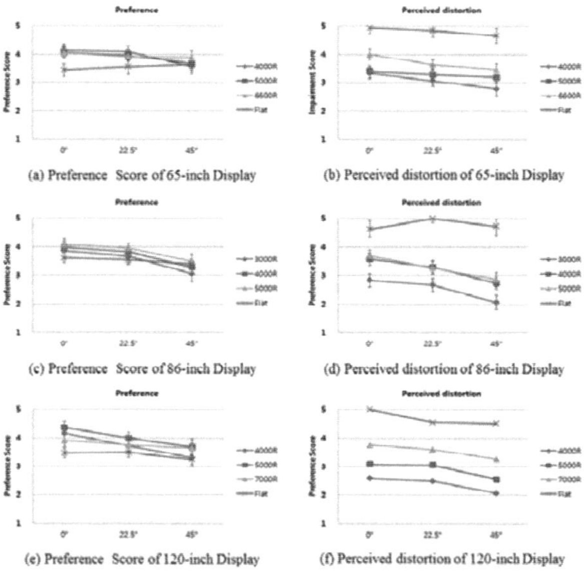

Figure 1. The results of visual assessment.

Table 2. Proper curvature for various-sized curved displays.

	55"	65"	77"	84"	98"	102"	120"~
D_F	3.13	3.11	3.11	3.35	3.34	3.33	3.31
T_{PQ}	3.54	3.53	3.51	3.56	3.54	3.54	3.57
Proper Curvature	4500–5000R			5500–6000R			6000–6500R

which are for preference and for distortion. Both the preference and distortion models can be determined as linear regression equation. We examined the proposed models based on coefficient of determination (R^2) analysis, which is a statistical measure of how well the regression model approximates the real data values. The R^2 values of the preference and distortion models are 0.77 and 0.92, respectively. It shows how the proposed models fit the real data.

We suggest that proper curvature values to meet the following conditions: The preference value (T_{PQ}) must be equal to or above the score 3.5 ("Fairly enough"), and the distortion value (D_F) must be equal to or above the score 3 ("Slightly annoying"). The proposed curvature values are described in Table 2.

3. References
[1] P. Emrath, "Spaces in New Homes", National Association of Home Builders (NAHB), 2013.
[2] HOMES, NA(National Archives): Department for Communities and Local Government, English Housing Survey, 2010.

Paper No S13.3: Optical Characterization of OLED Displays

Pierre Boher, Thierry Leroux, Véronique Collomb-Patton, and Thibault Bignon

ELDIM, 1185 rue d'Epron, Hérouville, France, E-mail: pboher@eldim.fr

Read the full article at DOI: 10.1002/jsid.369

Abstract

OLED displays are more and more used for many applications because of their interesting characteristics. Nevertheless, in spite of their high contrast ratio, wide viewing angle, and very fast response time, OLED displays are not perfect and require good manufacturing control to achieve optimized optical properties. In the present paper, we apply different types of optical characterizations to such displays (viewing angle, homogeneity, and response time) and we point out their specificities with regards to other types of displays. Since each blue, green, or red sub-pixel is an independent emitter of light, it is useful to study the light emission of each type of sub-pixel separately.

Emission homogeneity is studied on the entire surface of the displays and at the sub-pixel level using new multispectral imaging instrument. Viewing angle emission is measured with a multispectral Fourier optics instrument [1]. The two instruments used 31 band pass filters regularly distributed in the visible range to obtain multispectral data. The interest of the spectral information is that the exact shape of the light emission for each sub-pixel can be precisely determined and analyzed. For OLEDs, we use a simple double Gaussian model is used to extract model as reported in reference [2]. The wavelength position of the main emission peak and its intensity are particularly interesting to study for both type of measurements. In all the cases, at the sub-pixel level for pixels very closed to each other's, important luminance fluctuations are detected by high spatial resolution spectral imaging but the wavelength is quite stable [cf. figure 1(a)]. The overall homogeneity on the entire display surface extracted from the spectral imaging results is generally not perfect in terms of wavelength even for small size displays [cf. figure 1(b)].

The viewing angle emission of red, green, and blue sub-pixels presents complex spectral changes versus angle (cf. Figure 2). These changes that are related to interference fringes inside the OLED layered structure have generally small impact on color and luminance properties but can be used to check different structural parameters. Quantitative information on the optical thickness of active layer can be extracted knowing the exact structure of the OLED.

A new version of the Optiscope S.A instrument for response time characterization [3] is used in this study. To measure short response times lower than the line frame, it is mandatory to avoid averaging on many pixels. Consequently a very small measurement spot and a large angular aperture optics to collect light efficiently are needed. The new system integrates also a new analog to digital convertor working at 1 MHz frequency and allows accurate measurement of response times shorter than 10 µs. Impact of the display driving on the light emission can be easily measured working on a variable number of blinking lines.

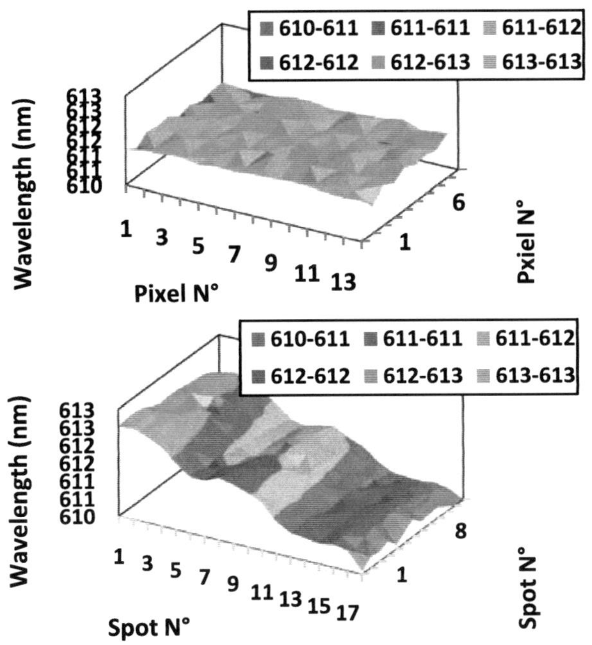

Figure 1. Wavelength of radiance maximum for red state on 14 × 10 pixels near center (top) and on the entire display surface (bottom).

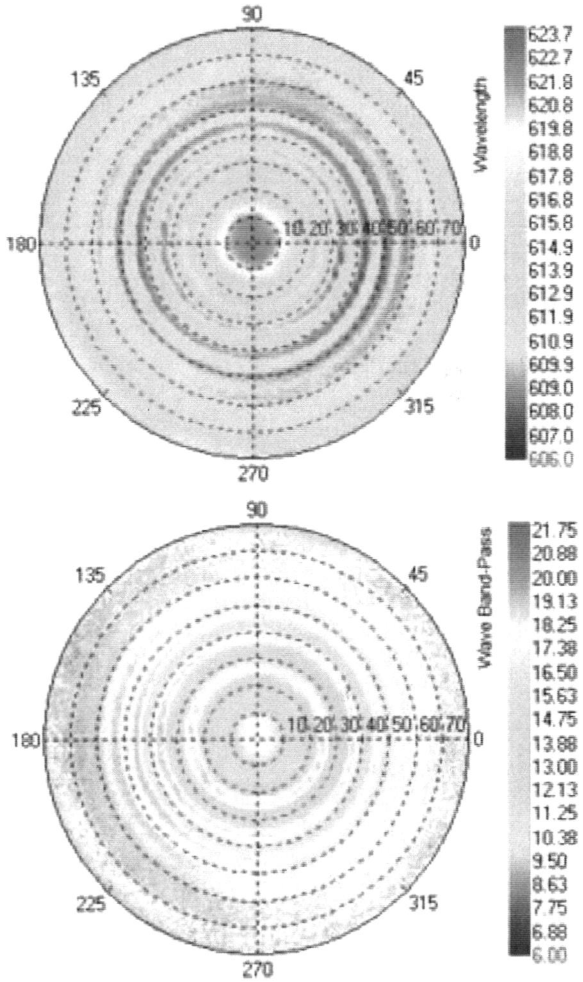

Figure 2. Wavelength position (top) and band pass (bottom) of AMOLED display for red state.

1. References

[1] P. Boher, T. Bignon, T. Leroux, D. Glinel, "New multispectral Fourier optics viewing angle instrument for full characterization of LCDs and their components", SID Meeting, Los Angeles, CA, 2008, p. 89.

[2] K. Man, I. Ashdown, "Accurate colorimetric feedback for RGB LED clusters", Proc. SPIE, Vol. **6337**, p. 633702, 2006.

[3] D. Glinel, P. Boher, T. Bignon, T. Leroux, "Precise response time measurement and analysis of liquid crystal displays", IMID Conference, Daegu, Korea, August 22–25, 2006, Paper P-14.

Paper No S13.4: Image Quality Simulations of Curved Displays

A. Marsal, A. Sycev, T. Kloth, C. Lehnert, and K. Blankenbach

Display Lab, Pforzheim University, Pforzheim, Germany, E-mail: kb@displaylabor.de

Abstract

The perceived image quality of curved displays depends significantly on viewing angle degradations. We developed a toolset for characterizing and simulation these degradations.

1. Introduction

Flexible—mainly curved—displays are the latest display trend in today's mass production. Those screens can have a concave or a convex shape (Figure 1, left) both horizontally or vertically. Viewing angle dependencies of LCDs (minor for OLEDs [1]) will cause image quality degradations; geometric distortions (not in focus here [2]) occur as well.

The motivation for our work was to simulate viewing angle degradations on the basis of corresponding measurements. This enables the judgment of pictures and GUI/HMIs without testing every redesign on the display. The other use is to calculate viewing angle requirements for displays on the basis of "allowed" degradations. We investigated flat and curved screens for perpendicular and off-axis geometry (Figure 1, right).

2. Measurements and Algorithms

On the basis of viewing (observer) angle measurements, we calculated via CIE Tristimulus and CIE 1976 LUV the color difference or modified the image grey levels acc. viewing angle effects. Measurements were performed with a SAMSUNG 55" UHD curved (R = 4.2 m) LCD. Figure 2 shows an example of the horizontal normalized ("1" for 0°) luminance characteristics over viewing angle measured in the center of the display. The shape of the curves depends on the grey level. Therefore color shifts for colors with different RGB grey levels will occur.

The easiest approach for simulations is to fit the viewing angle curves to a polynomial which provides the RGB subpixel luminance as being dependent from viewing angle and grey level. For other approaches we used LUTs derived from measurements. By using CIE formulas we can then calculate e.g. color co-ordinates and differences. This method needs low computing power and outputs a simulated image visualizing the viewing angle degradations like in Ref. 3. Furthermore we can calculate color differences which occur throughout the display. Parameters for all calculations are the observer geometry (distance and location) and the display's radius R (Figure 1, right). It is as well possible to compensate color shifts of known viewing angle degradations by RGB manipulation for a single observer.

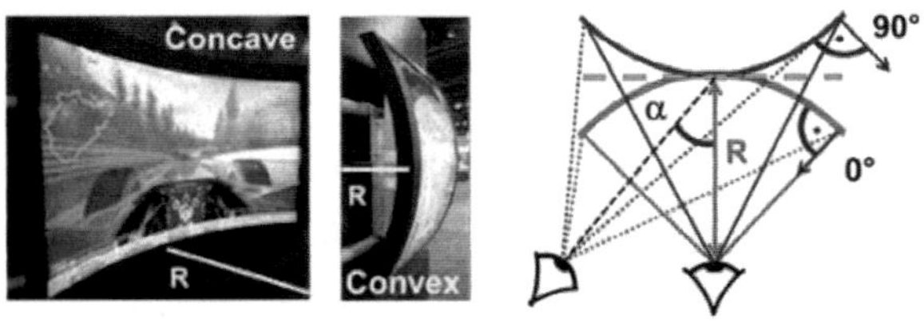

Figure 1. Curved displays (left) and viewer geometry (right).

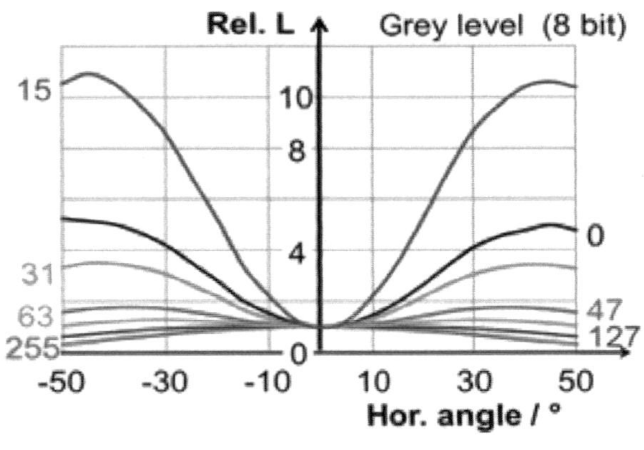

Figure 2. Gray level dependent luminance of a LCD.

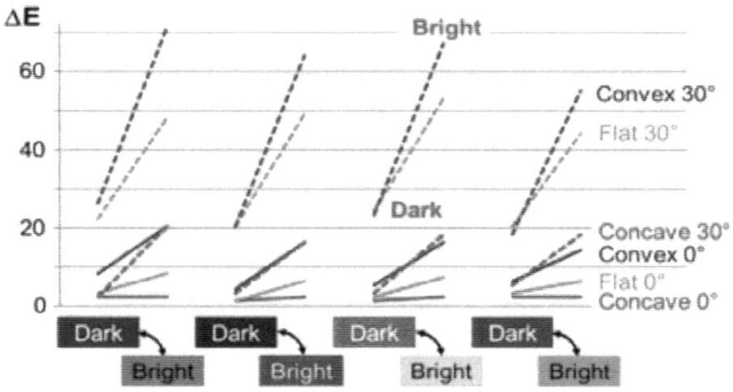

Figure 3. Color differences versus curvature of the display.

Figure 4. Result of simulation software for a convex display (img.bizhijidi.com/uploads/allimg/20141114/haitanpaidui-jiweijiu.jpg).

3. Results

The results presented here were calculated for the 55" LCD observed from focal point R/2 for on- ($\alpha = 0°$) and off-axis ($\alpha = 30°$). Figure 3 shows the CIE 1976 LUV color differences for 4 pairs (bright and dark) of selected colors. The colors are typical for many images and selected by RGB combinations of opposite viewing angle behavior (Figure 2). Brighter colors show higher maximum color differences. Due to its curvature toward the viewer, the concave display simulation shows the smallest ΔE and convex (curved away) the largest values of ΔE. Figure 4 shows the simulation for a convex screen ($\alpha = 0°$).

4. Summary

We developed a simulation toolkit for characterizing viewing angle effects of curved (and flat) displays using viewing angle measurements. The output is either the maximum color difference or a simulated image. The algorithm could apply vice versa to compensate known luminance and color shifts.

5. References

[1] E. F. Kelley, "Considering color performance in curved OLED TVs", SID ID, Vol. **29**, pp. 6–11, 2013.

[2] S. Hiller, D. Wollin, K. Blankenbach, "Novel algorithms for image warping of flexible LED video walls", Eurodisplay 2005, pp. 362–365, 2005.

[3] J. Kimmel, "Viewing properties of flexible AMOLEDs", SID ME Fall Meeting, 2014.

Paper No S14.1: OLEDs and QLEDs

Poopathy Kathirgamanathan (P. K. Nathan), Lisa M. Bushby, Muttulingam Kumaraverl, Seenivasagam Ravichandran, and Sivagnanasundram Surendrakumar

Brunel University London, Uxbridge UB8 3PH, United Kingdom, E-mail: p.kathirgamanathan@brunel.ac.uk

Abstract

The organic light-emitting diode (OLED) technology is now maturing. The unique physics and chemistry of quantum dots (QDs) result in a wider color gamut and increased stability over organic dyes meaning they have significant potential over organics in light-emitting devices. This article reviews the state of the art of OLEDs and quantum dot light emitting diode (QLEDs) followed by a comparison of devices fabricated with organic materials, in particular those of polymers, metal complexes (fluorescent and phosphorescent), and small molecules. Results of three devices: two red and one green are presented showing the excellent color coordinates that can be achieved from QD devices.

1. Introduction

Quantum dots (QDs) have become the subject of intense academic and industrial research over the past 15 years owing to their novel electronic, optical, and catalytic properties with much of this interest focused on their applications in display technology [1–3]. However, despite higher theoretical performance levels of so-called QLEDs, thus far efficiencies lag significantly behind those that have been achieved for organic light-emitting diodes (OLEDs). Nonetheless, results on reported devices indicate efficiencies for red, green, and blue devices are improving [4]. For instance, Mashford et al. [2] have reported a red QD (CdSe/CdS) device that reaches a peak efficiency of 19 cd/A and 25 lm/W, and Kim and Jang [3] have presented details of an inverted green device using CdSe/CdS/ZnS that achieved an impressive 28 cd/A and a power efficiency of 22 lm/W.

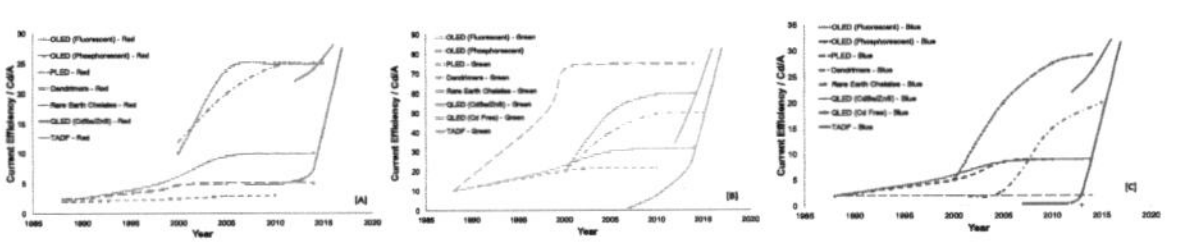

Figure 1. A comparison of typical device performance data based on fluorescent, phosphorescent, polymer, and QD emissive layers at 1000 cd m^{-2} is given in Table 1. It demonstrates that the performance of QD devices still lag behind those of OLEDs.

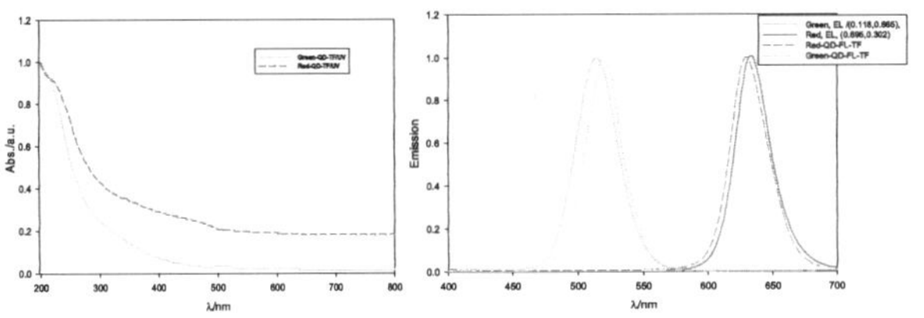

Figure 2. One of the device structures is shown in Figure 3 along with some of the materials used and an operating image of the device.

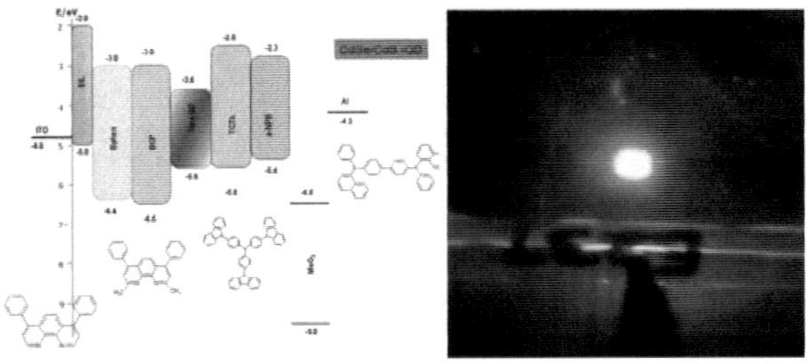

Figure 3. All the devices demonstrated low turn-on voltages, indicating well-charge-balanced devices. While the current efficiencies were lower than devices others have achieved, color coordinates were excellent (0.695, 0.302) and (0.697, 0.302) for the red devices and (0.118, 0.665) for the green and one of the red devices achieved a peak brightness of almost 4000 cd m^{-2}.

2. Background

Despite high theoretical performance levels of QLEDs in practice, thus far efficiencies still lag behind those for OLEDs, but as can be seen in Figure 1 and Table 1, there is a marked general trend toward improved efficiencies.

We prepared red and green devices using QDs provided by QD Vision. Preparatory studies found properties favorable for incorporation into devices, for example the QD formed homogeneous thin films that were transparent in the visible region of the spectrum, but that demonstrated narrow emission bands in the red and green areas of the spectrum as can be seen in Figures 2 and 3. We determined HOMO–LUMO levels of −5.6 and −3.4 eV for the red QD and −5.72 and −2.41 eV for the green.

3. Conclusion

The QDs- and rods-based light-emitting devices have the potential to become the next generation display materials because of their saturated colors, providing the life time of the devices could be improved to the levels of OLEDs.

4. Acknowledgement

We thank QD Vision for providing some QD samples.

5. References

[1] J. Lim, W. K. Bae, D. Lee, M. K. Nam, J. Jung, C. Lee, K. Char, S. Lee, "InP@ZnSeS, Core@Composition gradient shell quantum dots with enhanced stability", Chem. Mater., Vol.**23**, pp. 4459–4463, 2011.

[2] B. S. Mashford, M. Stevenson, Z. Popovic, C. Hamilton, Z. Zho, C. Breen, J. Steckel, V. Bulovic, M. Bawendi, S. Coe-Sullivan, P. T. Kazlas, "High-efficiency quantum-dot light-emitting devices with enhanced charge injection", Nat. Photonics, Vol.**7**, pp. 407–412, 2013.

[3] H.-M. Kim, J. Jang, "High-efficiency inverted quantum-dot light emitting diodes for display", Dig. Tech. Pap., Vol.**45**, p. 67, 2014.

[4] P. Kathirgamanathan, L. M. Bushby, M. Kumaraverl, S. Ravichandran, S. Surendrakumar, "Electroluminescent organic and quantum dot LEDs: The state of the art", IEEE J. Disp. Technol., Vol. **11**, No. 5, pp. 480–493, 2015.

Table 1. Selected typical performance data of OLED and QLEDS at 1000 cd m^{-2}

Color	Fluorescent molecules	Phosphorescent molecules	Polymers/dendrimers	Quantum dots
Red	(0.65, 0.35), 300–500 kh, 10 cd/A	(0.64, 0.36), 330 kh, 30 cd/A, 22 lm/W	(0.63, 0.37), 350 kh, 30 cd/A	
Red		(0.69, 0.31), 250 kh, 17 cd/A, 10 lm/W	(0.67, 0.32), 200 kh, 11 cd/A	(0.69, 0.31), 200 h, 15–20 cd/A, 15 lm/W
Green	(0.29, 0.61), 65 kh, 31 cd/A	(0.34, 0.62), 400 kh, 78 cd/A, 50 lm/W	(0.30, 0.63), 140 kh, 50 cd/A	(0.30, 0.68), 10 h, 12–35 cd/A, 10 lm/W
Blue	(0.15, 0.14), 50 kh, 10 cd/A, 5 lm/W	(0.18, 0.40), 20 kh, 50 cd/A, 30 lm/W	(0.15, 0.14), 20 kh, 6 cd/A	(0.16, 0.05), 1 h, 0.55 cd/A, 0.26 lm/W

Paper No S14.2: Degradation Behavior of Blue OLEDs

Xingtong Jiang, Pascal Volkert, and Chihao Xu
Chair of Microelectronics, Saarland University, Saarbruecken, Germany

Abstract

In this article, we investigate the degradation behavior of blue organic light-emitting diodes (OLEDs). Current–voltage–luminance characteristics were measured for various operational times. Analysis with respect to I–V drift and current efficiency degradation indicates that a compensation of OLED degradation may get feasible.

1. Introduction

Active-matrix organic light-emitting diode (AMOLED) as an active emitting display has been considered as the display technology of the future for many years. However, degradation is still one of the most challenging issues, which causes the image sticking problem for organic light-emitting diode (OLED) displays and limit their lifetime. Knowing and understanding the degradation behavior are therefore important to overcome the demerit, and allow a wide penetration of AMOLED displays in many applications like mobile phones, TVs, or wearable devices. The compensation of pixel-wise luminance loss could be practical, if the degradation behavior can accurately be estimated. Thus, the degradation behavior of blue OLEDs is investigated and analyzed in this article.

2. Test Condition

In this study, blue OLEDs with a size of 2.5 × 2.5 mm^2 from Novaled were tested. The samples are driven at a constant operating voltage (e.g., 4 V) at room temperature. The initial luminance was 2200 nits, $x = 0.13$ and $y = 0.12$. One advantage of a constant voltage is that it well simulates the operation condition of a digital driving scheme (cf. [1]). The current–voltage–luminance (*IVL*) characteristics were recorded over various operating voltages at different aging stages.

3. Results and Discussion

Under constant voltage stress, degradation composed of two parts has been observed, namely the current degradation and current efficiency degradation.

3.1. Current Degradation

Figure 1 shows *I–V* characteristic at different aging stages. The current decreases with the aging time. The current measured is highly sensitive to degradation of the OLED.

3.2. Current Efficiency Degradation

Figure 2 shows current efficiency as a function of voltage at different aging stages. With the increase of operational time, the current efficiency decreases. Furthermore, current efficiency depends on the operating voltages.

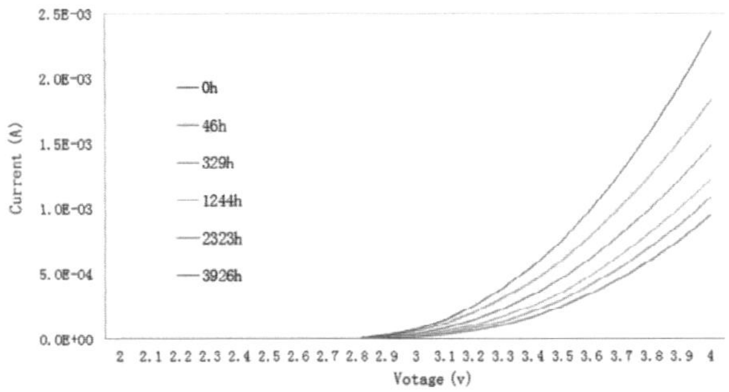

Figure 1. Current–voltage characteristic at different aging time.

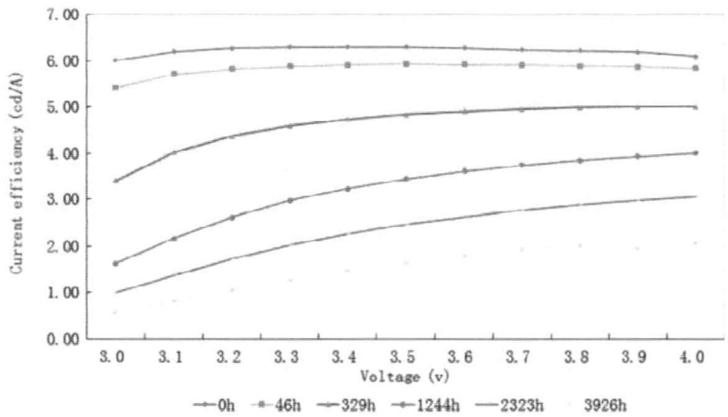

Figure 2. Current efficiency vs. voltage at different aging time.

Table 1. T_{80} in hours at different voltages

V	3.0	3.1	3.2	3.3	3.4	3.5	3.6	3.7	3.8	3.9	4.0
T_{80}	111.8	156.9	197.7	233.5	267.6	299.8	331.1	365.2	394.1	418.0	480.0

The trend is fitted by a simple function comprising the parameter T_{80}. The fitting function is as follows (cf. [2]):

$$\eta = \eta_0 / \left(1 + 0.25 \times \left(\frac{t}{T_{80}}\right)^{\alpha}\right) \quad (1)$$

The results are listed in Table 1. As an accelerated test condition (2200 nits) was applied, the numbers in Table 1 are relatively low. The degradation at different operating points differs, whereas the degradation at lower voltages is even stronger.

4. Conclusion

The degradation behavior of the blue OLEDs of Novaled is not singular or unique. The same trend could be observed for blue OLED devices provided by Merck, which were tested. The correlation between current degradation and current efficiency degradation was analyzed. A simple linear relationship between them may already lead to a first reasonable model, whereas the slope depends on the operation point (current or voltage amplitude). For digital driving, a specific compensation algorithm will be needed to consider this dependence. Since the operation point does not strongly vary when digitally driven, a good degradation model and specific algorithm may compensate the pixel-wise degradation artifacts like image sticking, so that the lifetime of an AMOLED display can be significantly extended.

5. Acknowledgement

We gratefully acknowledge the support from Novaled AG and Merck KGaA for providing the OLEDs test samples.

6. References

[1] P. Volkert, C. Xu, "Principle and validation of digital driving for AMOLED display", J. Soc. Inf. Disp., Vol. **22**, pp. 43–54, 2014.

[2] P. Kobrin, E. Boehmer, P. King, R. Fisher, S. Robinson, P. Green, "Time dependence of OLED luminance", Dig. Tech. Pap., Vol. **34**, pp. 539–541, 2003.

Paper No S14.4: Anisotropy in OLEDs

Michiel Callens,[1] Daisuke Yokoyama,[2] and Kristiaan Neyts[1]
[1]Ghent University, Belgium, E-mail: michiel.callens@elis.ugent.be; [2]Yamagata University, Japan

Abstract
In this paper, we discuss the effect of anisotropy on optical outcoupling in organic LEDs or OLEDs. We focus on different forms of anisotropy that can be found in OLEDs and the impact they can have on outcoupling efficiency. We discuss the emitter orientation and the anisotropy in the refractive indices of the electron transport layer, the hole transport layer and the emitting layer.

1. Introduction
Organic light-emitting diodes, or OLEDs, are luminescent devices consisting of a stack of thin organic layers. Each of these layers serves a specific purpose and when an appropriate combination of layers and emitters is used one can make these devices generate light with almost 100% internal efficiency. Even though light can be generated with such high efficiencies, only a relatively small portion can be extracted from the structure. Due to total internal reflection (TIR) at surfaces with media having a lower refractive index and coupling to plasmonic modes, a large portion of the light remains trapped inside the stack and is eventually absorbed.

In a traditional OLED the percentage of light that manages to escape the structure and is considered useful is usually limited to around 20%. Because losses are so high, there is a lot of potential for improvement. A plurality of solutions have been proposed to increase OLED efficiency, such as high-index substrates, grating-assisted outcoupling [1] and many others. We refer to the work of Br¨utting et al. [2] for an overview. In recent developments, Yokoyama et al. [3,4] showed that some organic materials show strong anisotropy in their refractive index and electrical properties. Historically, anisotropy was not taken into account in the optical design of OLEDs because the anisotropy was deemed very small. Although this is the case for many organic materials, there are materials (mostly having oblong or disk-like molecules) that show strong anisotropy. Typically, these organic layers are uniaxial with the c-axis perpendicular to the substrate.

2. Positive and Negative Anisotropy
Anisotropy is termed negative or positive depending on whether the extra-ordinary or ordinary refractive index is larger. For simplicity we will assume that all materials we discuss from now on are materials with the optical axis normal to the surfaces of the layers that make up the OLED, which corresponds to reality in most situations. We define the anisotropy as

$$\Delta n = n_e - n_o.$$

The strength and sign of the anisotropy is sufficient to describe the anisotropy since we assumed that the optical axis is fixed.

Whether positive or negative anisotropy will have a positive or negative effect on optical outcoupling is not obvious and has to be determined through numerical analysis.

3. The Effect of Anisotropy on Optical Outcoupling Efficiency
From numerical analysis of the device depicted in Figure 1, we found that the requirements for anisotropy depend on the position of the layer within the layered structure of the OLED. We found that they also depend on the orientation of the emitters and that opposing requirements are possible.

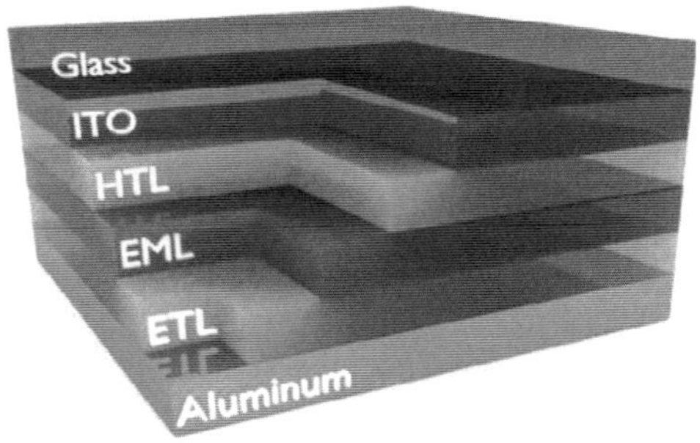

Figure 1. Schematic drawing of the OLED used in the numerical analysis. Consisting of a glass substrate, a tin-doped indium oxide (ITO) anode, a hole transport layer, an emitting layer (EML), an electron transport layer, and an aluminum cathode.

Anisotropic OLEDs were found to outperform their isotropic equivalents by 9% in terms of outcoupling efficiency for randomly oriented emitters with the anisotropy limited to ±0.2. Noteworthy is that improper use of anisotropic layers can deteriorate optical outcoupling by 8%. Horizontal and vertical orientation yield similar results, be it with different design requirements. This leads us to believe that anisotropy should be taken into account when designing the next generation of OLEDs. It can increase outcoupling for those who take it into consideration during the design and it can equally mean a drop in outcoupling efficiency for those who neglect it.

4. Acknowledgements
The authors would like to thank the Flemish Agentschap voor innovatie door wetenschap en techniek (contract IWT 120334) for funding.

5. References
[1] M. K. Callens, H. Marsman, L. Penninck, P. Peeters, H. de Groot, J. M. Ter Meulen, K. Neyts, "RCWA and FDTD modeling of light emission from internally structured OLEDs", Opt. Express, Vol. **22** (Suppl 3), pp. A589–A600, 2014.
[2] W. Brütting, J. Frischeisen, T. D. Schmidt, B. J. Scholz, C. Mayr, "Device efficiency of organic light-emitting diodes: Progress by improved light outcoupling", Phys. Status Solidi, Vol. **210**, pp. 44–65, 2013.
[3] D. Yokoyama, Y. Setoguchi, A. Sakaguchi, M. Suzuki, C. Adachi, "Orientation control of linear-shaped molecules in vacuum-deposited organic amorphous films and its effect on carrier mobilities", Adv. Funct. Mater., Vol. **20**, pp. 386–391, 2010.
[4] D. Yokoyama, "Molecular orientation in small-molecule organic light-emitting diodes", J. Mater. Chem., Vol. **21**, p. 19187, 2011.

Paper No S15.1: Monocular AR Display for Automobile Navigation and Safety Driving

Haruhiko Okumura,[1] Takashi Sasaki,[1] Aira Hotta,[1] and Kazumitsu Shinohara[2]

[1]Corporate Research & Development Center, Toshiba Corporation, Tokyo, Japan; [2]Graduate School of Human Sciences, Osaka University, Osaka, Japan

Abstract

We proposed and developed a novel monocular windshield augmented reality projector: WARP for AR and head-up display (HUD) applications. They use monocular vision that eliminates the depth cues caused by binocular parallax information. Our developed WARP system achieved not only a high hyper-reality performance with free depth perception and high visibility but also low eye-fatigue and wide field of attention.

1. Introduction

As one of the AR displays, a head-up display (HUD) superimposes the reflected display image and background space. For many years, it had been requested to set to the display image at any depth position of the driver's gaze point. When binocular parallax is used, the generation processing has to correspond to the parallax image to an observer's gaze point [1]. Therefore, a problem arises in that processing becomes complicated.

With our developed monocular HUD system, Windshield-refracted Augmented Reality Projector (WARP), the display image can be set to any depth position, which was difficult to achieve by the conventional approach.

2. Monocular Head-Up Display (HUD) Concept: WARP for Navigation

We found that monocular vision effects the reinforcement of space perception and the reinforcement of stereoscopic sense [2]. We used the depth perception enhancement by monocular vision for development of an HUD based on a new concept (WARP). It is important for WARP system to control perceived depth position of the display image, thus we have developed the method to control the depth perception position of the display image under monocular condition.

We have reported the depth perception position can be controlled up to 60m within an error of 30% by static display image with static perspective depth cues and can be controlled up to 120m within an error of 30% by dynamic display image with dynamic depth cues [3]. These results are obtained under the condition with no obstacles ahead on the load. However, in many cases, there are many cars may run ahead in the driver's way while driving. It has not been investigated the depth perception effects of the monocular HUD image in the case where the HUD image overlaps the preceding car or other obstacles. The objective of this study is to develop a perceived depth position control method in the case where there is a preceding obstacle in front of the car. We developed novel depth controllable method with which the perceived depth position of the HUD images can be controlled even in the case of a preceding obstacle, as shown in Figure 1.

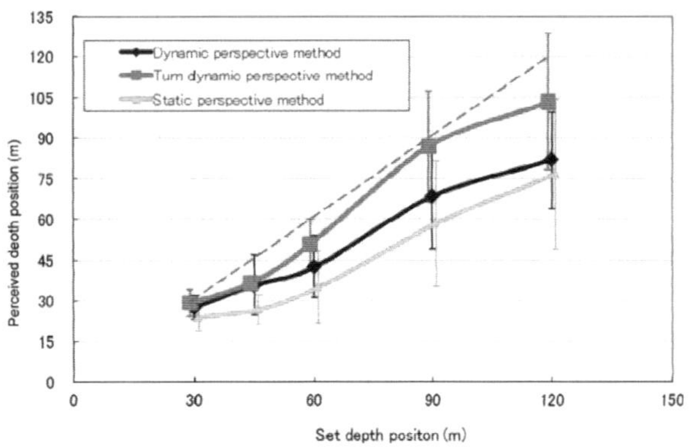

Figure 1. Perceived depth position under real space condition with a preceding obstacles.

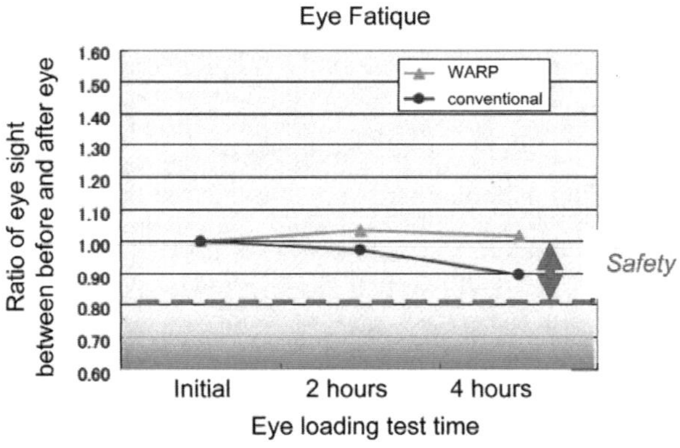

Figure 2. Long time eye fatigue tests for WARP.

3. Safety Test: Long Time Eye Fatigue Test

We made long time fatigue test to indicate safety performance of WARP. In the test, we watch two movies without caption for background image and only caption for superimposed HUD images .for two hours for each with one hour interval. Statistically speaking, surprisingly, eye fatigue for WARP was less than that of the conventional binocular HUD, as shown in Figure 2.

It indicated monocular observation reduces long time eye fatigue. It is expected that this phenomena can be explained by the hypothesis that moderate exercise of monocular vision emphasize eyesight.

4. References

[1] K. Nakamura, et.al, "Windshield display", Denso Tech. Rev., Vol. **10**, pp. 117–123, 2005.

[2] T. Sasaki et al., "Hyper-realistic display for automotive application", SID 2010, 64–2, 2010.

[3] A. Hotta, T. Sasaki, H. Okumura, "Depth perception effect of dynamic perspective method for monocular head-up display realizing augmented reality", IDW 2011, pp. 251–254, 2011.

Paper No S15.2: Exploring Crosstalk Perception for Stereoscopic 3D Head-Up Displays in a Crosstalk Simulator

S. Höckh,[1,2] A. Frederiksen,[1] S. Renault,[3] K. Hopf,[3] M. Gilowski,[1] and M. Schell[2,3]

[1]Robert Bosch GmbH, Gottingen, Germany, E-mail contact: simone.hoeckh@de.bosch.com; [2]Technische Universität Berlin, Berlin, Germany; [3]Fraunhofer Heinrich Hertz Institute, Berlin, Germany

Read the full article at DOI: 10.1002/jsid.368

Abstract

Envisioning a novel automotive stereoscopic 3D head-up display (HUD), we present a setup to simulate crosstalk including a new software solution. It constitutes a platform to explore the effects of stereoscopic crosstalk in the augmented reality (AR) viewing conditions of a 3D HUD. By means of this simulator, we investigate the variation of the visibility and acceptability thresholds of crosstalk over various parameters including contrast.

1. Motivation

Stereoscopic crosstalk is one of the most important parameters influencing the image quality of a stereoscopic system [1]. It can reduce the ability to fuse left and right view into a single 3D image, creates eye strain, and a lack of realism. Throughout the literature, quantitative data for the perception of crosstalk differ widely [1]. At past crosstalk investigations, common display technology was used which did not focus on the specific requirements of augmented reality scenarios. However, we are interested in the effects of crosstalk under the viewing conditions of a novel stereoscopic 3D head-up display (HUD). A HUD provides a virtual image superimposed with the real background, perceived under see-through condition, and used to augment reality.

2. Crosstalk Simulator Setup

We developed a setup with a visualization software based on the HHI Workbench3D framework and specifically adapted for crosstalk simulation. The hardware setup was realized by 3Dims GmbH and includes a projector capable of presenting stereoscopically perceived 3D images to an observer wearing shutter glasses. However, the images are projected onto a horizontal screen. A partly reflecting glass plate serves as a combiner allowing the observer to view the images as virtual images overlaid with the real background. The specially developed stereoscopic software can impose individual crosstalk to each created graphical object. For that, the user can adjust the amount of crosstalk while editing the 3D scene. Then the software renderer goes through three render passes, frame-by-frame: (i) coding individual crosstalk values for the left and right stereo views for all objects into a per-pixel lookup table, (ii) off-line rendering of both views, and (iii) merging the corresponding RGB color information from the one to the other view using the crosstalk values as written before in the lookup table. Finally, the resulting crosstalk-processed views are presented to the observer. As our device allows for the variation of many parameters associated with the perception of crosstalk, e.g. brightness, contrast, disparity, and image content, it is a very flexible tool for user trials on crosstalk disturbance.

3. Crosstalk Perception Study

We investigate the variation of the visibility and the acceptability thresholds of crosstalk in a human factor study based on 24 participants. The independent variables are the disparity sign, the object color (green or white), and the surrounding illumination (dark, intermediate, or bright), whereas the combinations of object color and illumination result in six different contrast values. For the visibility threshold, the object type (wide arrow or delicate line) constitutes an additional parameter. Our results show no influence of the disparity sign. We find the visibility

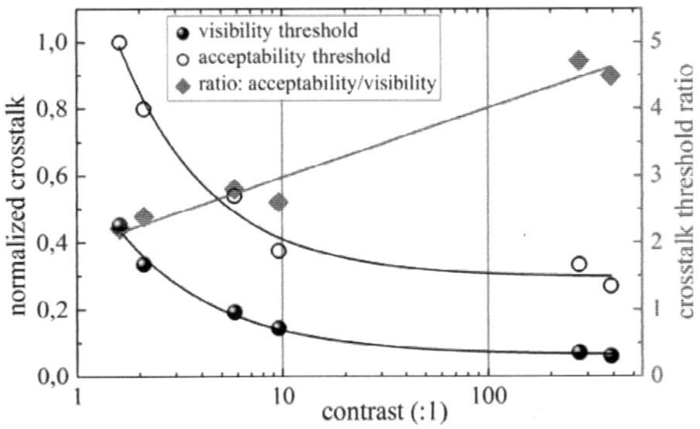

Figure 1. Variation of the visibility and acceptability thresholds and their ratio over contrast.

threshold to be lower for a delicate than for a wide symbol. Both thresholds decline with increasing contrast as illustrated in Figure 1.

For conventional stereoscopic displays, the visibility threshold is known to decrease with contrast [2]. Our results affirm this behavior for a see-through display. For a stereoscopic 3D HUD afflicted with crosstalk, they suggest preferring wide symbols. Since a high luminance means a high contrast with respect to the surroundings, our results indicate the choice of a moderate image brightness. In HUDs, luminance tends to be maximized depending on the lighting conditions to provide an appealing viewing impression. However, regarding the luminance requirements for a stereoscopic 3D HUD, our results suggest taking the perception of crosstalk into account. This may require a compromise between a bright image and a contrast leading to attainable crosstalk visibility and acceptability thresholds.

4. Conclusion

We present a simulator setup specifically adapted to determine crosstalk perception values valid for the envisioned application of an automotive stereoscopic 3D HUD. Our study indicates the behavior of the visibility and acceptability thresholds for stereoscopic see-trough displays demonstrating, inter alia, their decrease with rising contrast.

5. Acknowledgements

The project on which this work is based is funded by the German Federal Ministry of Education and Research, funding code 13N12602.

6. References

[1] A. J. Woods, "Crosstalk in stereoscopic displays: a review", J. Electron. Imaging, Vol. **21**, pp. 040902–040902, 2012.

[2] S. Pastoor, "Human factors of 3D imaging: Results of recent research at Heinrich-Hertz-Institut Berlin", Proceedings of 2nd International Display Workshop IDW'95, Vol. **3**, Hamamatsu, Japan, pp. 69–79, 1995.

Paper No S16.1: SVGA Bidirectional OLED Microdisplay for Near-to-Eye Projection

Uwe Vogel, Philipp Wartenberg, Bernd Richter, Stephan Brenner, Michael Thomschke, Karsten Fehse, and Judith Baumgarten

Fraunhofer Institute for Organic Electronics, Electron Beam and Plasma Technology FEP, Dresden, Germany, E-mail: uwe.vogel@comedd.fraunhofer.de

Abstract

The bidirectional microdisplay approach combines organic light-emitting diode (OLED) image display and silicon complementary metal-oxide-semiconductor image sensing in a single chip. Its application in smart glasses might enable gaze-controlled interaction. This is to present a new bidirectional OLED microdisplay featuring super video graphics array resolution for both image display and acquisition.

1. Introduction

Near-to-eye projection is the major approach to "Smart Glasses," which have gained lot of traction during the last few years. Microdisplays are key image generation components in this field. Thus, power consumption (directly related to battery lifetime) and user-interface are critical issues. Both topics can be addressed by bidirectional organic light-emitting diode (OLED) microdisplays. Microdisplays based on the OLED-on-silicon technology are predestinated for low power consumption because of the direct emitting behavior of the OLED. The special feature of the bidirectional display—the embedded image sensor—can be used for eye tracking in smart glasses, thus providing a hands-free approach to user interaction with the screen content and system.

2. Objective and Background

A key enabler is the OLED-on-silicon technology [1–3]. It uses a silicon wafer as a backplane toward the OLED pixels. Generally, the complementary metal-oxide-semiconductor (CMOS) backplane enables integration of further functions such as sensors. In a bidirectional OLED microdisplay, a photodiode is added to each pixel for light sensing and thus performs an embedded image sensor at the same resolution as the display.

Former designs of a bidirectional microdisplay had proven the concept of the integration of an image sensor into an OLED pixel matrix. Nevertheless, the resolution of the image sensor was always smaller than that of the display [1].

Data glasses are an example application of bidirectional OLED microdisplays. Inside such system, the display part delivers content to the user's eye, and the embedded image sensor serves for capturing the eye's image. By eye-tracking algorithms, the user's viewing direction can be calculated, and thus gaze-controlled interaction becomes feasible.

3. Results

The increased resolution of display and image sensor requires a higher bandwidth and thus a complete reconfiguration of the backplanes circuitries. To solve this issue, a novel system concept was developed and realized using leading edge mixed-signal integrated circuit design methodologies. This not only allows an increased resolution but also enables the addition of further functions to the chip which was done externally before, e.g., analog-to-digital conversion of the embedded image sensor data and exposure time control. The new super video graphics array (SVGA) bidirectional OLED microdisplay backplane was designed and manufactured using a 0.18 μm CMOS technology.

Display data are provided to the display via 24 bit RGB parallel interface including syncing. The pixel setup is RGBW, computing the white pixel's value on-chip.

Figure 1. SVGA bidirectional OLED microdisplay in self-capture mode.

The image sensor features a digital interface as well, enabling reduction of the complexity of external electronics and increased image sensor quality. The embedded analog-to-digital conversion allows simple implementation of additional image sensor features, e.g., exposure time control, which allows a correct function of the eye tracking in data glass applications under varying ambient light conditions.

A specific issue of the bidirectional pixel cell is the very close arrangement of OLED pixels and detecting photodiodes which results in a local optical cross-talk. In most applications, this can be resolved by a time-sequential control of the emission and detection phases. Nevertheless, it enables a very simple test mode of the integrated image sensor by capturing the image of the OLED display directly (Figure 1).

4. Acknowledgements

This work was partly funded by grants from the Federal Ministry for Education and Research (Bundesministerium f¨ur Bildung und Forschung, BMBF, 16SV3682) of the German government as well as by the Fraunhofer Internal Programs under Grant No. MAVO 823 279.

5. References

[1] U. Vogel, R. Herold, B. Richter, J. Baumgarten, K. Fehse, K. Leo, P. Schreiber, M. Sieler, "12.4: Interactive see-through augmented-reality smart display system", Dig. Tech. Pap., Vol. **42**, pp. 143–146, 2011.

[2] A. Ghosh, I. Wacyk, T. Ali, I. Khayrullin, O. Prache, S. Ziesmer, "High-brightness and high resolution AMOLED microdisplay", IDW'12 Digest, 2012, p. 1079.

[3] R. Asaki, S. Yokoyama, H. Kitagawa, S. Makimura, F. Abe, T. Yamazaki, T. Kato, M. Kanno, Y. Onoyama, E. Hasegawa, K. Uchino, "18.1: A 0.23-in. high-resolution OLED microdisplay for wearable displays", Dig. Tech. Pap., Vol. **45**, pp. 219–222, 2014.

Paper No S16.2: See-Through Multiaperture Near-to-Eye Display With Waveguide

Peter Schreiber, Matthias Lorenz, Peter Dannberg, and Frank Fuchs

Fraunhofer IOF Jena, Jena, Germany, E-mail: peter.schreiber@iof.fraunhofer.de

Abstract

We describe design and manufacturing of a multiaperture near-to-eye (N2E) display, establish design rules, and discuss relevant properties in comparison with traditional single-aperture devices. A grating-coupled waveguide shifts the image laterally toward the eye-motion box and enables see-through functionality using the zeroth diffraction order of the outcoupling grating.

1. Introduction

Traditional designs for near-to-eye (N2E) projectors employ a single-aperture eye piece—often realized as folded free-form optics to achieve a miniaturized system design—to observe a microimager [1]. Often, a subsequent pupil expander, which generates multiple, laterally displaced eye piece exit pupils, helps to enlarge the overall eye-motion box. Usually, such pupil expanders are realized using diffractive and light-guiding elements. In few cases, the pupil expander also acts as optical combiner, which superposes the projection with the observer's see-through view. The designs described above suffer from various drawbacks like system size and weight as well as difficulties of the manufacturing and assembly of the complex elements.

2. Multiaperture N2E Display

We propose a new approach to overcome these problems using a multi-aperture approach with split—but partially overlapping—FOV of the projected virtual image [2]. This rather simple system design consists of a microimager, a lens array (MLA), and a field lens (Figure 1).

As can be seen from Figure 1, the focal width of the field lens mainly determines the eye clearance, while the overall field of view results from the summation of the global FOV and the local FOV of individual array channels. Imager size and field lens focal width determine the global FOV, while the f/# of the lenslets basically controls the local FOV. The system length (from imager to field lens) nearly equals the focal width of the lenslets of only few millimeters. To achieve a large number of projected pixels, microimagers with a huge pixel number (preferably 4k $\times$ 2k or 2k $\times$ 1k) of very small pixels—preferably <4 μm—are required. The partially overlapping local FOV and the fill factor of the subimages on the microimager decrease the number of projected pixels to only 20–30% in both axes. Conversely, this redundancy helps, to correct for single pixel imager errors and enables application of RGB color filters channel-wise onto the lens array instead of pixel-wise onto the microimager. Preprocessing of the projected subimages enables control of virtual image projection distance and limited correction of possible low vision of the user.

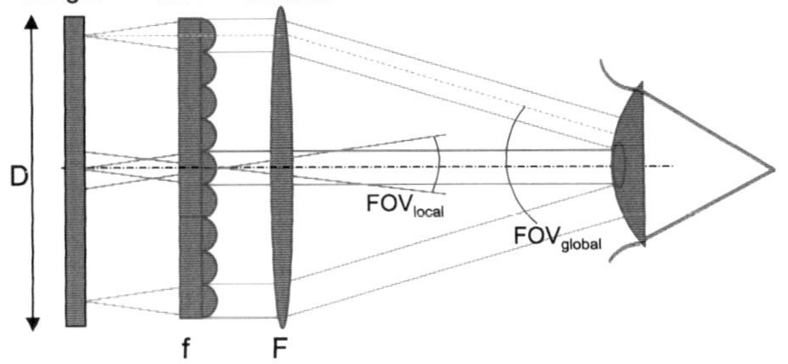

Figure 1. N2E display scheme without waveguide.

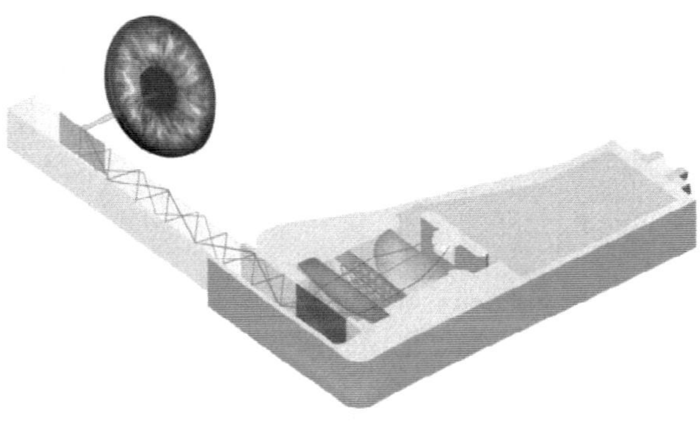

Figure 2. Lab sample schematic layout.

The lens array is manufactured by replication of comparatively large reflow microlenses (lens diameter about 1 mm) as polymer-on-glass element; the field lens is a simple planoconvex lens or could be "integrated" into the lens array, using off-axis lenslets. In our current demonstrator, a Cr-mask, buried under a condenser lens array (not shown in Figure 1), models the µ-imager.

3. Waveguide

If we combine the multiaperture eyepiece setup from Figure 1 with an image-shifting lightguide with diffractive incoupling and outcoupling features, we arrive with a—currently monochrome—miniaturized and unobtrusive system setup (Figure 2).

Like the lens array, the 455 nm period binary coupling gratings on the flint-glass lightguide are polymer-on-glass replica but in this case mastered by electron-beam lithography. Over an incidence angle range of $\pm5°$, the realized 455 nm period grating achieved tolerable variations of first diffraction order efficiency in the range of 12–25% and enabled see-through using its zeroth order with about 60% transmission.

4. Acknowledgements

We thank Stephanie Fischer and our former colleagues Marcel Sieler and Matthias Kraus for their contributions to array projection development and the German Federal Ministry for Education and Research for funding of the projects UIPicA and PRIAMOS.

5. References

[1] B. Kress, T. Starner, "A review of head-mounted displays (HMD) technologies and applications for consumer electronics", Proc. SPIE, Vol. **8720**, p. 87200A, 2013.

[2] P. Schreiber, M. Sieler, M. Kraus, "Projection display and method of projecting an overall image", WO 2013/144311.

Paper No P01: Nonspecular Reflectors Using One-Step Spray Coating for Brightness Enhancement in Reflective Displays

Su Pan and Hoi-Sing Kwok

State Key Lab on Advanced Displays and Optoelectronics, Department of Electronic and Computer Engineering, Hong Kong University of Science & Technology, Clear Water Bay, Kowloon, Hong Kong, E-mail: spanaa@ust.hk

Abstract

We proposed a novel method to fabricate nonspecular reflectors by spray coating system, which are applied to enhance brightness near normal view direction when light is obliquely incident. Fabrication parameters are optimized, and a 70 mm × 70 mm prototype is exhibited.

1. Introduction

Reflective displays are widely used in portable personal devices, like e-book, and other applications, such as electronic tags and labels. Reflective displays possess superiority of low power consumption as well as light weight and legibility under sunlight. There are several types of technology, including liquid crystal displays, such as super twist nematic LCDs, polymer dispersed LCDs, cholesteric LCDs, electro-wetting, electrophoretic and micro-electro-mechanical system. However, the light efficiency and contrast ratio is not satisfactory at this moment. Mirrors are usually used at the bottom in the reflective display as reflector. To avoid mirror lustrous, both front scattering films and internal diffusive reflectors (bump) are proposed, as well as to widen view angle. Due to the specular reflection, brightness along normal incidence is low when light is obliquely incident. Moreover, glares caused by the top surface overlap with images and results in poor contrast ratio, which is revealed in Figure 1. In this paper, we will describe an easy method to fabricate micro slant reflectors by one step spray coating.

2. Fabrication

The proposed fabrication method is demonstrated in Figure 2. α is desired slope of micro slant grating and β is tilt angle of the holder under spray coater. The oblique angle of illumination is assumed to be $-30°$. To enhance reflectance distribution near normal direction, slope of the desired slant reflector is set as about 15°.

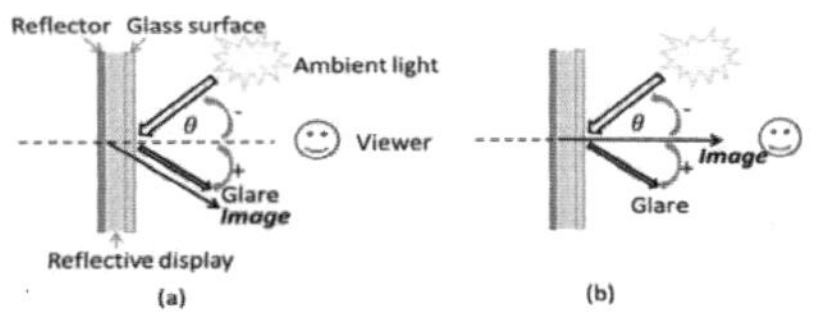

Figure 1. Reflectance distribution of reflective display when light is incident at oblique angle (a) mirrors (b) nonspecular reflectors.

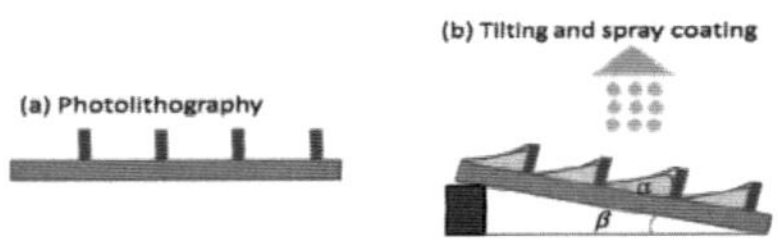

Figure 2. Demonstration of the proposed process. (a) Standard photolithography and deep reactive ion etching to "silicon walls". (b) Oblique spray coating.

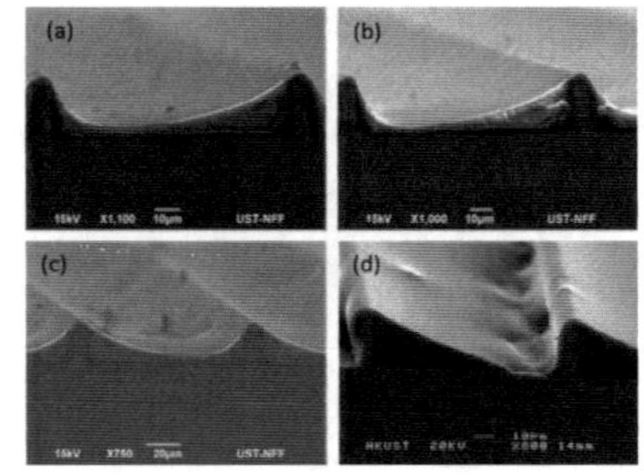

Figure 3. SEM pictures of cross section (a) 15°; (b) 20°; (c) 25°; and (d) 30°.

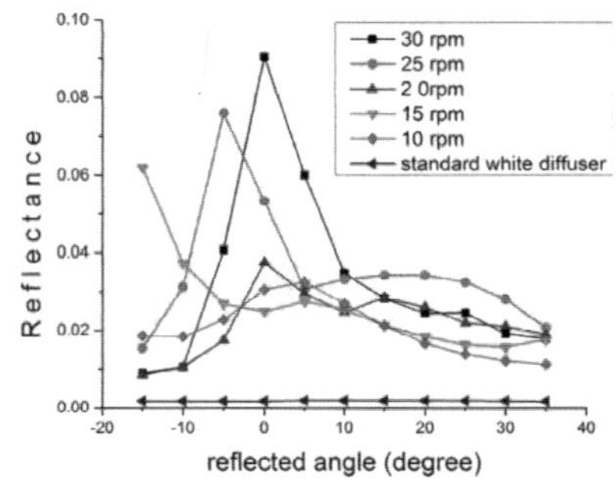

Figure 4. Reflectance of samples with different rotation speeds.

3. Results and Discussion

Slope of micro grating can be controlled by adjusting the angle of holder. Capability of 15°–30° slant grating is exhibited in Figure 4. For low inclined angle, slope of resist relief surface gradually changed. Straight hypotenuses are achieved for large slant angle. To achieve uniform slope, dose of resist should be precisely controlled to be just right, which corresponds to number of coating cycles. Figure 4 (a)–(d) elucidate change of surface profile as cycles increase. The tilt angle of the holder is set as 15°.

Figure 4 shows reflectance of nonspecular reflector of different rotating speed. As speed goes up, reflectance at normal view direction is improved. A 70 mm × 70 mm prototype is fabricated and compared with mirror and white paper.

4. Conclusion

A novel and easy method to fabricate efficient nonspecular reflectors is proposed by oblique spray coating. A 70 mm × 70 mm uniform prototype is demonstrated. Brightness at normal direction is enhanced 50× than standard white diffuser. Besides, scattering effect is obtained at the same time. We believe it is a good choice for reflective displays. Moreover, micro slant gratings have wide application in lens, beam steering, light-guiding plate, and many other areas.

Paper No P02: UV Penetration Depth in Hybrid-Aligned Reverse Mode Liquid Crystal Cell

Rumiko Yamaguchi, Tomoya Takatsu, and Koichi Inoue

Graduate School of Engineering and Resource Science, Akita University, Akita, Japan, E-mail: yrumiko@ipc.akita-u.ac.jp

Read the full article at DOI: 10.1002/jsid.319

Abstract

We have prepared reverse mode liquid crystal cells with a hybrid alignment by using polymer stabilized effect. In a polymerization process, a UV penetration depth in the cell from a vertical aligned side is estimated about two times longer than that from a planer aligned side, which results in a change of polymer morphology. The UV irradiation from the planer side gives a higher contrast ratio by the planer aligned polymer rich layer.

1. Introduction

A reverse mode with a transparent off-state and a scattering on-state has been proposed. Hikmet [1] has been reported the homogeneously aligned reverse mode cell which is prepared using a nematic LC with positive dielectric anisotropy and a reactive mesogen (RM). Reverse mode cells with 90° and 270° twisted nematic orientations have also been proposed to be lower driving voltage and to eliminate polarization dependence [2].

Recent years, a hybrid-aligned reverse mode cell has been reported [3]. The cell can be applied to a daylight transmission controllable window with an unsymmetrical incident angle property. In the hybrid-aligned cell fabrication process, we have two ways of UV irradiation to polymerize the RM. One is the irradiation from vertical and the other is from planer aligned sides. Liquid crystal and RM molecules have absorption anisotropy of UV light and the UV penetration depth should be different, as shown in Figure 1(a) and 1(b). In this report, therefore, we estimate the UV penetration depth of the cell when irradiated from vertical and planer aligned sides and clarify polymer morphologies and electro-optical properties.

2. Materials

The reverse mode LC cell was prepared using the RM of UCL-017 (DIC) and a tolane-type nematic LC of MLC2136 (Merck) with positive dielectric constant anisotropy. The RM was dissolved in the LC at concentration of 5wt%. The mixture was sandwiched between glass substrates coated with polyimide films for vertical and planer alignment. The cell thickness was 10 μm. We use a UV LED with an emission peak wavelength of 365 nm and a FWHM of about 13 nm. The cell was irradiated with UV light of 20 mW/cm^2 for 600 s at room temperature.

3. Results

We measured a UV absorption spectrum of the LC and RM mixture in Hexane. The absorption intensity at 365 nm is 0.5% of the peak absorption intensity at 309 nm. We refer absorption coefficient data of $\alpha_{//}$and $\alpha_{\perp}$ in some LCs with a tolane bridge reported by Wu et al. [4] and estimate about $\alpha_{//}$ of 3×10^3 and $\alpha_{\perp}$ of 4×10^2 cm^{-1} at 365 nm. The tilt angle of LC molecules in the hybrid aligned cell is supposed to be lineally increased (or decreased) from planer (vertical) to vertical (planer) alignment in the bulk. The UV penetration depth is calculated to be about 7.6 μm and 3.7 μm when the UV light enters from the vertical and planer sides as shown in Figure 1(a) and 1(b), respectively.

We measured electrostatic capacitance of the cell as a function of applied voltage and transform to the relative permittivity as shown in Figure 2. The driving voltage of the cell which is irradiated with the UV light from the planer aligned side is higher than that from the vertical aligned side. It is indicate that the planer-aligned polymer rich layer is formed near the substrate of the UV exposure side and higher applied voltage is needed to reorient the LC molecules. We confirmed an uneven distribution of the polymer by using SEM. The cell tunes to the scattering state by applying the voltage. The contrast ratio of the cell irradiated with the UV light from the planer aligned side is stronger, because the light is efficiently scattered in the planer-aligned polymer rich layer, not in the vertical aligned layer.

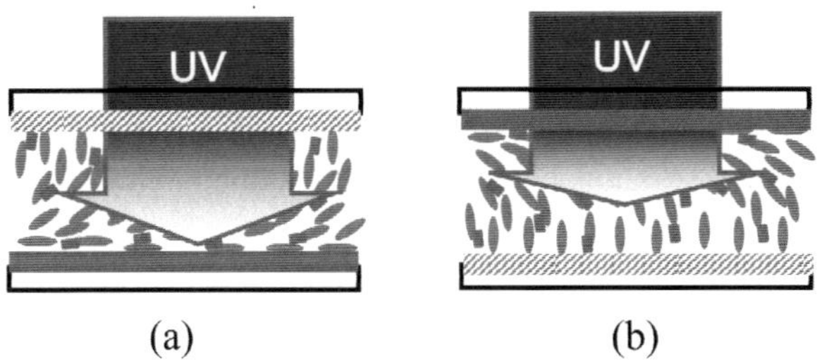

Figure 1. Schematic models of a hybrid-aligned LC cell and UV light penetration.

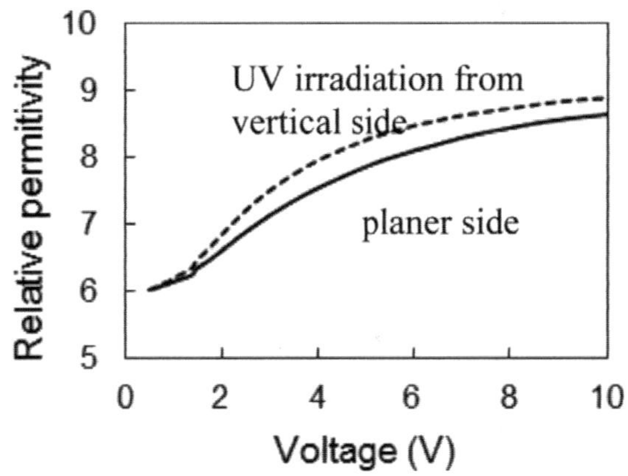

Figure 2. Relative permittivity as a function of applied voltage in hybrid-aligned reverse mode cells.

In conclusions, we calculate the UV penetration depth in the hybrid-aligned reverse mode cell. The penetration depth changes the polymer morphology and the electro-optical property.

4. References

[1] R. A. Hikmet, "Electrically induced light scattering from anisotropic gels", J. Appl. Phys., Vol. **68**, pp. 4406–4412, 1990.

[2] R. Yamaguchi, L. Xiong, "Reverse-mode liquid crystal gels with twisted orientation", Jpn. J. Appl. Phys., Vol. **49**, pp. 06023-1-06023-3, 2010.

[3] T. Takasu, R. Yamaguchi, "Switchable liquid crystal window for daylight control with asymmetrical incident angle", IDW'13, pp. 229–230, 2013.

[4] S.-T. Wu, E. Ramos, U. Finkenzeller, "Polarized UV spectroscopy of conjugated liquid crystals", J. Appl. Phys., Vol. **68**, pp. 78–84, 1990.

Paper No P03: Optical Switching of Scattering Mode Liquid Crystal Light Shutters

Ko-Ting Cheng,[1] Yen-Chen Liu,[1] and Andy Ying-Guey Fuh[2]

[1]Department of Optics and Photonics, National Central University, Chung-, Li City, 320, Taiwan, E-mail: chengkt@dop.ncu.edu.tw; [2]Department of Physics, National Cheng Kung University, Tainan 701, Taiwan

Abstract

We report that the isothermal phase transition induced by photoisomerization of azobenzene liquid crystals (azo-LCs) from trans- to cis-isomers results in the dissolution of poly(N-vinylcarbazole) (PVK) into azo-LCs. All-optically controllable and highly efficient scattering mode light modulators based on PVK films and its re-form mechanism were demonstrated.

1. Introduction

We combine the mechanisms of scattering mode light shutters using PVK morphologies, isothermal phase transition caused by photo-isomerization from *trans-* to *cis*-isomers, slow dark-relaxation and rapid photo-isomerization from *cis-* to *trans*-isomers to design all-optically controllable, and multistable devices. No thermal and/or electric fields are necessary in our work. PVK and azobenzene LCs (azo-LCs) are the key materials used to achieve our demonstration. The properties of PVK are reported in [1,2]. In this study, all-optically controllable and highly efficient scattering mode light modulators based on azo-LCs and PVK films are reported. The main mechanism involved includes the dissolution of PVK and azo-LCs resulting from isothermal phase transition, reformation of PVK films via slow/rapid phase separation by slow/rapid isomerization of azo-LCs. In addition to the described properties, such optical azo-LCs devices present high contrast ratio, polarization-independent scattering, multistability (or so-called gray-scales), and being polarizer free.

2. Experiments

The detailed processes involved can be found in [1,2]. The fresh filled cell presented clear transparency because of the uniformity of the PVK films. Excitation by green light will induce rapid phase separation of PVK and azo-LCs, and results in rough PVK surfaces and small-sized LC domains that highly scatter incident (visible) light. Here, high scattering can provide an efficient initial dark state. The fresh LC cell (*trans*-azo-LCs dominant) was illuminated with green light ($\lambda = 532$ nm) at an intensity of 252 mW/cm^2 for 120 s to obtain the initial scattering state. The UV and visible light sources used to photoisomerize the azo-LCs included a UV laser ($\lambda = 365$ nm) and a green laser ($\lambda = 532$ nm), respectively.

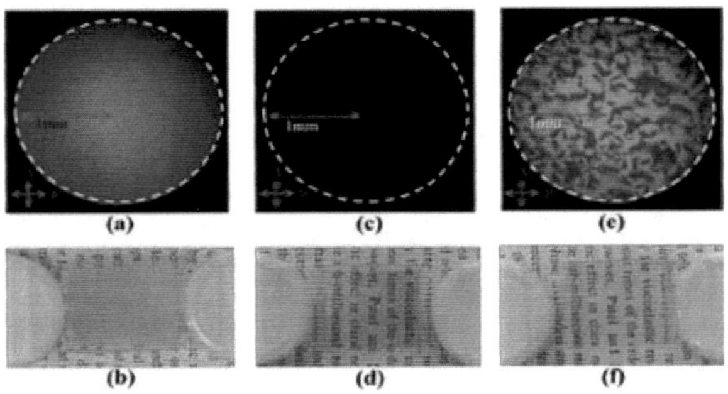

Figure 1. Images of the LC cell observed under a crossed-polarized optical microscope and photographed by a camera; (a), (b) Scattering state obtained by green light illumination. (c), (d) Transparent isotropic state achieved by UV light illumination. (e), (f) The isotropic phase LC cell after dark relaxation for 24 h, transferred to nematic phase.

3. Results and Discussion

The LC cell, shown in Figure 1(a), was then illuminated with UV light to transform *trans*-azo-LCs into isotropic *cis*-azo-LCs (isothermal phase transition). The temperature of the LC cell did not exceed the clearing temperature of the LCs in the *trans*-state; thus, isothermal phase transition may be inferred to occur after UV illumination (photoisomerization). The coated PVK partly dissolved into isotropic *cis*-azo-LCs. Figures 1(c) and 1(d), respectively, show a photograph of the LC cell as well as its image obtained by crossed-POM after treated of the cell with UV illumination. The mixture of PVK and *cis*-azo-LCs presented an isotropic state, as evidenced by the dark image under the crossed-polarizers shown in Figure 1(c). The isotropic LCs with a uniform refraction index show clear transparency [Figure 1(d)], and no light scattering resulting from the PVK surface can be observed. After the UV light was turned off, *cis*-azo-LCs began to slowly isomerize into *trans*-azo-LCs via dark relaxation, resulting in phase transition from isotropic to LC states as well as the slow phase separation of the PVK and azo-LCs because of the long lifetime of the *cis*-azo-LCs [3].

Based on the mechanism of phase separation and [1], the dimensions and roughness of the branch-like structures of reformed PVK increase with the increase of the cooling rate. Hence, long dark relaxation time caused the extremely low phase separation rates, so that the surface morphology of PVK was uniform and regular, associated with high transparency. Figures 1(e) and 1(f), respectively, show a photograph of the LC cell as well as its image obtained by crossed-POM after UV-illumination of the cell (7.4 mW/cm^2 for 120 s) after dark relaxation for 24 h. The LC phase appeared and generated large multidomains on the non-alignment treated PVK surfaces, as shown in Figure 1(e). The transparent state was permanently stable. Clearly, Figure 1 shows all-optical switching between bright (transparent) and dark (scattering) states.

4. Conclusions

The all-optically controllable and highly efficient scattering mode LC light modulator device is obtained by photoisomerization (UV) induced isothermal phase transition of LCs from a scattering device to a transparently isotropic one, during which the dissolution of PVK and *cis*-azo-LCs occurs. Green light illumination can be used to switch the LC cell from a transparent state to a scattering one, as well as the gray scales.

5. Acknowledgements

The authors would like to thank the Ministry of Science and Technology (MOST) of Taiwan for financially supporting this research under Grant Nos. MOST 103-2112-M-008-018-MY3.

6. References

[1] Y. D. Chen, A. Y. G. Fuh, K. T. Cheng, "Particular thermally induced phase separation of liquid crystal and poly(N-vinyl carbazole) films and its application", Opt. Express, Vol. **20**, pp. 16777–16784, 2012.

[2] Y. D. Chen, A. Y. G. Fuh, K. T. Cheng, "Optically and thermally controllable light scattering based on dye-doped liquid crystals in poly(N-vinylcarbazole) films-coated liquid crystal cell", Opt. Express, Vol. **24**, pp. 26252–26260, 2012.

[3] T. Ikeda, S. Horiuchi, D. B. Karanjit, S. Kurihara, S. Tazuke, "Photochemically induced isothermal phase transition in polymer liquid crystals with mesogenic phenyl benzoate side chains. 1. Calorimetric studies and order parameters", Macromolecules, Vol. **23**, pp. 42–48, 1990.

Paper No P04: Assessment of Liquid Crystal Display Image Defects by Pixel Capacitance Measurement based on Electrical Model for Panel Design

Yasuhiro Miyake,[1] *Atsuto Ota,*[2] *and Hidekazu Nishimura*[3]

[1]Keysight Technologies International Japan G.K., Japan; [2]True Step, Ltd., Japan; [3]Graduated School of System Design and Management, Keio University, Japan, E-mail: yasuhiro_miyake@keysight.com

Abstract

This article proposes the assessment of liquid crystal display (LCD) image defects based on electrical models which are also used for the design of liquid crystal (LC) cell panels. The effects of image defects on a LC pixel electrical model are analyzed, and the test method for assessing image defects using the electrical model is provided. Experimental results show the validity of the analysis and effectiveness of the proposed test method.

Figure 1. Charge map (write time (ms) = 0.5: left, 2: right).

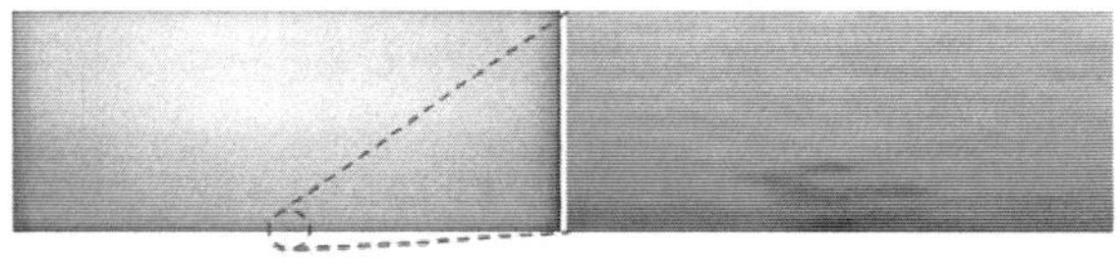

Figure 2. Charge map (magnified image at defect: right).

1. Introduction

In liquid crystal (LC) cell panel development, quantifying the orientation of LC molecules, determining the pixel transmission, to a LC capacitance value enables to integrate designs of two dissimilar properties: optical and electrical behaviors [1]. The requirements of high accuracy and fine pixels for panels are reflected into the circuit simulation at designing by expressing the activities of LC molecules as LC pixel capacitance and determining LC cell panel activities by the electrical model integrated with thin-film transistor (TFT) array. However, the electrical model of LC panel is not used for inspection in the manufacturing process; visual inspection has been the main method for detecting image defects. In our previous work, highly accurate LC pixel capacitance test method utilizing measured electrical charge was introduced and implemented [2,3]. In this article, effects of image defects on the electrical model are analyzed, and test method for assessing image defects in manufacturing process based on electrical models which are used for the design of LC cell panels is provided.

2. Electrical Model of LC Pixel

Smet's model is used for describing electrical characteristics of a LC pixel in this article [1]. Characteristics of C-t and C-V of LC capacitance C_{lc} are expressed as equations (1) and (2) in the model, where V is the externally applied voltage, τ is time constant indicating the response time of LC, V_T is the threshold voltage of the pixel, and $V_{m,c}$ is the capacitance modulation voltage. LC pixel capacitance value is calculated by adding a storage capacitance C_s to C_{lc} at a pixel.

$$V_i(t)=\sqrt{V^2\left(1-\exp\left(\frac{-t}{\tau}\right)\right)} \tag{1}$$

$$C_{lc}(V_i)=C_{\perp}+\frac{2}{\pi}(C_{\parallel}-C_{\perp})arctan\left(\frac{x+|x|}{2}\right) \tag{2}$$

with $x=(V_i-V_T)/V_{m,c}$.

3. Test Method for Detecting Visual Defects

3.1. Effects of Cell-Process Defects in the Model

Defects induced by TFT-array process can be electrically expressed as the device parameters or resistance changes. The effects of typical cell-process defects on Equations (1) and (2) are shown below. In Equation (1), polyimide (PI) film defects and excessive ions in LC increase τ whereas foreign materials in LC decrease $C_{\parallel}-C_{\perp}$ in equation (2) as the capacitance value of foreign materials is constant. As for the cell gap defect, wider the gap, smaller the $C_{\perp}$ and $C_{\parallel}$, or shorter the gap, bigger the $C_{\perp}$ and $C_{\parallel}$ in Equation (2).

3.2 Test Condition

The pixel capacitance test method consists of two operations: the voltage is written from the data lines to LC pixel, and electric charge stored by the LC pixel is measured to determine the capacitance value. Measurement results of each pixel aligned with the pixel orientation, called charge map, is used to detect image defects. By choosing adequate write time, defects affecting equation (1) can be differentiated in measurement results from normal pixels. An appropriate write voltage differentiates defects affecting Equation (2) likewise.

4. Test Results

Twisted-Nematic active matrix LC cell panels are used for the experiments. Figure 1 shows the measurement results of a panel with rubbing mura (PI film defects) at different write times. It shows that short write time with the changing orientation is the suitable measurement condition for detecting defective pixels. By using Equations (1) and (2) with the least squares method, τ in normal pixels and defective pixels are calculated to be 0.881 and 0.928 ms, respectively. In Figure 2, the measurement results of a panel having foreign material in the LC layer are shown. In this measurement, the voltage is chosen where the LC capacitance becomes $C_{\parallel}$ at longer write time. As a result, the capacitance of defective pixels is smaller than other areas (value of $C_{\parallel}-C_{\perp}$ is 10% smaller), which is observed as darker area in the charge map.

5. Conclusion

This article proposes assessment of image defects based on the common model with LC cell panel design, which enables to determine test conditions used in the manufacturing process in advance, namely at the design phase, and also enhances the efficiency in providing feedback of inspection results.

6. References

[1] H. D. Smet, J. V. D. Steen, D. Cuypers, "Electrical model of a liquid crystal pixel with dynamic, voltage history-dependent capacitance value", Liquid Crystals., Vol. **31**, pp. 705–711, 2004.

[2] Y. Miyake, A. Ota, H. Nishimura, "Cell panel electrical test for evaluating the electrical characteristics of liquid crystal displays", J. Inform. Display, Vol. **16**, pp.17–21, 2015.

[3] Y. Miyake, K. Chikamastu, J. Mizoguchi, "New electrical test method for LCD cell-manufacturing process", J. Soc. Inform. Display, Vol. **16**, pp. 83–87, 2008.

Paper No P05: Increasing the Dynamic Range of LC Displays

Peter Cirkel, Lieven Penninck, and Rimmert Wittebrood

TP Vision, Innovation Site Europe, Technologiepark-Zwijnaarde 19, 9052 Gent, Belgium

Abstract

This article describes a method to extend the dynamic range of an LCD display by increasing the room for backlight boosting by hardware and algorithms.

1. Introduction

As a reaction on OLED TVs coming to the market, LCD TVs are equipped with features similar to OLED, like wide color gamut, ultra-slim design, and high contrast. The high contrast feature is closely related to another feature which is hitting the market now: High-dynamic range. In this article, we give an overview of technologies we use for the implementation of high-dynamic range in LCD TV.

2. Dynamic Range

The dynamic range of an LCD panel is naturally limited by its contrast of about 5000 at best for a VA panel. Under slight viewing angles this number quickly drops to lower values. Backlight dimming can be used to increase the dynamic range temporally and/or spatially. In this way the dynamic range of the LCD panel is increased by a factor equal to the dimming range of the backlight. This increase in dynamic range however has its limitations depending on the backlight dimming method used.

3. Backlight Dimming and Boosting

The limitations in the dynamic range of the backlight are twofold. First of all the backlight only has a limited number of segments and the backlight value varies due to thermal fluctuations. Therefore, dimming has to be balanced against the introduction of visible artefacts. Second, when the backlight is at its maximum brightness it can overheat. In order to cope with these limitations the hardware and driving algorithm can be adjusted in different ways as follows:

		Temperature measurement		
Adjustment of intensity		No	Global	Local
	Global		x	
	Local		x	

For edge lit backlight the number segments is only one or a few, so the adjustment of intensity can only be done globally. On the other hand in a direct lit backlight the number of segments can be >100 and local dimming and boosting can be done.

In this article, we mainly focus on the case of a local dimming and boosting backlight, and at global or local control of temperature.

4. Limiting Factors

The light sources of choice for modern LCD backlights are LEDs, which basically can be boosted to high brightness if the temperature is kept under control. Thermal control in a backlight is thus very important. The temperature can be limiting in different ways. First of all the LED junction temperature can be limiting. If this temperature is too high the LED lifetime will be reduced to an unacceptable level. This temperature is closely related to the thermal resistance of the LED package. There are continuous efforts to reduce this resistance. In particular the introduction of flip-chip packages has such an effect. The next limiting factor is the solder joint temperature. Failure of the solder joint can occur because of two reasons: solder creep and diffusion of solder material away from the joint. From these two, solder creep is the most important. Unlike the LED lifetime the solder creep will depend on the number of heating/cooling cycles rather than the absolute temperature. Another factor which can limit the boosting of LEDs is the touch temperature on the outside of LCD display. In particular for very slim designs it is a challenge to isolate the heat generated in the LEDs from parts of the display which can be touched by the user and are therefore not allowed to get too hot [1].

5. Temperature Model

Measurements on the touch temperature, for different displays show that its time dependence follows a slow single exponential behavior. Physically this corresponds to the heating and cooling of a heat sink, which can be modeled by a simple thermal resistor-capacitor network. For the LED solder and junction the data can be fit to a double exponential. In addition to the slow effect of the heat sink there is a fast effect of heating up the LED and solder/PCB only. Using these inputs the following overall thermal resistance network was constructed:

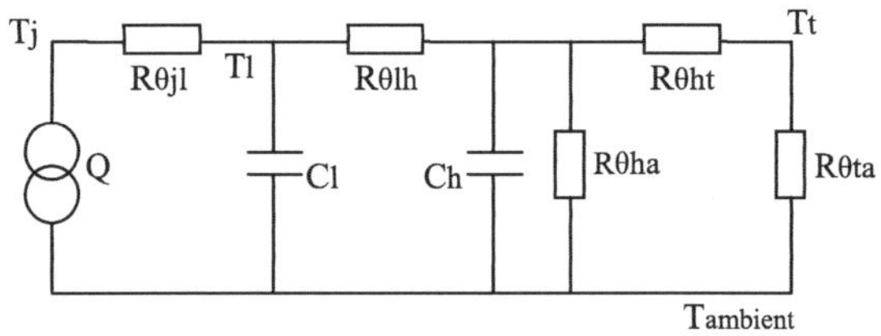

This thermal resistance network is used to optimize the display's dynamic range. By increasing the $R\theta ht$ from 15 to 35 K/W we significantly improve the room to boost the luminance.

6. Life Time Algorithm

In order to be able to boost the luminance of the backlight further, the thermal resistance network model is also used to predict and control the actual temperatures. This works in two ways. First by measuring the actual ambient temperature at a reference point, the reserve at other points in the display can be calculated. In this way the use of a worst case ambient temperature can be avoided. This is useful for locations in the display that may not exceed a certain temperature, such as the touchable parts. Second, by keeping track of the temperature at the lifetime critical points in the display (LED junction, solder joint), boosting is optimized by discounting the time that these points are relatively hot by moments that these points are relatively cool when relatively dark content is displayed. In this way an algorithm is constructed with a prediction block, based on the thermal resistor network, to model the parameters to be tracked. The results of this block are fed to a control block which steers the display so that all constraints are met.

7. Reference

[1] P. Cirkel, L. Penninck, "Design and perception of an edge lit HDR display", IDW '14, 2014.

Paper No P06: Preserved Color Gamut and High Color Stability by Local Dimming for LC-Panels

Daniel Schäfer and Chihao Xu

Institute of Microelectronics, Saarland University, D-66123 Saarbruecken, Germany,
E-mail: daniel.schaefer@lme.uni-saarland.de

Abstract

The light leakage and the color shift of an liquid crystal display (LCD) and especially vertically aligned (VA) panel drastically increases with viewing angle. Particularly for dark images the color gamut gets poorer and the color remarkably shifts with change of viewing angle. In this article, we investigate the impact of local dimming in respect of color gamut and color shift. The results by applying the sorted sector covering (SSC) local dimming algorithm in respect of color gamut and color shift are impressive. Not only the static contrast, but also the color gamut and stability are significantly enhanced, so that the image displayed is much more vivid and colorful.

1. Introduction

The color of an liquid crystal (LC) pixel is altered by the light leakage which is mostly gray tending blue. For dark pixels, the light leakage substantially superposes the color of the pixel. The problem gets severe, if the viewing angle is not zero [1]. In recent years, local dimming is applied for TVs for suppression of the light leakage and enhancement of contrast and black level. The impact of local dimming on the color gamut has not been investigated yet.

2. The SSC Local Dimming Algorithm with Pixel Compensation

The sorted sector covering algorithm [2] is a local dimming approach developed by the Institute of Microelectronics of Saarland University. It calculates the necessary brightness for every pixel using the light spread function of each LED. This yields decreased LED values and therefore a darker backlight b_p. In the next step, the values of the pixels (t_p) get increased to reach the requested brightness i_p.

$$t_p = \min\left(\frac{i_p}{b_p}, 1\right) \cdot t_{max} \geq t_{original}$$

For this investigation, we use this algorithm to validate the color gamut and color stability related to a dimmed backlight and thus reduced light leakage.

3. Color Gamut and Color Stability

It is well known that color is decreasing at rising viewing angle because light leakage is increasing. This effect is especially viewable for low gray values because of the worse signal to noise ratio.

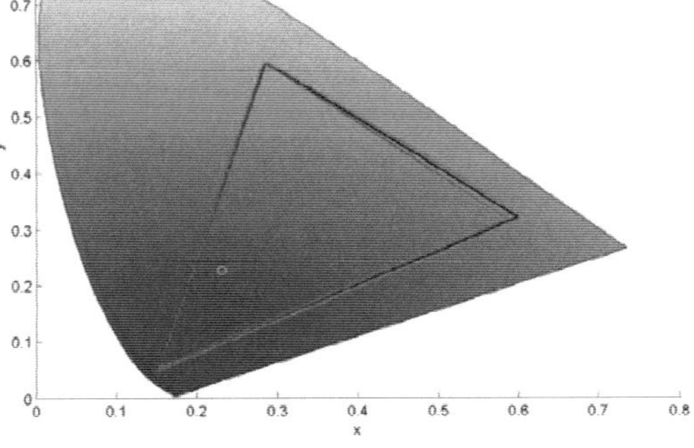

Figure 1. Original color gamut over the viewing angle.

A Hisense 50 Inch 4K TV was characterized. The contrast ratio is 4400. The x, y values of the light leakage is listed in Table 1.

Figure 1 shows the x-y-color-space. The white cycle represents the color of light leakage and the three triangles the color gamut of the panel for the viewing angle from 0° to 45°. For this measurement, the display is working in a nondimming mode at pixel values of 24% uniform. The blue primary is unchanged because of

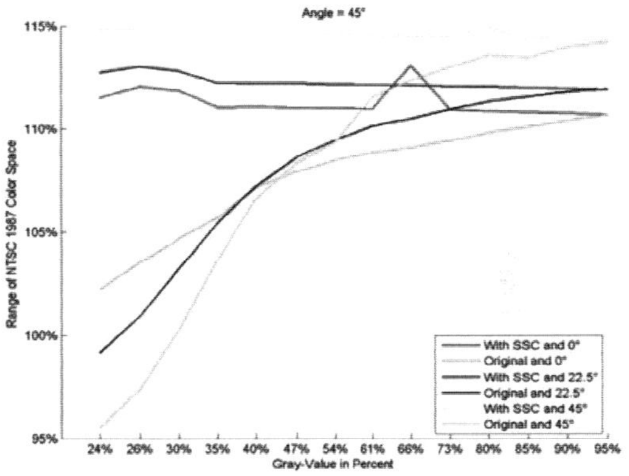

Figure 2. Color gamut for various viewing angles.

Table 1. Color coordinates of light leakage.

x = 0.27307	y = 0.22660

the blueish color of the light leakage. The contrast decreases with the angle and therefore the red and green primary move in direction to the light leakage color.

This causes a 7% reduced color gamut standardized to the NTSC 1987 color space. Figure 2 shows the complete characterization results with varying viewing angle and gray values for dimmed and undimmed operations.

The difference between dimmed and undimmed operation is for low gray values remarkable. The dimmed color gamut remains constant, because the transmission of pixels are due to pixel compensation high. The signal-to-noise ratio remains high. Even for an angle of 22.5°, the color gamut is for 13% larger than undimmed. A side effect is higher color stability for dark colors, if the viewing angle is changed. This effect is particularly perceivable at dark red or green areas.

4. Conclusion

In this article, it can be proven by measurements that local dimming is an appropriate method to preserve the color gamut without any need of expensive amendments for the panel's hardware. For our panel, we reach up to 19% higher color gamut. Furthermore the color stability for dark colors is increased too. Combined with enhanced contrast, local dimming makes dark images like movie much more vivid and colorful.

5. References

[1] S. Park, K.-H. Park, J.-H. Lee, J. H. Yoon, B. K. Kim, B.-H. Yu, K.-H. Kim, T.-H. Yoon, "Dark-state color shift and gray scale inversion in an in-plane switching liquid display device", J. Opt. Soc. Korea, Vol. **16**, pp. 409–413, 2012.

[2] D. Schäfer, T. Jung, C. Xu, "Enhanced local pixel compensation with clipping suppression and global luminance preservation", SID Digest, Vol. 43, pp 473–476, 2012.

Paper No P07: Saliency-Based Backlight Regulation Method for LCD Display

Jae Sung Park, Insung Hwang, and Nam Ik Cho

Seoul National University, Seoul Korea, E-mail: gogojs8902@gmail.com

Abstract

This paper presents a backlight unit (BLU) control method of the liquid crystal display devices for improving the quality of visually important regions in a scene. The proposed method dims and boosts the levels of the BLU blocks according to the saliency map and pixel distribution of input images. Simulation results indicate that users can feel improved visual quality without the increase of power consumption.

1. Introduction

Liquid crystal displays have been the dominant display systems in recent years, which need efficient backlight unit (BLU) and its control for high-quality image display. Hence, there have also been various backlight control methods, mostly backlight dimming and pixel compensation. Specifically, backlight dimming algorithms find the appropriate brightness levels of blocks and compensate the reduced brightness by increasing the pixel levels of the input image. In this paper, it is noted that most of the existing methods do not consider the psychological aspects of human visual system (HVS) in controlling the BLU, but just resort to the low-level image features from the pixel values in a block. Hence, we propose to control the BLU according to the saliency map of the scene, where the salient regions are found considering the HVS properties. Unlike the conventional methods that only dim some of the BLU regions, the proposed method boosts the brightness of BLU in the salient regions while suppressing the others for reducing or keeping the power consumption level.

2. Related Works

There is a local dimming method that keeps salient regions while dimming other regions for power saving purpose [1]. On the other hand, our method employs more elaborate method for finding salient region and boosts the salient area while dimming other regions with the power regulation algorithm.

3. Saliency-Based Local Backlit Control

The proposed method first finds the area that can be dimmed and then compute the amount of power to boost the salient regions. The backlight of salient region is then boosted considering the power consumption level.

3.1. Initial Backlight Dimming Gain

The features of an input image such as pixel mean and max values are analyzed block by block to determine the initial local backlight dimming gains.

3.2. Backlight Boosting Gain

We adopt a saliency detection algorithm to identify important and informative parts in a scene [2]. The block-wise saliency gain obtained by the algorithm is used to boost the backlight level of each block.

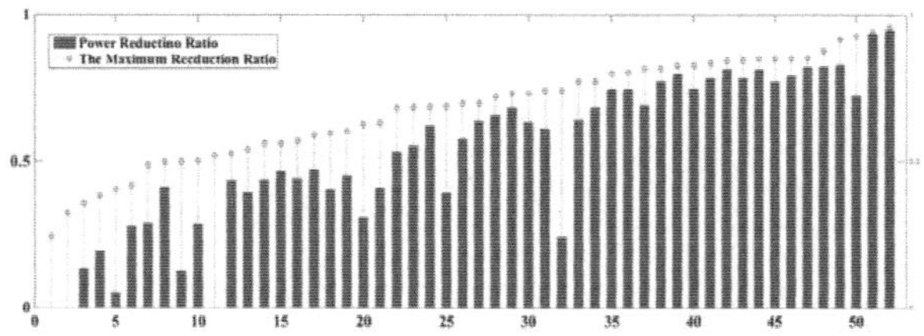

Figure 2. Normalized power reduction ratio.

3.3. Adaptive Gain Control

The maximum power consumption is set to the level of "no-operation" on the BLU. That is, the total amount of power for the backlight boosting cannot be larger than the power saved by dimming. The distribution of pixel levels in each block is also considered to adjust the initial gain, because too much dimming can cause the saturation problem. In addition, difference between the neighboring blocks is also considered to suppress the block artifacts. It is noted that our power regulation problem has the analogy to the bit-rate control of video encoders, and hence we adopt the rate control algorithm of MPEG2 TM5 for our power consumption control.

4. Experimental Results

We consider a display system with 20 × 12 backlight blocks and 255-level brightness. Figure 1(a) shows a sample input, and the results of Figure 1(b) dimming gains at the first step, Figure 1(c) saliency gains, and Figure 1(d) the final backlight levels. Also, we simulate the power reduction ratio using various images of different average signal level as shown in Figure 2. The pink colored markers mean the maximum power decrease ratio and blue bars indicate power reduction ratio of the sample images. The power consumption level is also well regulated in general images. The simulation results support that we can expect contrast enhancement in salient regions and unnoticeable quality degradation in other areas without power increase.

5. Conclusion

We have proposed a backlight control algorithm for improving the visual quality of images considering the HVS properties. Power consumption is also regulated so that the proposed system consumes equal or less power than before, by developing a control algorithm based on the bit rate control strategies of video encoders.

6. References

[1] C. H. Lee, W. H. Shaw, H. I. Liao, S. L. Yeh, H. H. Chen, "Local dimming of liquid crystal display using visual attention prediction model", *Proceeding of 20th ICCCN*, Maui, Hawaii, 2011, pp. 1–6.

[2] C. Yang, L. Zhang, H. Lu, X. Ruan, M.-H. Yang, "Saliency detection via graph-based manifold ranking", CVPR, Portland, OR, 2013, pp. 3166–3173.

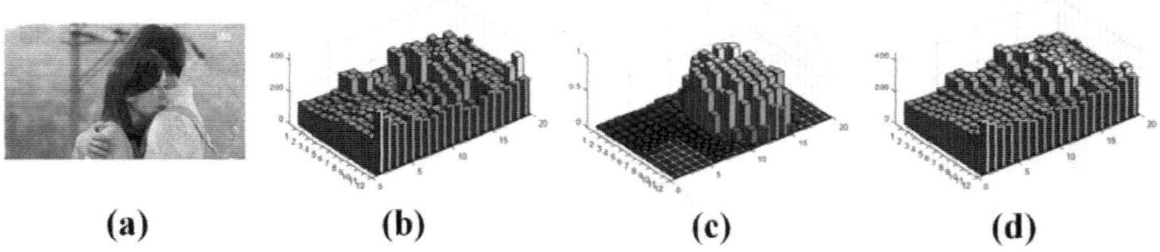

(a) (b) (c) (d)

Figure 1. Backlight adjustment result.

Paper No P08: Study of the Bend Oriented Liquid Crystal Phase Grating

Zhang Shuyuan,[1] Yu Tao,[1] Zhang Jiahe,[1] Zhang Bo,[1] Zhao Jinggang,[2] and Zhang Lina[2]

[1]Department of Physics, DaLian Maritime University, China, E-mail: zsy890103@sina.com;
[2]DaLian DKE LCD Ltd., China

Read the full article at DOI: 10.1002/jsid.317

Abstract

A bend-oriented liquid crystal phase grating was presented in this paper. The diffraction efficiency and the response time were studied and compared to the same parameters in parallel-oriented liquid crystals phase grating. The result showed that the bend-oriented liquid crystal phase grating behaves a higher diffraction efficiency than the comparative parallel-oriented ones and 20 times shorter in response time.

1. Introduction

The liquid crystal phase grating exhibits the attractive property of the tunable diffraction, low driving voltage, low power consumption, small volume, and so on. Recently, it was studied broadly [1]. The popular liquid crystal grating's response time was several ten times of milliseconds. It was difficult to satisfy the application. It was studied widely to develop a fast response liquid crystal grating in recent years. Ge Zhu reported a blue phase liquid crystal grating [2] that had the response time of 860 μs. A. K. Srivastava reported the ferroelectric liquid crystal grating that had a response time of 20 μs [3]. However, the blue phase liquid crystal grating used the special material and needed high driving voltage. Ferroelectric liquid crystals have some problems about the complex alignment technology and the bistable electro-optical performance. The desired fast liquid crystal grating will use nematic liquid crystals and its cell gap will be higher than 3 μm. In this paper, we presented a bend-oriented liquid crystal grating. It could avoid the "backflow" effect and have a fast response speed. We also found that its diffraction efficiency was higher than the parallel one. This study has a potential in the development of a fast nematic liquid crystal grating with a less difficult process.

2. Device Structure and Fabrication

In order to obtain a bend oriented liquid crystal grating, we used one substrate with the ITO interdigital electrode which has a width of 15 μm and a period of 30 μs. The other substrate has a plate ITO electrode. When the driving voltage was applied to the electrode, the period electric field was built in the liquid crystal layer. The liquid crystal will be shown a period refractive index to form a phase grating. In order to achieve the bend oriented liquid crystal, the pretilt angle on the substrate should be higher than 5°. We used the mixture polyimide of the parallel alignment and vertical alignment to achieve a pretilt angle of 7°. The substrate was rubbed by a rubbing machine. The two substrates were assembled with a plastic film spacer with a thickness of 10 μm. The rubbing direction of the bend oriented devices was parallel. The cell gap of the each device was measured by the optical method before injected the liquid crystal. The E7 liquid crystal was injected the devices. By comparison, the parallel alignment liquid crystal grating was made with the same parameters.

3. Testing and Results

The devices were tested using a standard optical diffraction experiment system. The light source is the 650 nm laser diode. The light pass through a polarizer to achieved the extraordinary ray. The liquid crystal grating was applied by the 1 kHz alternating current square waveform in which the amplitude could be controlled from 0 V_{rms} to 10 V_{rms} by the computer. The first and second order diffraction light intensities were measured by the Si-photo-detector and were acquired by the computer. To obtain the bend-oriented liquid crystal, the device was applied by 10 V_{rms} at first for 10 min. Then the voltage fell to the bias voltage of 2.5 V_{rms} quickly. By comparison, the same parameters as the parallel-oriented grating was applied with the same bias voltage. The results showed that the bend-oriented liquid crystal grating's diffraction efficiency was higher than the parallel one about 5%. It was 28% in this work. The bend-oriented liquid crystal grating's response time was 5.6 ms, which was defined as $T_{on}+T_{off}$. After the difference of the cell gap was corrected, it was 20 times shorter than the parallel one.

4. Discussion

A general bend-oriented liquid crystal devices have a response time low to 1 ms. In this work, our result was longer than the general one, because we used the high viscosity liquid crystal material (E7) and the thick liquid crystal layer. If the low-viscosity material and high Δn liquid crystal will be used, the thinner layer of liquid crystal also could be achieved. The response time will decay to sub-millisecond. In addition, the bend oriented liquid crystal grating's diffraction efficiency was higher than the parallel one, because the liquid crystal deformation of bend-oriented grating is smaller than the parallel grating in the area between the two interdigital electrodes.

5. Conclusion

We presented a bend-oriented liquid crystal grating. It has higher diffraction efficiency than the parallel-oriented liquid crystal grating with same structure and same liquid crystal. The response time is 20 times shorter than the parallel one. Our work could be applied in the production of fast response time and high diffraction efficiency liquid crystal phase grating.

6. Acknowledgements

We would like to thank the Mrs. Li Xiaolian of the Dalian University of Technology of China for her help and advantage discussion.

7. References

[1] C. M. Titus, P. J. Bos, "Efficient polarization-independent, reflective liquid crystal phase grating", Appl. Phys. Lett., Vol. **71**. pp. 2239–2241, 1997.

[2] G. Zhu, J. Li, X. Lin, H. Wang, W. Hu, Z. Zheng, H. Cui, D. Shen, Y. Lu, "Polarization-independent blue-phase liquid crystal grating driven by vertical electric field", J. SID, Vol. **20**. pp. 341–346, 2012.

[3] A. K. Srivastava, W. Hu, V. G. Chigrinov, A. D. Kiselev, Y.-Q. Lu, "Fast switchable grating base on orthogonal photo alignments of ferroelectric liquid crystals", Appl. Phys. Lett., Vol. **101**, pp. 031112-1-031112-4, 2012.

Paper No P09: Electrically Tunable Grating Using Holographic Polymer Templated Blue Phase Liquid Crystal

Chao Ping Chen,[1] Zhenghong He,[2] Yan Li,[1] and Yikai Su[1]

[1]National Engineering Lab for TFT-LCD Materials and Technologies, Department of Electronic Engineering, Shanghai Jiao Tong University, Shanghai 200240, China; [2]School of Physical Science and Technology, Southwest University, Chongqing 400715, China

Abstract

In this paper, we demonstrate an alternative approach to fabricating an electrically tunable holographic polymer-templated blue phase liquid crystal grating. This grating is obtained by preforming a polymer grating template, and then refilling it with the blue phase liquid crystal. Compared with conventional holographic polymer dispersed liquid crystal gratings, its driving voltage can be reduced to 43 V, while maintaining sub-millisecond response time.

1. Introduction

Tunable gratings based on holographic polymer dispersed liquid crystal (HPDLC) have been extensively studied for achieving low driving voltage, high diffraction efficiency, and fast response time. Sarkar et al. reported that the driving voltage can be decreased from 9.0 to 2.5 V/μm by using partially fluorinated monomers, but its decay time is slowed from 1.6 to 18 ms [1]. Jang et al. reported a HPDLC that is fabricated with the chemically incorporated graphene oxide, by which the driving voltage is reduced from 70 to 25 V. However, its decay time is slightly slowed from 3.2 to 4.8 ms [2]. In this paper, we propose a holographic polymer templated blue phase liquid crystal (HPTBPLC) grating, which is fabricated by refilling the blue phase liquid crystal (BPLC) into a grating template that is pre-formed by the holographic exposure [3].

2. Experiments

In experiments, the mixture for the polymer template comprises 21.9 wt %: 7.5 wt %: 1 wt %: 0.6 wt %: 69 wt % of TMPTA monomer (Aldrich): *N*-vinylpyrrollidone (Aldrich): *N*-phenylglycine (Aldrich): Rose Bengal (Aldrich): nematic liquid crystal (BP-06, $\Delta n = 0.158$, $n_{\text{iso}} = 1.56$, $\Delta\varepsilon = 34.2$, Jiangsu Hecheng). The BPLC for refilling is composed of LC host (BP-06) at 96.5% and chiral dopant (R5011, Jiangsu Hecheng) at 3.5%.

3. Results and Discussion

3.1. Driving Voltage

Diffraction efficiency (DE) versus applied voltages of HPDLC and HPTBPLC gratings is plotted in Figure 1. The DE is defined as a ratio of the power of the first-order diffraction to the total output power. For HPDLC grating, DE = 15% and driving voltage is 200 V at room temperature. For HPTBPLC grating, DE = 14.7% and driving voltage is 43 V at 70.5°C. The relatively low DE for HPTBPLC comes from the small refractive index contrast. The refractive index of the polymer matrix is 1.527, and $n_{\text{iso}} = 1.56$ for the BPLC. If n_{iso} could be increased to 1.59, the maximum phase modulation will reach π, at which DE is 33%. Moreover, for getting higher DE, smaller grating period and larger cellgap are both desired.

3.2. Response Time

The measured response time is shown in Figure 2, where the red dashed curve and blue solid curve represent the first-order transmittance of HPDLC and HPTBPLC gratings, respectively. The rise and decay time measured at room temperature are 341 and 424 μs for the HPDLC grating, respectively. While for the HPTBPLC grating, the rise and decay time measured at 70.5°C are 610 and 890 μs, respectively.

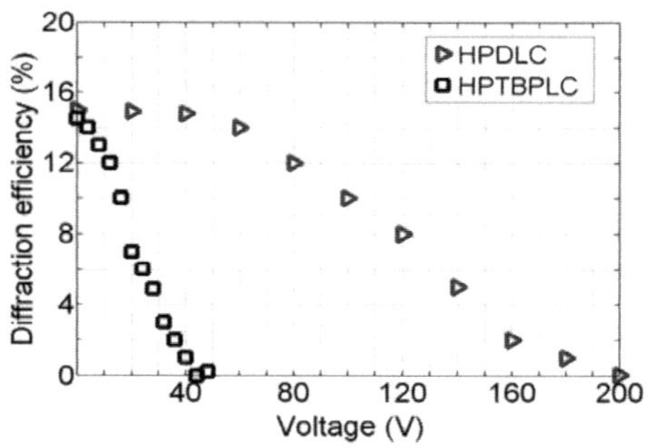

Figure 1. Measured DE versus driving voltage.

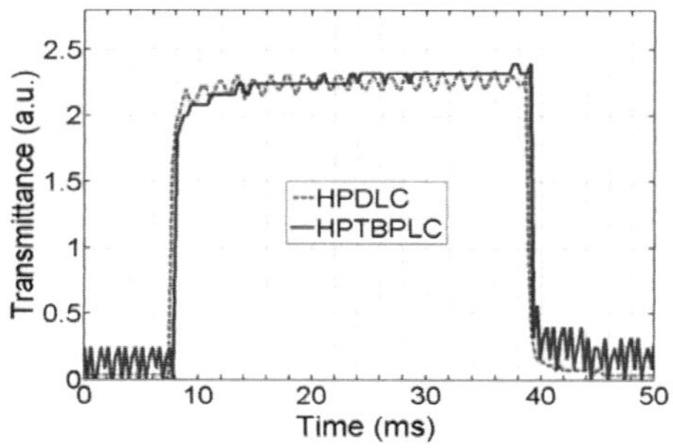

Figure 2. Measured response time of grating switching.

4. Conclusion

We have demonstrated a tunable HPTBPLC grating. This method is eligible in lowering the driving voltage to tens of volts, while maintaining sub-millisecond response time.

5. Acknowledgements

This work is sponsored by 973 Program (2013CB328804), NSFC (61307028), and Science & Technology Commission of Shanghai Municipality (13ZR1420000).

6. References

[1] M. D. Sarkar, J. Qi, G. P. Crawford, "Influence of partial matrix fluorination on morphology and performance of HPDLC transmission gratings", Polymer, Vol. **43**, pp. 7335–7344, 2002.

[2] M. W. Jang, B. K. Kim, "Low driving voltage holographic polymer dispersed liquid crystals with chemically incorporated graphene oxide", J. Mater. Chem., Vol. **21**, pp. 19226–19232, 2011.

[3] Z.-H. He, C.-P. Chen, J.-L. Zhu, Y.-C. Yuan, Y. Li, W. Hu, X. Li, H.-J. Li, J.-G. Lu, Y.-K. Su, "Electrically tunable holographic polymer templated blue phase liquid crystal grating", Chin. Phys. B, Vol. **24**, p. 064203, 2015.

Paper No P10: Influence of Dye Molecular Structure on Liquid Crystal Anchoring Energy

N. N. Barabanova,[1] V. V. Belyaev,[1] D. L. Bogdanov,[1] A. K. Dadivanyan,[1] A. P. Nazarov,[1] O. V. Noah,[2] and V. G. Chigrinov[3]

[1]Moscow Region State University, Russian Federation, E-mail: vic_belyaev@mail.ru; [2]Moscow State University, Russian Federation; [3]Hong Kong University of Science and Technology, China, Hong Kong

Abstract

Theoretical description of the photoalignment process details is an urgent task to make the LC alignment more perfect and develop displays with new functions. In this paper we describe formation of photoaligning dye dimers and influence of their molecular structure on both polar W_θ *and azimuthal* W_φ *anchoring energy.*

1. Introduction

Properties of liquid crystals while applying them in electronic paper, displays and other optoelectronic devices strongly depend on the value of polar W_θ and azimuthal W_φ anchoring energy, as well as on the ratio W_θ/W_φ. Liquid crystal (LC) photoalignment (oriented LC is orientation by laser irradiation in an LC – dye system) is a promising and powerful tool to create new displays, e-paper, and other opto-electronic devices. Theoretical description of the photoalignment process details is an urgent task to make the LC alignment more perfect and develop displays with new functions.

Some problems of such theory are reviewed in [1,2]. In [3,4], a model of liquid crystals and dyes orientation by the laser radiation taking into account the anisotropy of the molecules optical polarizability has been proposed. Influence of both electric and magnetic field of the light wave was considered. The value of anchoring energy should be strongly affected by the structure of the used dye. However this problem did not investigated.

2. Dye Dimerization Evaluation

It is shown in the presented work, that when using dyes SD-1, CD-1, DR-23, which can form flat dimers via hydrogen bonds, the ratio W_θ/W_φ grows with increasing order parameter S, but at the same time, the using of the dyes which cannot form dimers results in independence of the ratio W_θ/W_φ on the S value.

The change of the dimerization entropy was calculated and was equal to 40-50 kJ/(mol*K). Dimerization energy was calculated by Hartree-Fock energy with the using of GAMESS program package. It was equal to 50-110 kJ/mol. In this case, the change of the free energy ΔG in dimerization process alters from 20 to 90 kJ/mol. According to this value ΔG, the amount of dimers in the system is several orders greater than the amount of separate molecules.

3. Influence of Dye Structure on Anchoring Parameters

It was shown, that for planar orientation arising in the case of SD-1, CD-1, DR-23 dyes forming flat dimers the resistance accompanying the change of a polar angle ϑ is essentially higher than at the change of azimuthal angle φ. Therefore the value of polar energy W_θ is essentially higher than the azimuthal W_φ. Using dyes BY and CBY, which do not form dimers, results in the formation of the LC – dye system, where values of W_θ and W_φ are nearly the same. This fact can be explained as the result of minor difference between molecular sizes in directions orthogonal to the axis of easy rotation.

The values of the polarization tensor diagonal components of the CD-1 dimer were calculated with the valent-optical scheme. Optical polarization exaltation, as the result of bonds conjugation was taken into account. The energy of interaction of dye dimers with an electric component of electromagnetic wave was calculated. The amount of dye molecules cooperatively oriented in the electric field of laser irradiation was estimated. Angle distribution function for molecules as a function of radiation electric field intensity, dimer polarization anisotropy and the amount of cooperatively orient dimers was calculated.

4. Acknowledgements

The work was supported by Russian Foundation for Basic Researches, grants #14-07-00574-a and #14-47-03608 (with Moscow Region Government).

5. References

[1] V. Chigrinov, S. Pikin, A. Verevochnikov, V. Kozenkov, M. Khazimullin, J. Ho, D. D. Huang, H.-S. "Diffusion model of photoaligning in azo-dye layers", Kwok/Phys. Rev. E, **69**, 061713, p. 1–9. 2004.

[2] V. Chigrinov, V. Kozenkov, H.-S. Kwok. *Photoalignment of Liquid Crystalline Materials*, Wiley-SID Series Display Technology, New York, 2008.

[3] N. N. Barabanova, V. V. Belyaev, D. L. Bogdanov, A. L. Bugrimov, V. G. Chigrinov, A. K. Dadivanyan, Ye. A. Rodionova, "Distribution of Dye and Mesogen Molecules Orientation in Photoaligning Layer vs. Aperture of Polarized Light Beam", Mol. Crystals Liquid Crystals,Vol. **596**, pp. 76–81. (2014).

[4] N. N. Barabanova, V. V. Belyaev, D.L. Bogdanov, A.L. Bugrimov, A.K. Dadivanyan, M. A. Osipov, V. G. Chigrinov, "Orientation of dyes under the action of laser irradiation", Bull. Moscow Region State University. Series Physics-Mathematics, No. 1, 2015.

Paper No P11: Nanoparticles- and Ionic Liquid-Modified Liquid Crystal Systems for Spatial Light Modulators

M. Czajkowski,[1] J. Cybinska,[1,2] J. Klajn,[1] J. Feder-Kubis,[3] M. Gordel,[3] and K. Komorowska[1]

[1]Wroclaw Research Center EIT+, Wroclaw, Poland, E-mail: maciej.czajkowski@eitplus.pl; [2]University of Wroclaw, Wroclaw, Poland; [3]Wroclaw University of Technology, Wroclaw, Poland

Abstract

We present some approaches for modulation of light by hybrid liquid crystal materials. Mixtures of liquid crystals with chiral ionic liquids are used for modulating the incident light amplitude by alternative electric field. Hybrid cells of liquid crystals with inner surfaces, being modified by metallic and semiconductor nanoparticles, are used for phase or amplitude modulation of light. Those groups of the materials used for modification of liquid crystal cells are promising for construction of efficient light switches and modulators.

1. Introduction

Liquid crystals (LC) are often used for modulation of light because of their anisotropic refractive properties. Usually the effective birefringence is modulated by means of electric field and the LC cell is placed in crossed-polarizers system to observe changes of the transmitted light.

In this communication, we present approaches of light modulation in two different systems: first—usage of liquid crystal doped with chiral ionic liquid modulated by alternative electric field for amplitude transmission modulator without application of crossed-polarizers system; second—hybrid liquid crystal cells with inner surfaces modified with nanoparticle materials, used for modulation of birefringence by light appropriate for nanoparticle absorption band.

2. Amplitude Light Modulation in Liquid Crystal Doped with Chiral Ionic Liquid

Several mixtures of LC with chiral ionic liquid were prepared. Cholesteric textures of mixtures were observed under the polarized microscope. Alternating voltage applied to the sample causes appearance of microscopic liquid crystalline structures that scatter the transmitted light, causing drop off the overall transmission, through the sample (Figure 1).

The transmission of the mixtures can be modulated by applied alternative voltage, usually at two ranges of frequencies: tens of Hertz and several megahertz.

3. Photorefractive Effect in Hybrid LC Cells with Nanoparticle-Modified Surfaces

Semiconductor $CuInS_2$ nanoparticles, gold nanospheres, and gold nanorods were used for enhancing the photorefractive effect in liquid crystal cells. Cells with modified surfaces and volume mixtures of liquid crystal with nanoparticles were prepared, and the electrorefractive and photorefractive characteristics and dynamics were measured.

Reversible photorefractive switching of transmission of the light can be observed in hybrid liquid crystal cells (Figure 2). Studies of the stability of the effect were performed.

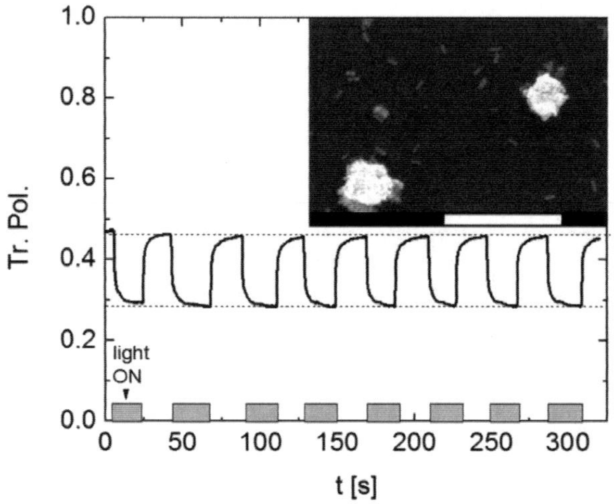

Figure 2. Modulation of light transmission in crossed-polarizers setup by tuning birefringence by light in hybrid liquid crystal cell with gold nanorods deposited on both inner surfaces (inset picture, white bar is equal distance 500 nm).

The approaches may be useful in liquid crystal systems in nondisplay applications, such as smart windows, filters modulators used for communication without usage of electric field, e.g., for all-optical switches.

4. Acknowledgements

The research was supported by Wrocław Research Centre EIT+ within the project "The Application of Nanotechnology in Advanced Materials"—NanoMat (POIG.01.01.02-02-002/08) financed by the European Regional Development Fund (Operational Programme Innovative Economy, 1.1.2.)

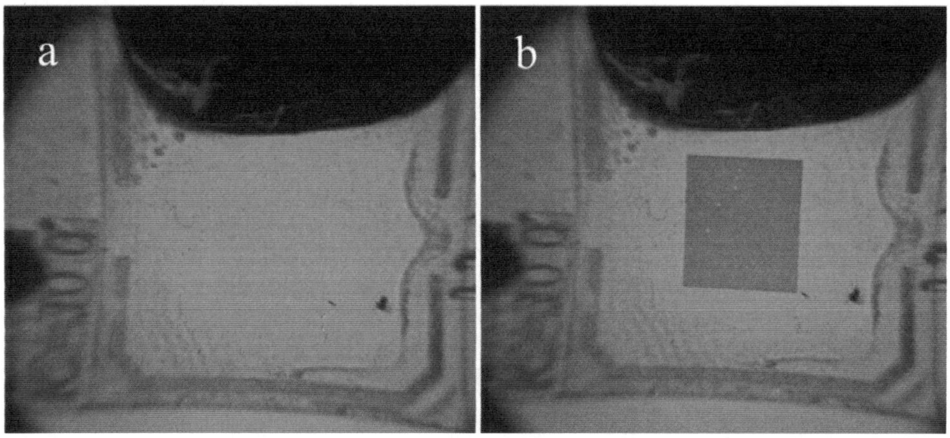

Figure 1. Light amplitude modulation in mixture of W1825 with 5,4% chiral imidazolum derivative 1.7.Sacc: (a) without and (b) with applied MHz alternating voltage (±10V).

Paper No P12: Transparent Conductive Electrode Based on Hydrogen Doped Zinc Oxide for OLED Application

Shuming Chen and Sisi Wang

Department of Electrical and Electronic Engineering, South University of Science and Technology of China, Shenzhen 518055, People's Republic of China, E-mail: chen.sm@sustc.edu.cn

Abstract

A transparent and conductive electrode based on hydrogen (H) doped ZnO has been proposed for active-matrix (AM) display applications. With optimal H plasma power and treat time, the resultant ZnO:H exhibits a low sheet resistance of 200 ohm/sq at a thickness of 150 nm. The demonstrated transparent and conductive ZnO:H can serve as electrode for LCD or OLED as well as S/D electrode for ZnO TFT. With proposed ZnO:H electrode, two photomask steps can be reduced in the fabrication of ZnO TFT-based AM backplanes.

1. Introduction

ZnO-based transparent conductors have received considerable attention because of its attractive features like high transparency, low cost and high conductivity. Moreover, ZnO is a good semiconductor, which can serve as channel layer for thin-film transistors (TFTs). ZnO-TFTs treated by hydrogen (H), argon (Ar) or NH3 plasma exhibit significantly improved performance due to effective reduction of the contact resistance. If the resistance of ZnO:H films is sufficiently low, they can potentially serve as pixel electrode for displays. With ZnO:H films simultaneously serving as S/D electrodes for TFTs and pixel electrodes for OLED/LCD, two photomask steps can potentially be reduced.

In this paper, we investigate the possibility of using ZnO:H films as electrodes for OLEDs. With optimal H plasma power and treatment time, the resultant ZnO:H exhibits a low sheet resistance of 200 ohm/sq at a thickness of 150 nm. The transparent conductive ZnO:H can work as anode for normal OLEDs or as cathode for inverted OLEDs. OLEDs with ZnO:H electrodes exhibit comparable performance compared with that using ITO electrodes. With proposed ZnO:H electrodes, the cost of the ZnO-based active-matrix (AM) backplane can potentially be reduced due to elimination of the ITO and reduction of the processing steps.

2. Results and Discussion

The as-deposited 150 nm ZnO films were transferred to a RIE machine for H plasma treatment. To optimize the resistance of the doped films, the plasma power was varied while the treatment time was kept for 5 min. As shown in Figure 1(a), the sheet resistance of the ZnO:H films decreases very quickly with increasing plasma power. For example, the sheet resistance decreases from $>10^7$ ohm/square to $\sim$ 200 ohm/square when the plasma power increases from 100 to 300 W.

The reduced sheet resistance by treating ZnO with H plasma is mainly due to the introduction of H. It is reported that H can serve as electron donors for ZnO. Secondary ion mass spectrometry (SIMS) was used to probe the H concentration and distribution profiles. As shown in Figure 1(b), the films treated with the H plasma exhibit higher H intensity when compared with that of the as-deposited films, revealing that the reduced sheet resistance is resulted from the hydrogen dopants.

Encouraged by the low resistance of the ZnO:H films, we then explore their possibility of serving as pixel electrode for OLEDs. Normal OLEDs with structures glass/ITO or ZnO:H anodes/MoO3 8 nm/NPB 60 nm/CBP:Irppy3 10%, 20 nm/TPBi 40 nm/LiF 1 nm/Al and inverted OLEDs with structures glass/ITO or ZnO:H cathodes/Yb 5 nm/TPBi 40 nm/CBP:Irppy3 10%, 20 nm/NPB 60 nm/MoO3 8 nm/Al were fabricated. Figure 2 shows the current density-voltage-luminance characteristics of the devices. The devices with ZnO:H electrodes exhibit comparable performance with that using ITO electrodes. For example, for the normal OLEDs, both devices turn on at 3 V and reach 100 cd/m^2 at 4 V.

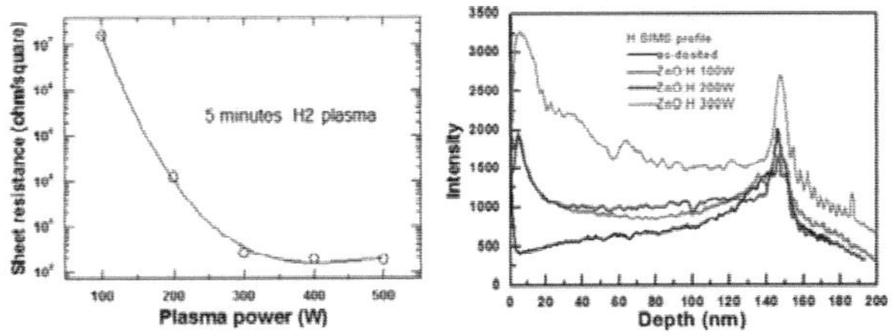

Figure 1. (a) Sheet resistance of the ZnO:H as a function of plasma power. (b) The SIMS profiles of the ZnO:H transparent films.

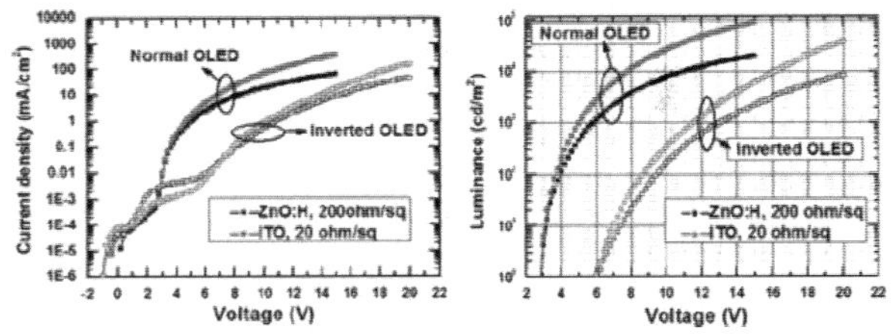

Figure 2. (a) Current density-voltage characteristics and (b) luminance-voltage characteristics of the OLEDs with ZnO:H and ITO electrodes.

3. Conclusion

In conclusion, we have demonstrated transparent conductive films based on ZnO:H. The demonstrated transparent and conductive ZnO:H can serve as pixel electrode for LCD or OLED as well as S/D electrode for ZnO TFT. With proposed ZnO:H electrode, two photomask steps can be reduced in the fabrication of ZnO TFT-based AM backplanes.

4. Acknowledgements

This work was supported by the National Natural Science Foundation of China under Grant No. 61405089, and by the Innovation of Science and Technology Committee of Shenzhen under Grant No. JCYJ20140417105742713.

Paper No P13: Measurement of Ultra-Low Water Vapor Permeability Through Barrier-Coated Flexible Films With Varying Temperature and Humidity for OLED

Byung Il Choi,[1] Sang-Wook Lee,[1] Sang Bong Woo,[1] Jong Chul Kim,[1] and Sang Joon Seo[2]

[1]Korea Research Institute of Standards and Science, Daejeon 305-340, Korea, E-mail: cbi@kriss.re.kr; [2]SSKU Advanced Institute of Nano Technology, Sungkyunkwan University, Suwon 440-746, Korea

Abstract

As organic light-emitting diodes (OLEDs) and other optoelectronic materials are very vulnerable to moisture and oxygen, securing proper encapsulation is critical in the development of flexible OLED displays and other flexible electronic devices. This problem is typically solved by the use of barrier-coated polymeric films that are composed of alternating organic/inorganic multilayers. Precision devices testing for water vapor permeability in ultra-low range were developed in KRISS using water containing tritium. These devices are under operation to measure the range covering (10^{-7} to 10^{-2}) g·m^{-2}·day^{-1}. In this study, various studies on water vapor permeability through barrier-coated flexible films were conducted with varying temperature and humidity, and it was observed that effects of temperature and humidity were significant. Permeability was increased a few hundred times and 15 times when increasing temperature from 23 to 80°C, and relative humidity (rh) from 6 to 72% rh, respectively. These results can provide valuable information on the reliability evaluation of flexible electronics products.

1. Introduction

Flexible displays such as organic light-emitting diodes (OLEDs) are the next-generation display which can be bent, crooked, and/or rolled without any damage to the image. This can be accomplished by using thin, light, and flexible substrates such as plastic films instead of glass substrates. However, one of the major challenges in using polymeric films in displays is the protection of OLED materials from damage by moisture and oxygen. To assure adequate lifetime stability for most OLED devices, the water vapor transmission rate (WVTR) required for substrates to sufficiently protect OLEDs is reported to be less than 10^{-6} g·m^{-2}·day^{-1}. For this reason, it is absolutely necessary to measure the WVTR in this ultra-low range to evaluate plastic barrier substrates. Recently, the use of tritium to measure extremely low water vapor permeability has been reported [1–3].

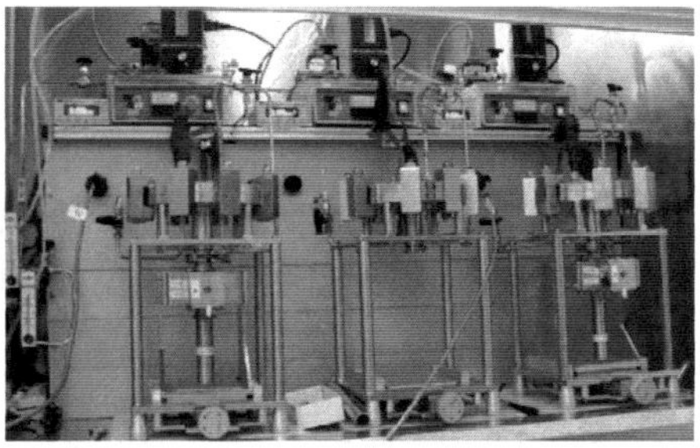

Figure 1. Measurement system for water vapor permeability.

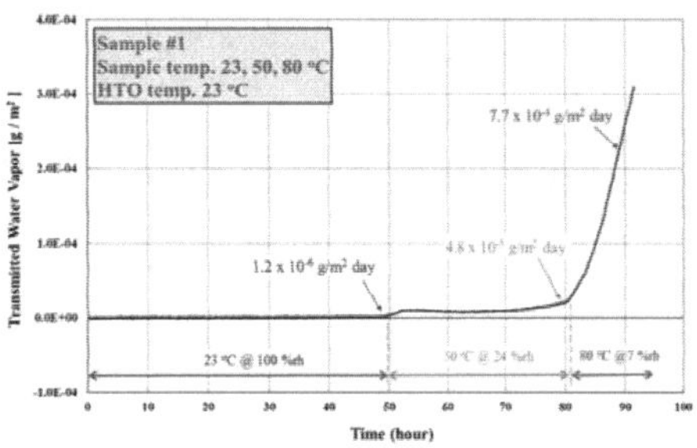

Figure 2. Effect of humidity on water vapor permeability.

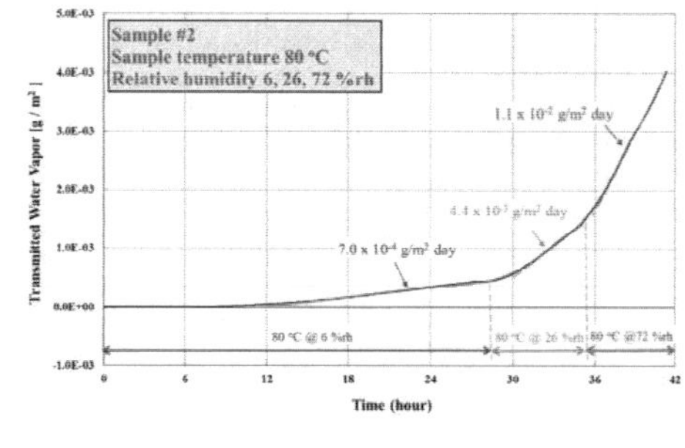

Figure 3. Effect of temperature on water vapor permeability.

2. Measurement Device

To support industrial needs, precision devices measuring water vapor permeability in ultra-low range were developed in KRISS in 2008, using water containing tritium, a radioactive isotope. Three devices are under operation to measure the range covering (10^{-7} to 10^{-2}) g·m^{-2}·day^{-1} (Figure 1).

3. Experiment Results

Effects of temperature and humidity on water vapor permeability through barrier-coated plastic films were investigated. Figure 2 shows a measurement of water vapor permeability with varying sample temperature from 23 to 50°C and then 80°C, which gives 100, 24, and 7% rh on the sample surface, respectively, at the fixed vapor pressure. The permeability seemed rapidly increasing from 1.2×10^{-6} g·m^{-2}·day^{-1} at 23°C to 7.7×10^{-4} g·m^{-2}·day^{-1} at 80°C.

Figure 3 shows the result of water vapor permeability with varying relative humidity from 6% to 26% rh and then 72% rh, where the sample temperature was kept constant at 80°C. The permeability was nearly proportional to relative humidity, varying from 7.0×10^{-4} g·m^{-2}·day^{-1} at 6% rh to 1.1×10^{-2} g·m^{-2}·day^{-1} at 72% rh.

4. References

[1] R. Dunkel, R. Bujas, A. Klein, V. Horndt, "Method of measuring ultra water vapor permeation for OLED display", Proc. IEEE, Vol. **93**, 1478–1482, 2005.

[2] B. I. Choi, H. S. Nham, S. B. Woo, J. C. Kim, "Ultralow water vapour permeation measurement using tritium for OLED displays", J. Korean Phys. Soc., Vol. **53**, 2179–2184, 2008.

[3] B. I. Choi, S. B. Woo, J. C. Kim, S. H. Kim, S. J. Seo, "Determining ultra-low moisture permeation measurement for OLED encapsulation", J. Korean Phys. Soc., Vol. **61**, 2032–2035, 2012.

Paper No P14: Key Technology of 8G In-Line Deposition System for OLED TV

Myungwoon Choi, Kownkuk Yu, Okchul Jeon, Sangmin Lee, Sungmoon Kim, Hyungmin Kim, Jeongguk Seo, and Kwangho Jeong

YAS Co. Ltd., 477-1 Geumseung-ri, Tanhyeon-myeon, Paju-si, Gyeonggi-do, 412-843, Korea, E-mail: oeld21@yasoled.com

Abstract

In this report, the new production line for organic light-emitting diode (OLED) display to overcome hurdles in OLED TV production is described. Instead of conventional cluster system, we adopted in-line system with linear nozzle source (LNS), gluon chuck, and speed buffer (SB) system. The thickness uniformities of organic layers evaporated are well controlled within 3% over the area of 2200 × 2500 mm^2. The glass was horizontally moved from chuck chamber to dechuck chamber by gluon chuck with glass sagging less than 3 mm. Using SB systems, the distance between masks can be controlled by 10 mm. The efficiency of the system is obtained about 60%. Most effective in-line system is developed and applied to the mass production of OLED TV.

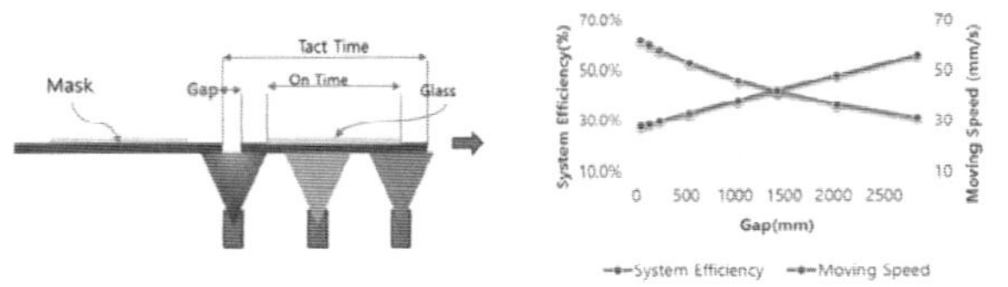

Figure 2. System efficiency variation with the gap distance between masks.

1. Introduction

Organic light-emitting diode (OLED) display has been considered as an ideal flat panel display (FPD) because of high image qualities and various display forms compared to the existing other FPDs [1]. During the last decade, great efforts and investments from universities, institutes, and companies have focused on issues that barriers for OLED TV displays to be commercialized.

2. Result and Discussions

Key concepts of the system are horizontal moving, upward deposition, and high-speed in-line transportation. The size of substrate is 2200 × 2500 mm^2. The system concept is easily expanded or downsized for other substrates without essential modifications. The first system delivered to customer is now operating for mass production.

2.1 In-Line System for OLED TV

2.1.1In-Line System. In-line type deposition system is developed to maximize system efficiency and productivity for OLED TV mass production. The schematic drawing of the in-line deposition system is shown in Figure 1. When the pretreated glass enters in the system, the glass attached to gluon chuck to moves horizontally. For the next processes, Gluon chuck flips in the flip chamber. And then a mask and a gluon chuck are aligned in the alignment chamber. Before the deposition, the gap between mask and mask can be controlled by 10 mm. After finishing organic layer deposition, the mask is changed to the metal mask. And then metal deposition processes are conducted. The glass is detached in dechuck chamber, and chuck plate returns to chuck chamber. The glass moves to encapsulation chamber. Organic and metal mask can be circulating through return path. Each process will be done within 80 s.

2.2 Source and Gluon Chuck for Glass Handling in 8G In-Line System

Linear nozzle source (LNS) for 8G in-line system is developed with divide crucible. Each Crucible is controlled by separated heating unit.

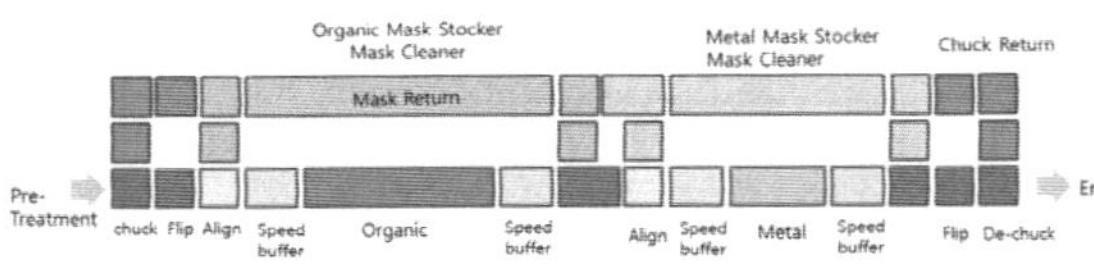

Figure 1. Layout of in-line deposition system for OLED TV.

The distance of LNS to glass is 250–400 mm depending on the process. Its uniformity is less than 3% and material efficiency is larger than 70%. Low sagging metal-based material such as aluminum is used in glass handling chuck to prevent sagging. Large size glass can be handled by gluon chuck and electrostatic chuck. The principle of gluon chuck is Van der Waals force between Gluon material (pressure sensitive adhesive) and glass. Using this force, we can hold an 8G glass and move chamber to chamber. We design the sagging of gluon chuck less than 3 mm.

2.3 Gap Control and Alignment System

During deposition, the evaporation source is always ON in in-line system that time the glass is on top of the source (Figure 2).The system is OFF when there is no glass on top of the source in OLED system. To design effective OLED production system, we have to minimize the OFF time in in-line system. Alignment process will be done without moving of glass, but deposition process will be done with a speed of that in in-line system. Therefore, the gap between mask and mask control system must be adopted for a highly efficient production system. If there is a larger gap (2800 mm), the system efficiency of the system will be reduced 50% of that of the minimum gap (10 mm).

Requirement of alignment in mobile OLED product is less than 3 μm. But in the case of OLED TV, required alignment specification is less than 30 μm. To obtain that accuracy of alignment in 8G system, we have to minimize the distance between glass and mask. Using the gluon chuck, we can control the distance less than 3 mm.

3. Conclusion

Key technology of OLED TV mass production system is low production cost and high productivity. The system should utilize high material efficiency source, glass handling tool for horizontal moving, and gap control system for system efficiency. 8G glass can be used for OLED TV production, but more lager glass should be used for competitiveness of OLED TV.

4. Acknowledgements

We thank LG Display for providing verification and opportunity to supply our works in production system.

5. Reference

[1] C.-W. Han, J.-S. Park, Y.-H. Shin, M.-J. Lim, B.-C. Kim, Y.-H. Tak, B.-C. Ahn, "Invited paper: Advanced technologies for large-sized OLED TV", SID Symp. Dig. Tech. Pap., Vol. **45**, pp. 770–773, 2014.

Paper No P15: Enhancement of Extraction Efficiency in OLED with Multi-Cathode Structure Prepared on a Plastic Substrate

Akiyoshi Mikami and Shuhei Doi

Kanazawa Institute of Technology, Japan, E-mail: mikami@neptune.kanazawa-it.ac.jp

Abstract

Light extraction of organic light-emitting device has been successfully enhanced by preparing on a plastics substrate. We describe optical design method of mode conversion for reducing optical losses in wave-guide and evanescent modes by introducing a new cathode and a plastic substrate. The phosphorescent green light emitting device exhibits higher light extraction by a factor of 2–3.

1. Introduction

Organic light-emitting device (OLED) are now widely recognized as a potential application for flexible displays and general lighting. However, the external quantum efficiency (EQE) of conventional devices remains 20–25% in spite of high internal efficiency because of poor light extraction. One of the reasons is quite a large losses induced by waveguide effect including surface plasmon (SP) coupling in a metal cathode [1]. We found that the combination of refractive index controlled plastic substrate and a multi-cathode structure (MLC) is effective for the increase of substrate and air modes. The objective of this work is optical design of waveguide and evanescent modes for the possibility of enhanced light extraction.

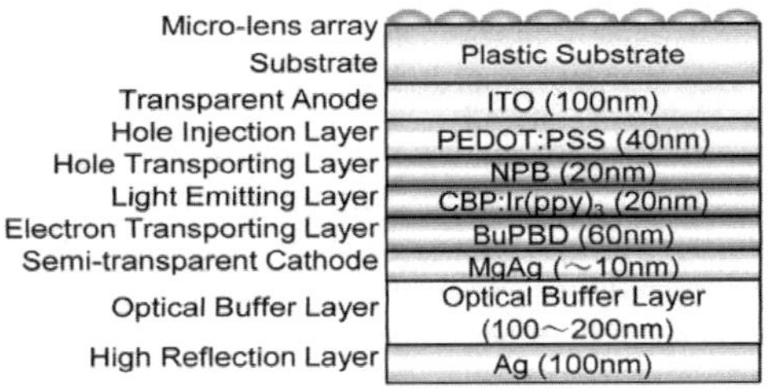

Figure 1. A device structure of green OLED with a multi-cathode structure deposited on a plastic substrate.

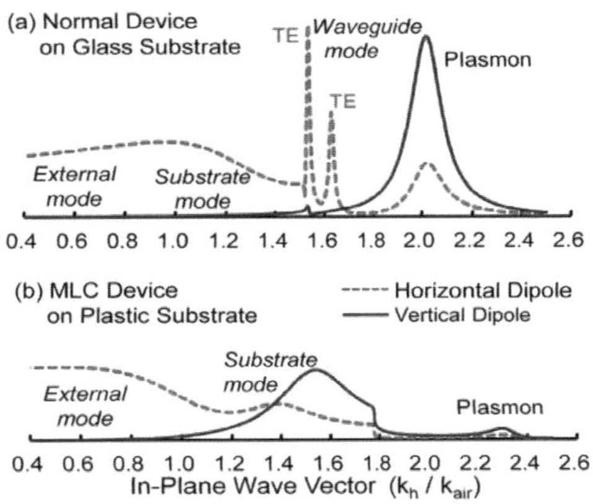

Figure 2. Optical power spectrum of a dipole emission as a function of in-plane wave vector. (a) Normal device and (b) This work's MLC device on a plastic substrate.

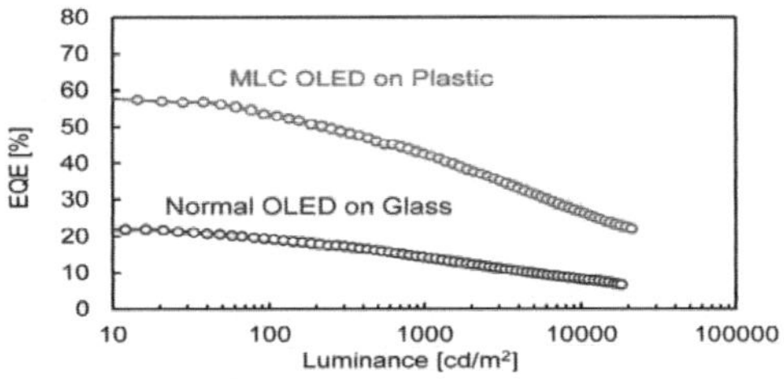

Figure 3. EQE versus luminance characteristics in green PH-OLEDs with different cathode and substrate.

2. Device Structure

Figure 1 shows a typical device structure of green phosphorescent OLED used in this experiment. The device basically consists of ITO bottom electrode, PEDOT:PSS hole injection layer, NPB hole-transporting layer, CBP emissive layer doped with $Ir(ppy)_3$ emitting guest, Bu-PBD electron transporting layer and semi-transparent MgAg cathode. The MLC includes an optical compensation (OC) layer and high reflection Ag layer on the back-side of thin MgAg cathode [2]. Transmittance of plastic substrate is about 90%, and its refractive index is between 1.60 and 1.75 in the visible light region.

3. Optical Analysis

Figure 2(a) and 2(b) are calculated power spectrum in k-space for the normal devices with thick MgAg cathode (100nm) on the glass and this work's device with multi-cathode on the plastic. In the normal device, surface plasmon pole appears at 2.02 of *k*-space in the vertical dipole moment together with two waveguide TE lines in the horizontal dipole. In contrast, both of plasmonic and waveguide modes almost disappears and broad substrate and external modes becomes dominant instead in the MLC device. This means that the waveguide mode including evanescent wave is successfully converted to the propagation mode by employing MLC on the plastic substrate. According to the detail optical analysis, it is found that the significant reduction of SP-loss is due to the optical capping effect by the OC layer. In addition, almost all of waveguide modes are converted to the substrate mode by adjusting refractive-index anisotropy of plastic sheet with various waveguide modes. The sum of external and substrate modes reaches to approximately 90%.

4. Device Performance

We have experimentally confirmed the effect of MLC device on a plastic by using a green OLED shown in Figure1. A comparison of EQE of this work's device with the normal OLED is shown in Figure 3. The maximum EQE are 58% and 22%, respectively.

5. References

[1] K. A. Netzs, "Simulation of light emission from thin-film microcavities", J. Opt. Soc. Am. Vol. **15**, p. 962, 1998.

[2] A. Mikami, "Optical design of enhanced light extraction efficiency in organic light emitting device with an optically controlled surface plasmon coupling", J. Light & Visual Environment, Vol. **37**, pp. 62–65, 2013; DOI: IEIJ130000502

Paper No P16: Efficient ITO-Free Organic Light-Emitting Diodes Based on Highly Conductive Polymer Electrodes

Yong Hyun Kim,[1,2] Jonghee Lee,[2,3] Lars Müller-Meskamp,[2] and Karl Leo[2]

[1]Department of Display Engineering, Pukyong National University, Busan, Korea, E-mail: yhkim113@pknu.ac.kr; [2]Institut für Angewandte Photophysik, Technische Universität Dresden, Dresden, Germany; [3]OLED Research Team, Electronics and Telecommunications Research Institute (ETRI), Daejeon, Korea

Abstract

We demonstrate low-cost, efficient indium tin oxide (ITO)-free organic light-emitting diodes (OLEDs) with improved stability based on conductive, transparent poly(3,4-ethylenedioxythiophene):poly(styrenesulfonate) (PEDOT:PSS) electrodes. The device structures are carefully optimized by tuning the thickness of doped transport layers and electrodes based on optical simulations. The performance of PEDOT:PSS-based OLEDs reaches that of ITO-based reference devices. Furthermore, we present efficient ITO-free white OLED based on internal light extraction system combined with the PEDOT:PSS electrodes.

1. Introduction

The development of transparent electrodes is of great importance for realizing the full advantages of organic light-emitting diodes (OLEDs) such as being cheap and flexible [1]. The commonly used indium tin oxide (ITO) as a bottom electrode remarkably increases device costs due to limited indium supply and the inherent brittleness of the material which hinders the applications in flexible devices. Therefore, alternative electrodes are extensively investigated to replace ITO. Among various alternative electrodes, poly(3,4-ethylenedioxythiophene):poly(styrenesulfonate) (PEDOT:PSS) is regarded as an especially promising alternative electrode due to its high conductivity and transmittance, excellent flexibility, and low-cost processing. Here, we present high performance ITO-free OLEDs with PEDOT:PSS electrodes which show comparable performance to the ITO-based OLEDs. The ITO-free white OLEDs based on PEDOT:PSS electrodes on internal light extraction systems show a greatly improved efficiency as well [2].

2. Results and Discussion

We simulate the external photon flux of OLEDs for optimizing the device structure. To investigate the effect of the device structure on the performance of OLEDs, different hole transport layer (HTL) and PEDOT:PSS thicknesses are studied. It is observed that the thicknesses of the HTL and the bottom electrodes strongly influence the photon flux of devices. ITO-based OLEDs show the highest external quantum efficiency (EQE) of 11.9% at a HTL thickness of 80 nm. For the PEDOT:PSS-based devices, the OLEDs with a 60-nm-thick PEDOT:PSS electrode show the highest EQE of 12.1% at a HTL thickness of 180 nm. The higher performance of PEDOT:PSS-based OLEDs is mainly due to the weak microcavity effect, which decreases organic waveguided mode. Moreover, a long lifetime of the PEDOT:PSS-based OLEDs is achieved by tuning the electrode thickness. These results indicate that thickness tuning for both HTLs and electrodes is of great importance to maximize the amount of light extraction for OLEDs.

In addition, a highly efficient OLEDs based on internal light extraction system and PEDOT:PSS electrodes are developed using a simple and easy manufacturing process. The metal oxide embedded nanostructures combined with PEDOT:PSS electrodes exhibit a good refractive index matching from the organic layers to the substrate and provide excellent light scattering effects. This novel architecture results in a 2.9-fold enhanced EQE for white OLEDs and leads to excellent color stability over a broad range of viewing angles.

3. Conclusion

In summary, we demonstrate low-cost, efficient ITO-free OLEDs with highly conductive PEDOT:PSS electrodes. The PEDOT:PSS-based OLEDs achieve comparable performance to the ITO-based OLEDs. The high performance is attributed to the careful optimization of the device stack, supported by optical simulation. The structure engineering performed in this work, which improves efficiency and stability of OLEDs with a highly conductive polymer electrode, is beneficial for realizing low-cost, flexible, and long living OLEDs applications. Furthermore, we show a novel concept to strongly improve the performance of white OLEDs based on a combination of readily fabricated internal light extraction system composed of a metal oxide nanostructure and a highly conductive low refractive index PEDOT:PSS electrode.

4. Acknowledgements

This work was funded by the European Union (EFRE), the Fraunhofer Gesellschaft, and the Free State of Saxony as part of the Dresdner Innovationszentrum Energieeffizienz. J. Lee acknowledges the Alexander von Humboldt Foundation and the IT R&D program of MSIP/KEIT (Grant No. 10041416).

5. References

[1] Y. H. Kim, J. Lee, S. Hofmann, M. C. Gather, L. Müller-Meskamp, K. Leo, "Achieving high efficiency and improved stability in ITO-free transparent organic light-emitting diodes with conductive polymer electrodes", Adv. Funct. Mater., Vol. **23**, p. 3763, 2013.

[2] Y. H. Kim, J. Lee, W. M. Kim, C. Fuchs, S. Hofmann, H.-W. Chang, M. C. Gather, L. Müller-Meskamp, K. Leo, "We want our photons back: Simple nanostructures for white organic light-emitting diodes outcoupling", Adv. Funct. Mater., Vol. **24**, p. 2553, 2014.

Paper No P17: Highly Efficient Green Phosphorescent Top-Emitting Organic Light-Emitting Diodes with IZO/Ag/IZO Reflective Electrode

Jeonggi Kim, Songi Han, and Jin Jang

Department of Information Display and Advanced Display Research Center, Kyung Hee University, Korea, E-mail: jgkim@tft.khu.ac.kr

Abstract

In this paper, we report that IZO/Ag/IZO multilayer could be used as reflective electrode for top emitting OLED. A further investigation on top emitting OLED with cohost EML demonstrates better charge injection and improve efficiency. The device showed a maximum current efficiency of 130 cd/A, a maximum power efficiency of 144 lm/W. Moreover, the efficiency roll off was small long-lasting to 20,000 cd/m^2 with current efficiencies of 111.8 cd/A at 10,000 cd/m^2 and 102.6 cd/A at 20,000 cd/m^2, respectively.

1. Introduction

Indium-tin-oxide (ITO) is the most commonly used transparent conductive oxide (TCO) material due to its excellent properties such as high conductivity and transparency. However, the complex fabrication and easy cracking upon bending make it unsuitable as electrode in flexible OLEDs. Indium-zinc oxide (IZO) have been attracting a lot of attention because of high optical transparency, good conductivity, very smooth surface roughness, and low deposition temperature [1] in comparison with ITO. Recently, other group proposed TCO/Ag/TCO multilayer structures with much lower resistance as a good candidate for transparent conducting electrodes [2].

In this work, we report the IZO/Ag/IZO multilayer with good flexibility as reflective electrode for top-emitting OLED (TOLED) and fabricated an ultrahigh efficiency TOLED with the IZO/Ag/IZO electrode.

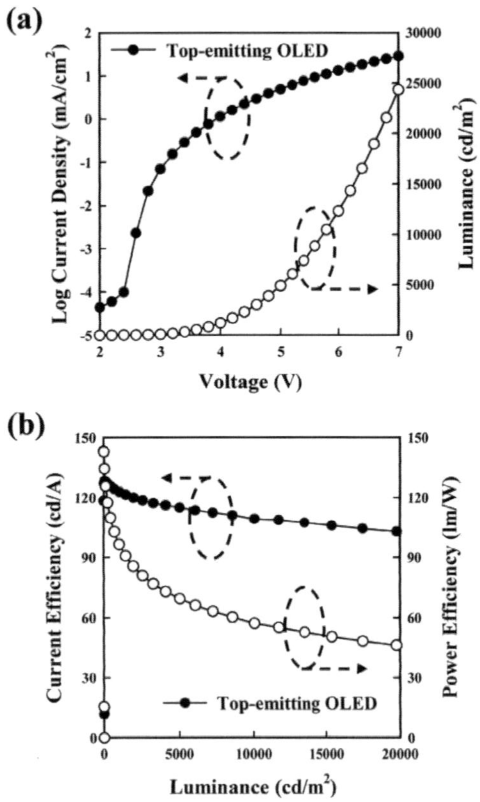

Figure 1. (a) Current density-voltage-luminance (J-V-L) characteristics and (b) current and power efficiencies-luminance charactersitics of the TOLED.

2. Experimental Section

First, the bottom TCO is IZO that was deposited by sputtering at room temperature on pre-cleaned glass. After the sputtering of the bottom TCO layer, an Ag reflective interlayer was deposited by thermal evaporation on the bottom TCO layer with thickness of 100 nm. Subsequently, IZO as top TCO layer was deposited by sputtering at room temperature on the Ag interlayer. Then, 1,4,5,8,9,12-hexaazatriphenylene-hexacarbonitrile (HAT-CN) was used as a hole injection layer (HIL) and N,N-di (naphthalene-1-yl)-N,N-diphenylbenzidine (NPB) was used as a hole transport layer (HTL) and 4,40,400-tris(N-carbazolyl)-triphenylamine (TCTA) was used as an exciton blocking layer (EBL). Co-deposited TCTA and 2,2,2-(1,3,5-benzenetriyl) tris-(1-phenyl-1Hbenzimidazole) (TPBi) with 3:7 ratio and doped with 12 wt.% Ir(ppy)3 were used as an emission layer (EML) to take advantage of the exciplex forming character of the materials [3]. TPBi was used as an electron transport layer (ETL) and LiF, Al, and Ag as a transparent top cathode. A 80-nm-thick NPB layer deposited on the Ag cathode was used as capping layer (CPL).

3. Conclusion

In this work, we report the IZO/Ag/IZO multilayer with good flexibility as reflective electrode for top-emitting OLED (TOLED) and fabricated an ultrahigh efficiency TOLED based on commonly used organic materials. The maximum current efficiency can reach 130 cd/A and remain at 111.8 cd/A at 10,000 cd/m^2 and 102.6 cd/A at 20,000 cd/m^2. The power efficiency can reach as high as 144 lm/W.

4. Acknowledgements

This work was supported by the Human Resources Development program (Grant No. 20134010200490) of the Korea Institute of Energy Technology Evaluation and Planning (KETEP) grant funded by the Korea government Ministry of Trade, Industry and Energy.

5. References

[1] N. Naghavi, A. Rougier, C. Marcel, C. Guery, J. B. Leriche, J. M. Tarascon, "Characterization of indium zinc oxide thin films prepared by pulsed laser deposition using a $Zn_3In_2O_6$ target", Thin Solid Films, Vol. **360**. pp. 233–240, 2000.

[2] M. Sawada, M. Higuchi, S. Kondo, H. Saka, "Characteristics of indium-tin-oxide/silver/indium-tin-oxide sandwich films and their application to simple-matrix liquid-crystal displays", Jpn. J. Appl. Phys., Vol. **40**, pp. 3332–3336, 2001.

[3] J.B Kim, J. H Lee, C. K Moon, K. H. Kim, J. J. Kim "Highly efficient inverted top emitting organic light emitting diodes using a horizontally oriented green phosphorescent emitter", Org. Electr., Vol. **15**. pp. 2715–2718, 2014.

Paper No P18: Study of Interfacial Treatment on the Metal-Oxide Electron Transport Layer in the InP Quantum Dot Light-Emitting Diodes

J. Kim,[1] I. Jang,[2] C. Ippen,[3] Y. Kim,[3] W. K. Kim,[1] A. Wedel,[3] S. K. Park,[2] and C. J. Han[1]

[1]Korea Electronics Technology Institute, Gyeonggi-do, Korea, E-mail: jiwank@keti.re.kr; [2]Chung-Ang University, Seoul, South Korea; [3]Fraunhofer Institute for Applied Polymer Research, Potsdam, Germany

Abstract

In this article, we describe the effect of ethanolamine (EA) surface treatment on the inverted InP quantum dot light-emitting diodes (QD-LEDs) with inorganic metal oxide layers. The efficiency of the inverted QD-LEDs was significantly enhanced by EA treatment and optimization of the ZnO annealing temperature.

1. Introduction

Colloidal quantum-dots based light-emitting didoes (QD-LEDs) have been highly spotlighted as the next generation display due to unique properties of colloidal quantum dots (CQDs) such as narrow full width at half maximum (FWHM), color tunable luminescence, and cost-effective solution processability [1]. Although the performance of state-of-the-art QD-LEDs is now catching up with that of organic light-emitting diodes (OLEDs), most QD-LEDs were fabricated with cadmium (Cd) based CQDs. QD-LEDs with an inverted structure recently have been studied due to their promising results over conventional structure. In this study, InP-based multishell QDs were used as an emissive layer and metal oxides were used for charge transport layers of inverted QD-LEDs due to robust and stable characteristics. For efficient charge recombination in InP QD emissive layer and better device efficiency, ethanolamine (EA) surface treatment was performed on top of the ZnO ETL. The performance of inverted QD-LEDs was improved efficiently by EA surface treatment and following optimization of the ZnO annealing temperature.

2. Experimental Procedure

The sol-gel derived ZnO solution was spin-coated on the cleaned ITO substrate. The temperature of underlying hotplate was increased up to 130, 150, and 200°C to observe the effect of annealing temperature. After that, 5 wt% of EA diluted in 2-methoxyethanol (2-ME) was spin-coated on ZnO layer. InP/ZnSe/ZnS QDs was spin-coated for emissive layer on EA treated surface. After these solution processes, the hole transport layer (HTL) of 4,4'-N,N'-dicarbazole-biphenyl (CBP) (60 nm), HIL of MoO3 (10 nm), and Al (150 nm) anode were deposited sequentially by thermal evaporation. Finally, the encapsulation glass was covered to passivate QD-LED from ambient air containing water vapor and oxygen.

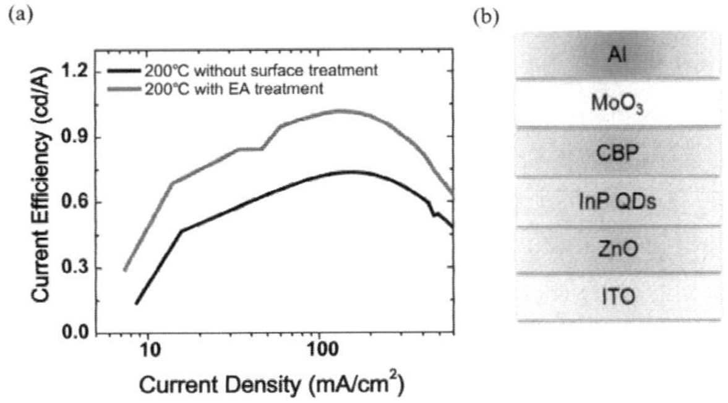

Figure 1. (a) Cross-sectional structure and (b) current efficiency-voltage of InP QD-LED.

3. Results and Discussion

Figure 1(a) shows the schematic structure of the inverted QD-LEDs. Device structure is composed of ITO glass as a cathode/sol-gel derived ZnO as an ETL/InP based multishell QDs as an emissive layer/CBP as a HTL/MoO_3 as a HIL/Al as an anode. By using the inverted structure, in contrary to the conventional structure, electrons and holes are injected into the InP QDs through the ZnO sol-gel film (ETL) and CBP (HTL) from ITO (cathode) and Al (anode), respectively. In this inverted structure, the underlying ZnO ETL can efficiently facilitate electron injection from the ITO cathode and also block the holes.

Since organic charge transport materials in the OLED devices can be easily influenced by oxygen and water, the robust metal oxides (ZnO and MoO_3) are better for the charge transport layers of the inverted QD-LEDs. EA surface treatment on top of the ZnO ETL was performed to obtain better surface morphology and device efficiency. After that, the effect of annealing temperature of ZnO ETL was investigated by measuring the electrical and optical properties of QD-LEDs. Figure 1(b) shows electrical and optical characteristics of QD-LEDs without and with surface treatment. Current efficiency was increased with EA treatment over 1 cd/A. Surface profiles of ZnO film were investigated to observe the surface roughness according to the EA surface treatment. The roughness of ZnO was decreased at all annealing temperatures after the EA treatment.

4. Conclusion

The QD-LEDs with inverted structure were fabricated using Cd-free InP based QDs. Inorganic charge transport layers such as ZnO sol-gel and MoO_3 were used as an ETL and HIL, respectively. For the surface modification, ethanolamine solution was spin-coated on top of the ZnO ETL. The surface roughness of ZnO layers was reduced and the luminance and efficiency of QD-LEDs were efficiently improved by EA surface treatment.

5. Acknowledgements

This work was supported by the Industrial Strategic Technology Development Program (10044876) funded the Ministry of Trade, Industry and Energy (MOTIE, Korea) and Dual Use Technology Program funded by Civil Military Technology Cooperation Center (CMTC, Korea).

6. Reference

[1] L. Qian, Y. Zheng, J. Xue, P. Holloway, "Stable and efficient quantum-dot light-emitting diodes based on solution-processed multilayer structures", Nat. Photonics, Vol. **5**, pp. 543–548, 2011.

Paper No P19: Characteristic of Thermal Behavior and Optical Performance of AC Powder Electroluminescence Panel under Controlled Temperature

Wen Zhi Yu,[1] Shuai Zhang,[1] Jin Wah Ronnie Teo,[2] Chuan Seng Tan,[1] and T. K. S. Wong[1]

[1]School of Electrical and Electronic Engineering, Nanyang Technological University, Singapore, E-mail: WZYu@ntu.edu.sg; [2]A*STAR Singapore Institute of Manufacturing Technology, Singapore

Abstract
The self-heating phenomenon and optical performance of the powder-based AC electroluminescence panel under controlled temperature have been investigated. Both the self-heating temperature and the temperature coefficient of luminance were found to increase with drive voltage and frequency.

1. Introduction
As the only mature technology for large area flexible flat light sources, AC powder electroluminescence (ACPEL) has wide applications including back-lighting of liquid crystal displays, mobile phone keyboards, signage, advertising, and entertainment. Despite decades of research, the extension of ACPEL lifetime and high efficacy are still major issues to be resolved. The effect of the temperature of the working environment on these devices has also not been well studied. The objectives of this work are twofold. First, the self-heating effect is studied under different excitation conditions. Second, in order to show the effect of the self-heating temperature on the luminance, the EL panel is maintained at different temperature by a thermal controller. The luminance of the EL panel at different temperatures is measured and analyzed.

2. Experiment Description
The 10 × 10 cm^2 ACPEL panel with ZnS:Cu,Cl phosphor (Gwent Group, UK) was fabricated by screen printing on indium tin oxide (ITO) coated PET substrate. A Pacific Power Source 105AMX with a triangular AC voltage output was used to excite the device and luminance was measured by PR-655 spectroradiometer. The temperature rise was measured by a thermocouple pasted on the panel surface.

3. Results and Discussion
Figure 1 shows the temperature of the ACPEL panel due to self-heating increases with both the root-mean square (rms) voltage (V) and the drive frequency (f). At f = 1 kHz, the increase is 67%. For a constant luminance of 50 cd/m^2 (see inset), the self-heating temperature decreases from 27 to 24.5°C with increasing frequency and decreasing rms voltage.

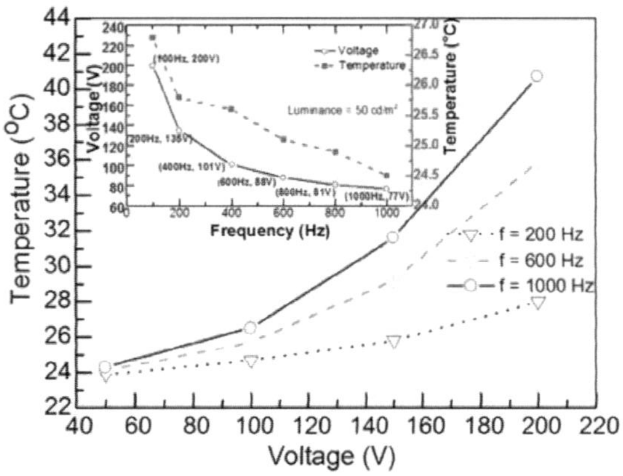

Figure 1. EL panel self-heating effect characteristics.

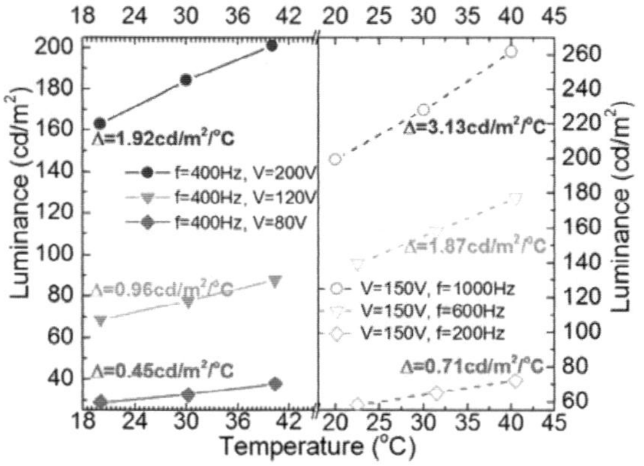

Figure 2. Luminance versus temperature relationships for constant frequency (left) and constant voltage (right).

Table 1. Fitted parameters a and b for L-V equation.

Temperature (°C)	Parameter a	Parameter b
20	6955.9	43.5
30	7990.2	43.5
40	8934.8	42.5

In Figure 2, the luminance (L) is linearly proportional to the control temperature for constant rms voltage and frequency. However, the temperature coefficient of luminance Δ is increased for higher rms voltage and higher frequency. The measured luminance-voltage (L-V) characteristics (not shown) can be described by the Equation [1]:

$$L = a\exp\left(-b/V^{1/2}\right)$$

By using least square curve fitting of the L-V data, the parameters a (cd/m^2) and b (V$^{1/2}$) at three temperatures were found (Table 1). The parameter: $a \approx 4992 + 98.9T$, where T is the temperature in Celsius and b is almost constant. The extracted Δ at 80, 120, and 200 V are 0.762, 1.86, and 4.72 cd/m^2/°C, respectively, in qualitative agreement with the trend shown in Figure 2 (left).

4. Acknowledgements
The authors gratefully acknowledge A*STAR SIMTech, Singapore for providing the funding for this research.

5. Reference
[1] A. G. Fischer, "Electroluminescent lines in ZnS powder particles. II. Models and comparison with experience," J. Electrochem. Soc., Vol. **110**, pp. 733–748, 1963.

Paper No P20: Effects of the Channel Thickness on Characteristics of Ga-Doped Zinc Oxide Thin-Film Transistors Fabricated on Glass

Dedong Han,[1] Suoming Zhang,[1] Jing Wu,[1] Yingying Cong,[1] Lingling Huang,[1] Yi Zhang,[1] Pan Shi,[2] Wen Yu,[2] Shengdong Zhang,[2] Xing Zhang,[1] and Yi Wang[1,3]

[1]Institute of Microelectronics, Peking University, Beijing 100871, China, E-mail: handedong@pku.edu.cn; [2]Shenzhen Graduate School, Peking University, Shenzhen 518055, China; [3]Beijing Engineering Research Center for Active Matrix Display, Beijing 100871, China

Abstract

In this paper, high-performance fully transparent bottom-gate type Ga-doped zinc oxide thin-film transistors (GZO TFTs) have been successfully fabricated on glass substrate. The effects of channel thickness on the electrical performances of GZO TFTs are researched. We study to improve the performance of bottom gate Ga-doped Zinc Oxide Thin Film Transistors by optimizing the active layer process. Optimized TFTs exhibit excellent electrical properties, with high I_{on}/I_{off} current ratio of 1.3 × 10^9, saturation mobility (μ_{sat}) of 99 cm^2/Vs, subthreshold swing (SS) of 77mV/decade and threshold voltage (V_{th}) of 2.2 V. The variation trend of I_{on}/I_{off}, μ_{sat}, SS, and V_{th} against channel thickness is analyzed in detail. The experimental results suggest that the performance of GZO TFT can be improved effectively by optimum channel thickness.

1. Introduction

Recently, ZnO-based thin-film transistors have demonstrated excellent optical and electrical properties and offer great promise for the next generation display applications, such as active-matrix organic light-emitting diodes (AMOLEDs) displays, transparent displays, flexible displays, etc. As we know, a-Si TFTs have been the key components of the flat-panel-displays. However, with the development of high resolution, high frame-rate, and high-size displays, the performance of a-Si TFTs are not enough to satisfy the demand of industry. What is more, LTPS TFTs have poor uniformity for the non-uniform grain sizes in the poly-Si channel layer. Among all kinds of ZnO-based materials, indium gallium zinc oxide (IGZO) is considered as the most promising materials because of its high mobility, transparency and good electrical performance [1]. But In element is toxicant, rare on earth and going to be exhausted, so many researchers turn to other doping in Zinc Oxide (ZnO) such as Al-doped ZnO, Sn-doped ZnO, Ga-Sn-doped ZnO. In this paper, we choose Ga-doped ZnO (GZO) as channel material because it has many advantages. Ga is abundant on earth. Besides, Ga atom acts as substitutional impurity when it replaces the zinc ions, releasing a free electron into the conduction band to increase the electrical conductivity.

2. Experiment

In this fabrication, Ga-doped zinc oxide thin-film transistors are fabricated on glass substrate as shown in Figure 1. First, a 100 nm indium tin oxide (ITO) film was deposited as a gate electrode in pure Ar atmosphere on the glass. Then, a 150 nm SiO_2 dielectric layer was coated by plasma-enhanced chemical vapor deposition (PECVD) at 100°C. The channel layer is deposited at RT by RF Magnetron Sputtering with different GZO thicknesses which are 15, 20, 25, 30, 40, and 50 nm as the active channel. At last, the S/D electrodes were patterned and a 100nm ITO layer was deposited as S/D contact.

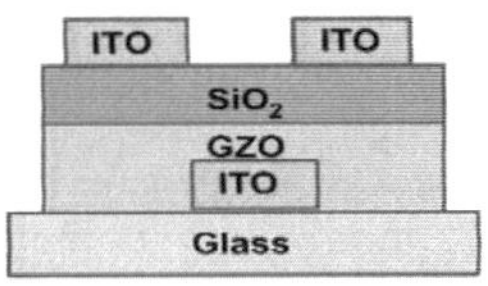

Figure 1. The structure of bottom-gate GZO TFT.

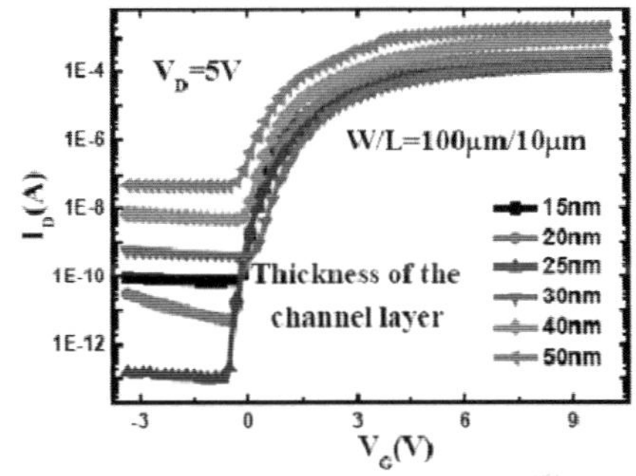

Figure 2. The transfer characteristics of GZO TFT with different channel thickness.

3. Results and Discussions

Figure 2 indicates the transfer characteristics of Gallium-doped ZnO TFTs the devices with respect to the thickness of channel layer: 15, 20, 25, 30, 40, and 50 nm. It can be seen, compared with the TFT which using different channel thickness, the GZO TFT with 25 nm channel thickness exhibit excellent electrical properties such as high I_{on}/I_{off} of 1.3 × 10^9, saturation mobility of 99 cm^2/Vs, Subthreshold swing of 77 mV/decade and threshold voltage of 2.2 V. The results indicate that characteristics of Gallium-doped ZnO TFTs depend on channel layer thickness very much.

4. Conclusion

We studied the effect of channel thickness on the characteristics of GZO TFT. The fully transparent GZO TFT with optimum channel thickness exhibit excellent electrical properties and is promise for the next generation transparent display applications.

5. Acknowledgements

This work was supported in part by the National Basic Research Program of China (973 program, no. 2011CBA00600) and by the National Natural Science Foundation of China (no. 61275025).

6. Reference

[1] K. Nomura, H. Ohta, K. Ueda, T. Kamiya, M. Hirano, H. Hosono, "Thin-film transistor fabricated in single-crystalline transparent oxide semiconductor", Science, Vol. **300**, pp. 1269−1272, 2003.

Paper No P21: Organic Thin-Film Transistors Using V-Shaped Organic Semiconductor With Various Interfacial Layers

Safizan Binti Shaari,[1,2] Shigeki Naka,[1] and Hiroyuki Okada[1]

[1]Graduate School of Science and Engineering, University of Toyama, Toyama, Japan, E-mail: safizanshaari@yahoo.co.jp; [2]School of Microelectronic Engineering, Universiti Malaysia Perlis, Perlis, Malaysia

Abstract

Organic Thin-Film Transistor (OTFTs) using V-shaped organic semiconductor with various insulating interfacial layers (IILs) were investigated. The mobility and threshold voltage of OTFT without interfacial layer were 0.70 cm²/Vs and 1.2 V, respectively. However, by using various interfacial layers, OTFT with CT4112 exhibit high performance of mobility up to 1.2 cm²/Vs and low threshold voltage −4.3 V was obtained.

1. Introduction

Organic Thin-Film Transistors (OTFTs) has been studied for decades and sparked myriad of applications, such as in integrated circuit, display panels and radio frequency identification (RFID). However, many challenges and problems need to be solved in order to increase the specific performance of OTFTs. Many studies have been focusing on improving the performance of OTFTs, especially, by controlling the crystal growth of devices and interfacing alignment between the organic semiconductor and the dielectric substrate. In our previous report, we have studied OTFTs using pentacene as an organic semiconductor with various insulating interfacial layer (IIL). The exact behavior mechanism of organic material system and interfacial layer combination and their effect to the device characteristics have been a major research focus. In this study, we have investigated and fabricated OTFTs with various interfacial layers, such as, second polymer materials, self-assembled monolayers (SAMs) and high-k materials. In this context, we have selected a novel V-shaped organic semiconductor, dinaphtho[2,3-b:2′,3′-d]thiophene (C6-DNT) as an active layer. Other researchers reported that average mobility was achieve 3.6 cm²/Vs by vapor-deposition method of V-shaped organic materials [1]. This material is particularly attractive us due to its potential for large-area applications. Therefore, we have studied and reported in this time.

2. Experiment

A heavily doped n-type Si-wafer was used as a substrate with a thickness of SiO_2 of 100 nm. Silicon was cleaned in an ultrasonic bath with acetone, alkaline solution and DI water. Then, the IIL was coated on the substrate. Dielectric surface layer is treated with SAM; polymethylmethacrylate (PMMA), CT4112 (Kyocera Chemical), CYTOP (Asahi Kasei) and organic insulating layer; octadecyltrichlorosilane (OTS) and hexamethyldisilazane (HMDS). For high-k materials which are Ta_2O_5 and Si_3N_4 layer were deposited by sputtering on SiO_2/Si through a shadow mask. The thickness of high-k materials was 100 nm, respectively. After the formation of IIL, the contact angle was measured to analyze the changes in surface condition. After that, the C6-DNT was evaporated through a metal mask to a thickness of 50 nm with substrates temperature to approximately 90°C. Then, source and drain were evaporated with a thickness of 50 nm. The channel length and width is 500 μm and 1.5 mm, respectively.

3. Results and Discussions

Mobility (μ) and threshold voltage (V_{TH}) are compared for various interfacial layers are shown in Figure 1.

The OTFT without interfacial layer has the field-effect mobility of 0.70 cm²/Vs, threshold voltage of 1.2 V and on/off ratio of 10^6. By inserting the IIL, particularly by using SAM and organic insulating layer, the threshold voltage of the OTFT were shifted to negative voltage. Among various interfacial layer, SiO_2 with CT4112 was significantly improved the mobility from 0.70 to 1.2 cm²/Vs and threshold voltage shifting from positive voltage to negative voltage. It can be speculated that there exist negative charges elsewhere, for example, insulator/insulator and/or insulator/organic material interface to induce such effect. These results also shows that device characteristics is influenced by the various interfacial layers, due to the presence intermolecular interaction on the charge transports occur via a hopping mechanism at grain boundaries of organic semiconductor and dielectric interfaces.

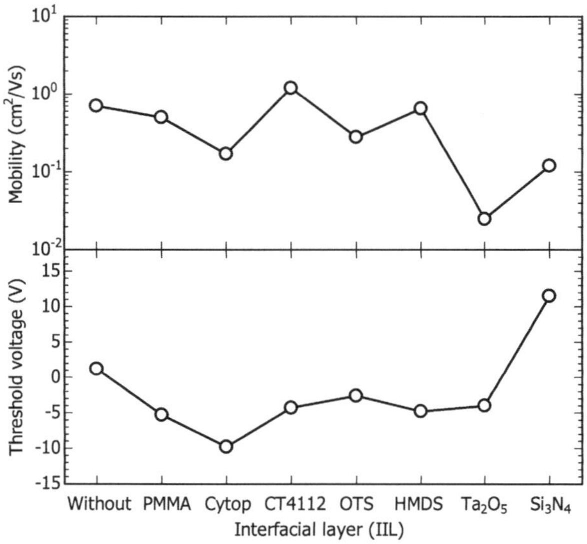

Figure 1. Comparison of threshold voltage and carrier mobility for various interfacial layers.

4. Conclusions

We had studied OTFTs using new material C6-DNT and thoroughly compared against mobility and threshold voltage performances with various interfacial layers. This study will continue with further investigations on structural properties of C6-DNT by using AFM observation and XRD to clarify the details of the transport mechanism between organic semiconductor and dielectric layer.

5. Reference

[1] T. Okamoto, C. Mitsui, M. Yamagishi, K. Nakahara, J. Soeda, Y. Hirose, K. Miwa, H. Sato, A. Yamano, T. Matsushita, T. Uemura, J. Takeya, "V-shaped organic semiconductors with solution processability, high mobility, and high thermal durability", Adv. Mater., Vol. **25**, pp. 6392–6397, 2013.

Paper No P22: A Study on the Characteristics of IZO-TFTs with High-k $HfSiO_x$ Gate Insulator Annealed in Various Conditions

Yoo Seong Lim,[1] Yong Jin Im,[1] Seung Soo Ha,[2] Chan Hee Park,[1] Min-hyung Jang,[1] Seung-il Choi,[2] Ji-in Park,[1] and Moonsuk Yi[1]

[1]Department of Electronics Engineering, Pusan National University, Busan, Republic of Korea, E-mail: msyi@pusan.ac.kr; [2]Department of Advanced Integrated Circuit, Pusan National University, Busan, Republic of Korea

Read the full article at DOI: 10.1002/jsid.323

Abstract

In this work, we investigate the enhanced performance of IZO-based TFTs with HfSiOx gate insulators. HfSiOx gate insulators, annealed at various conditions, are deposited by co-sputtering of HfO_2 and Si. The HfSiOx structural properties are investigated using AFM, XRD, and XPS techniques. Furthermore, the electrical characteristics are analyzed to investigate the effect of annealing conditions. We obtain optimal results for TFTs with HfSiOx gate insulators annealed for 1 h at 100°C, with a saturation mobility of 1.2 cm^2/V·s, threshold voltage of 2.2 V, I_{on}/I_{off} ratio of 2.0 × 10^6, and insulator surface roughness of 0.187 nm RMS.

1. Introduction

The crystallization of HfO_2 increases leakage current and deteriorates the surface characteristics. However, its variant, hafnium silicate (HfSiOx) has excellent thermal stability allowing it to maintain its amorphous structure at temperatures higher than 500°C, thus suppressing increase in the leakage current. [1–3]. In the present paper, we describe the fabrication of amorphous indium zinc oxide (a-IZO)-based TFT gate insulators (HfSiOx), patterned onto transparent substrates and conduct characterization and analysis by investigating varying annealing temperature conditions. These are carried out in the presence and absence of an inert gas. We find that the different annealing temperatures used have a further effect on both the physical and electrical properties of our HfSiOx films.

2. Results and Discussion

We fabricated a-IZO TFTs and measured their electrical characteristics. Figure 1 shows the drain current vs. gate voltage (I_D–V_G) characteristics of the a-IZO TFTs with V_{DS} = 10 V.

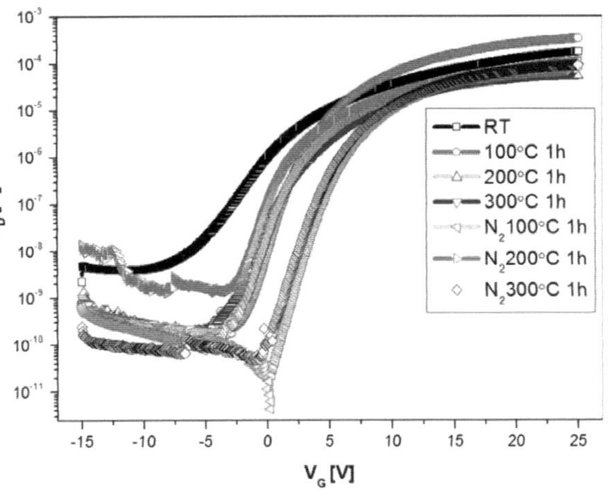

Figure 1. Transfer characteristic curves of a-IZO TFTs at various annealing temperatures, with the V_{DS} set to 10 V.

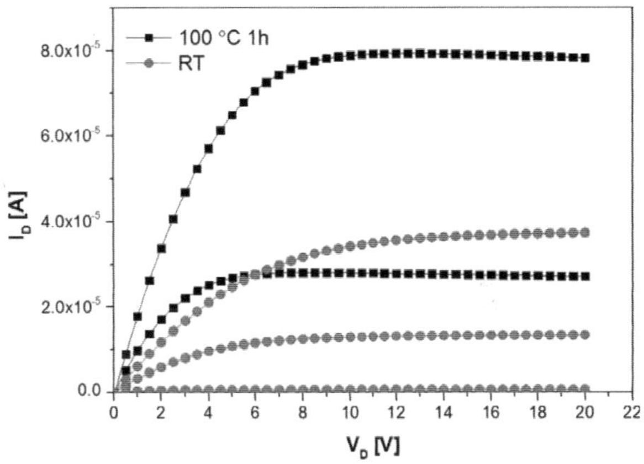

Figure 2. The output characteristic curves of the a-IZO TFTs at RT and 100°C with the V_D of (0, 6, and 10 V) 1 h annealing step for HfSiOx.

Figure 2 shows the drain current–drain voltage (I_D-V_D) characteristics of a-IZO TFTs based on the HfSiOx dielectrics at RT and 100°C. Figure 2 (RT) shows that saturation is difficult as the voltage is increased. In contrast, Figure 2 (100°C) shows that the output characteristics exhibit strong saturation and a clear pinch off. From Figure 1, it can be confirmed that the off-current does in fact decrease as a result of the annealing process. In particular, after 1 h at 100°C, we obtain best results with a saturation mobility 1.2 cm^2/V s. With the data examined, we can confirm that the oxide TFT performance is significantly improved.

3. Acknowledgements

This research was supported by the creative human resource development program for IT Convergence, BK21+ (Brain Korea 21 Plus).

4. References

[1] P. Punchaipetch, G. Pant, M. A. Quevedo-Lopez, C. Yao, M. El-Bouanani, M. J. Kim, R. M. Wallace, B. E. Gnade, "Low-temperature deposition of hafnium silicate gate dielectrics", IEEE J. Quantum Electron, Vol. **10**, p. 89, 2004.

[2] P. Punchaipetch, G. Pant, M. Quevedo-Lopez, H. Zhang, M. El-Bouanani, M. J. Kim, R. M. Wallace, B. E. Gnade, "Hafnium silicate formation by ultra-violet/ozone oxidation of hafnium silicide", Thin Solid Films, Vol. **425**, p. 68, 2003.

[3] G. Pant, P. Punchaipetch, M. J. Kim, Robert M. Wallace, Bruce E. Gnade, "Low temperature UV/ozone oxidation formation of $HfSiO_N$ gate dielectric", Thin Solid Films, Vol. **460**, p. 242, 2004.

Paper No P23: Effect on Electrical Performance TiO_x Doped InZnO Thin-Film Transistor (TFT)

Chanhee Park,[1] Yooseong Lim,[1] Seungsoo Ha,[2] Yongjin Im,[1] Minhyung Jang,[1] Seung-il Choi,[2] Ji-in Park,[1] and Moonsuk Yi[1]

[1]Department of Electrical and Computer Engineering, Pusan National University, Republic of Korea, E-mail: msyi@pusan.ac.kr; [2]Department of Advanced Circuit Interconnection, Pusan National University, Republic of Korea

Read the full article at DOI: 10.1002/jsid.321

Abstract
We investigated the electrical performance of TiO_x-IZO Thin-Film Transistor (TFT) changing the target composition ratio of IZO, and Radio-Frequency (RF) power of Titanium target. Titanium and IZO target were co-sputtered by using RF magnetron co-sputtering system. The samples were postannealed in the air, at 300°C for 1 h. When the formation of TiO_x-IZO rises in the film, it causes the oxygen vacancy in the film not to generate, and to suppress the carrier concentration.

1. Introduction
Thin-Film Transistor (TFT) based on amorphous silicon is widely used in the display industry, such as Liquid-Crystal Display (LCD). However, the amorphous silicon TFT has poor stability and low mobility. In order to solve these problems, Transparent Oxide Semiconductor (TOS) is used to fabricate TFT. TOS used Oxide-TFT has high electrical performance, low cost of fabrication, and high transparency. It can be used in large area display, and transparent display [1].

IGZO, which is composition of IZO and Gallium, is the most typical Oxide-TFT in the display industry. But the cost of Gallium is so expensive because of its deposits in the Earth. To substitute Gallium, which has suppressing effect of carrier concentration in IZO, Titanium is the alternative material. Just like Gallium, Titanium has similar effect on the Oxide-TFT due to its low standard electrode of −0.53V [2].

In this article, we fabricated the TiO_x doped IZO TFT changing the RF power of Titanium target and IZO composition ratio, one is In_2O_3 60 wt%, ZnO 40 wt%, and the other is In_2O_3 90 wt%, ZnO 10 wt%.

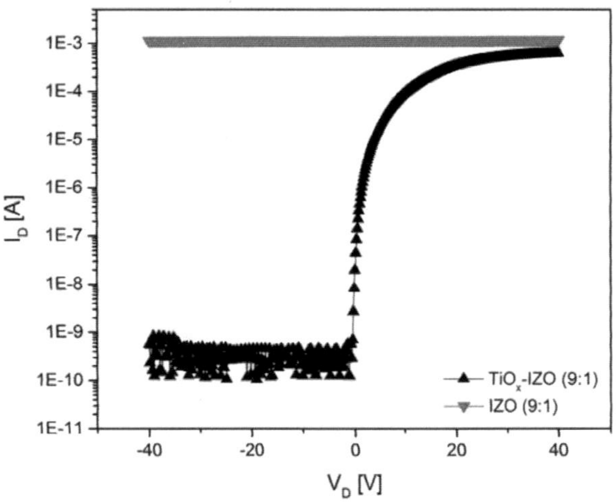

Figure 1. The curves of transfer characteristic about the only IZO and TiO_x-IZO TFT (In_2O_3: ZnO = 90 wt%: 10 wt%).

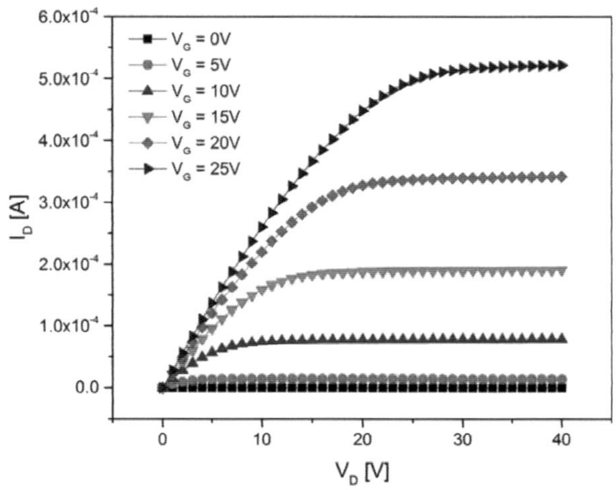

Figure 2. The curves of output characteristic about the TiO_x-IZO TFT (In_2O_3: ZnO = 90 wt%: 10 wt%).

2. Results and Discussion
The electrical performance of the TiO_x-IZO sputtered TFT is measured by using Elecs EL423 semiconductor test and analyzer. As shown in Figures 1 and 2, the transfer and output characteristic curves, we found that Threshold voltage (V_{th}) is 0.48V, saturation mobility (μ_{sat}) is 10.14 cm^2/Vs, I_{on}/I_{off} ratio is 4×10^6, and Subthreshold voltage Swing (S.S) is 0.37 V/dec. In addition, the TiO_x-IZO TFTs operated in the N-Channel enhancement mode with low I_D, and saturation behavior [3] whereas only IZO (In_2O_3: ZnO = 90 wt%: 10 wt%) sample operates just like electrode because of too many carrier concentration in IZO. It means that Titanium in IZO suppresses the carrier concentration and effect on electrical performance.

3. Acknowledgements
This research was supported by the creative human resource development program for IT Convergence, BK21+ (Brain Korea 21 Plus).

4. References
[1] Y. J. Im, S. J. Kim, J. H. Shin, S. S. Ha, C. H. Park, M. S. Yi, "Improvement in the electrical performance of Ge-doped InZnO thin-film transistor", J. Nanosci. Nanotechnol., Vol. **15**, pp. 1-5, 2015.

[2] S. H. Lee, D. C. Paine, "Metallization selection and the performance of amorphous In-Zn-O thin film transistors", Appl. Phys. Lett., Vol. **104**, p. 252103, 2014.

[3] D. K. Cho, S. H. Woo, J.I. Yang, D. H. Lee, Y. S. Lim, D. K. Kim, S. M. Park, M. S. Yi, "High performance thin film transistor with HfSiOx dielectrics fabricated at room temperature RF-magnetron sputtering", Electron. Mater. Lett., Vol. **9**, pp. 381–384, 2013.

Paper No P24: Effect of Mechanical Strain on Charge-Transfer V_T-Shift Compensation Circuits for Flexible AMOLED Displays

Nikolas P. Papadopoulos, Czang-Ho Lee, Manoj Sachdev, and William S. Wong

Department of Electrical and Computer Engineering, University of Waterloo, Waterloo, ON, N2L 3G1, Canada,
E-mail: npapadop@uwaterloo.ca

Abstract

A 4-thin-film transistor (TFT) voltage-programmed pixel circuit is fabricated using low-temperature (170°C) hydrogenated amorphous silicon (a-Si:H) TFTs process on flexible polyethylene naphthalate substrate. The electrical stability of the 4-TFT circuit was characterized under mechanical strain and flat (unstrained) conditions. The compensated drive current degraded approximately 5% under electrical bias and tensile strain. This result was similar to pixel circuits fabricated at high temperature (300°C) on rigid glass substrates.

1. Introduction

The operation of flexible electronics under mechanical bending provides additional degradation mechanisms in the electrical stability of the transistors and circuits. a-Si:H thin-film transistors (TFTs) on flexible substrates have decreased electrical stability under applied uniaxial strain. These changes are mostly reversed upon removal of the mechanical strain. In addition, the long-term electrical stability of a-Si:H TFTs under applied tensile strain is reduced compared to the flat unstrained condition [1]. These issues can greatly affect the operational lifetimes of flexible displays when running under applied mechanical stress.

Recently, we proposed a 4-TFT pixel circuit which has been shown to have excellent compensation capabilities for a-Si:H TFT-based backplanes [2,3], but its application in flexible electronics is unknown and untested. Therefore, to investigate the effectiveness of the 4-TFT pixel circuit in improving drive current stability, circuit samples were fabricated on flexible polyethylene naphthalate (PEN) substrates and are characterized under electrical bias stress with mechanical strain. In this article, we describe the integration and performance of the 4-TFT charge-transfer ΔV_T-compensation pixel circuit on flexible platforms. Circuit samples were tested under electrical stress in unstrained (i.e., flat substrate) and tensile strain conditions for 24 h.

2. Pixel Circuit Operation and Results

Inverted-staggered bottom-gate back-channel etched (BCE) a-Si:H TFTs and circuits were fabricated on 3-in. PEN substrates and tested under long-term bias stress and mechanical strain. The 4-TFT pixel circuit and the driving signals are shown in Figure 1.

The comparison between the measurement results from the 4-TFT and the typical 2-TFT pixel circuit samples for active-matrix organic light-emitting diode (AMOLED) displays demonstrates that the 4-TFT pixel circuit is effective in compensating the ΔV_T of the drive TFT and improving the stability of the organic light-emitting diode (OLED) drive current under both electrical bias and mechanical strain, as shown in Figure 2.

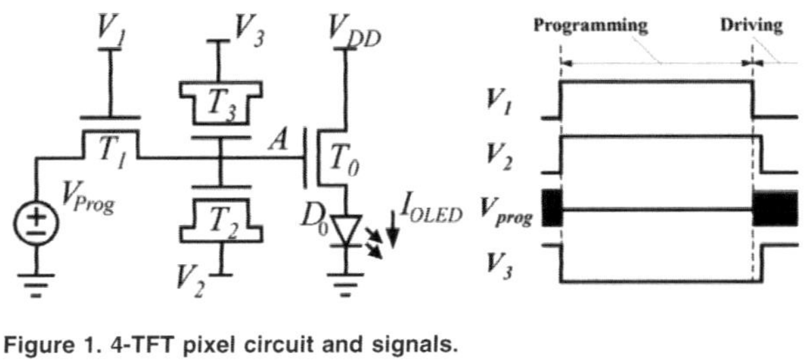

Figure 1. 4-TFT pixel circuit and signals.

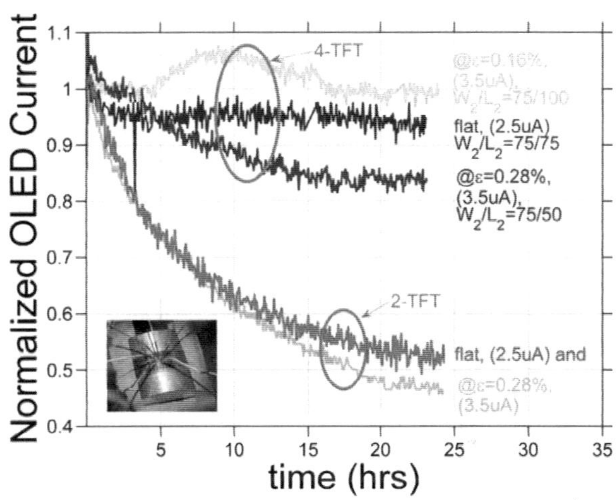

Figure 2. Experimental results of 24 h electrical bias tests of the 4-TFT pixel circuit under tensile mechanical strain and flat unstrained conditions.

The degradation of the OLED current in 24 h is more than 50% for the typical 2-TFT pixel circuit in flat or under tensile strain, where the OLED current from 4-TFT degrades less than 18% in all cases demonstrated and for up to 0.28% of tensile strain. The higher OLED current degradation for the larger strain is attributed to the different geometry of transistor and orientation of T_2 and the rate of degradation of the transistor due to the mechanical strain.

3. Acknowledgements

The authors acknowledge the Giga-to-Nanoelectronics (G2N) Centre at the University of Waterloo for the fabrication of circuits on PEN substrates, and the CMOS Design and Reliability Group of University of Waterloo for the testing infrastructure. This work was partially funded by the NSERC Discovery Grant.

4. References

[1] M. J. Chow, A. A. Fomani, M. Moradi, G. Chaji, R. A. Lujan, W. S. Wong, "Effects of mechanical strain on amorphous silicon thin-film transistor electrical stability", Appl. Phys. Lett., Vol. **102**, p. 233509, 2013.

[2] M. Yang, N. P. Papadopoulos, W. S. Wong, M. Sachdev, "A novel voltage-programmed pixel circuit utilizing ΔV_T-dependent charge-transfer to improve stability of AMOLED display", J. Display Technol., Vol. **9**, pp. 957–964, 2013.

[3] M. Yang, N. P. Papadopoulos, C.-H. Lee, W. S. Wong, M. Sachdev, "A novel voltage-programmed pixel circuit with ΔVT-shift compensation for AMOLED displays", Custom Integrated Circuits Conference (CICC), IEEE, 2013, pp. 1–4.

Paper No P25: The Nanocomposite on the Base of Liquid Crystal Material with Aluminum Nitride for Sulfur Dioxide Optical Sensor

Orest Sushynskyi, Taras Prystay, and Zinoviy Mykytyuk

Lviv Polytechnic National University, Ukraine, E-mail: orestsy@yahoo.com

Read the full article at DOI: 10.1002/jsid.380

Abstract

In this paper, we study the influence of sulfur dioxide (SO_2) on spectral characteristics of the nanocomposite on the base of cholesteric liquid crystal with aluminum nitride (AlN). The changes in spectral characteristics as the result of the interaction of SO_2 with AlN nanotubes was demonstrated. We propose to use this nanocomposite as the material of the primary transducer of SO_2 optical sensor.

1. Introduction

Sulfur dioxide (SO_2) is the one of the six main atmospheric pollutants [1]. Sulfur dioxide gas is toxic. At low concentrations (0.6 mg/m^3), this gas causes reflex changes in the functional state of the cerebral cortex [2].

We investigated the spectral characteristics of nanocomposite on the base of CLC2101L cholesteric liquid crystal (CLC) with single-wall aluminum nitride (AlN) nanotubes. Aluminum nitride is the one-dimensional (1D) nanostructure, including crystalline nanowires, nanotubes and faceted conventional single-layer nanotubes. This material is actively studies with future possibilities to use in the elements of the electronic gas sensors [3]. Band structure of AlN nanotubes can be modified by means of adsorption of various gases. This feature is useful to their potential use as electronic gas sensors. It is assumed that the single-wall AlN nanotubes can be administered as an electronic sensor to detect molecules of SO_2.

The advantage of such sensors is their high sensitivity. Because of this, we propose to use a single-wall AlN nanotube introduced in liquid crystal materials as a sensitive material of primary transducer of SO_2 optical sensor.

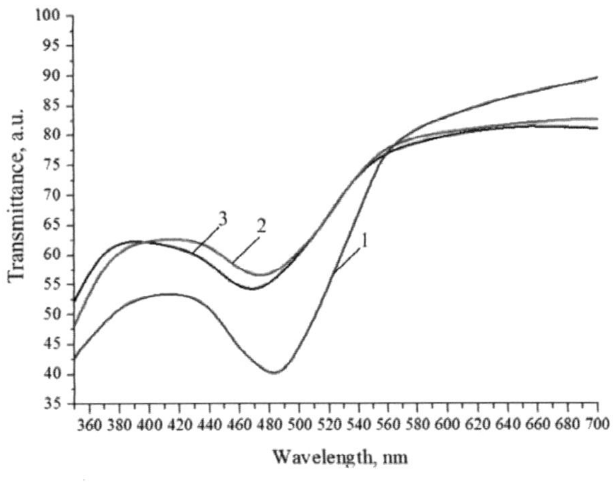

Figure 1. Spectral dependences of the studied nanocomposites: curve 1 is the pure CLC matrix, curve 2 is the CLC matrix with AlN nanotubes and curve 3 CLC matrix with AlN nanotubes under SO_2 influence.

2. Experiment

The concentration of AlN nanotubes in the CLC material is 0.15, 0.29, 0.46 wt%. As the liquid crystal matrix the CLC2101L heat-stable CLC was chosen. Spectroscopic studies of CLC2101L CLC in the temperature range 22–30°C have a transmittance minimum at a 482 nm of wavelength.

The AlN—a material with covalent bonds and a hexagonal crystal structure. The spatial group of this structure is $C_{6v}^4 - P6_3mc$. This material is characterized by resistance to very high temperatures in inert atmosphere.

Technology of nanocomposites preparation is presented in the paper [4]. Sulfur dioxide was obtained by using the chemical reaction of hydrochloric acid with sodium hydrosulfite:

$$NaHSO_3 + HCl - NaCl + SO_2 + H_2O$$

The functional diagram to study of harmful gases described in paper [4] was used to investigate the influence of SO_2 in CLC matrix with AlN nanotubes.

The analysis of experimental spectral characteristics was carried out in the range of 250–800 nm and it was showed that the introduction the single wall AlN nanotubes in to the CLC matrix are shift the transmittance minimum is towards short values of wavelengths. Under the influence of SO_2 with concentrations of 20–400 mg/m^3 we observed the further shift of the transmittance minimum towards short values of wavelengths. The Figure 1 are shown the spectral dependences of the studied nanocomposites, in particular curve 1 is the pure CLC matrix, curve 2 is the CLC matrix with AlN nanotubes and curve 3 CLC matrix with AlN nanotubes under SO_2 influence.

In case of introduction the AlN nanotubes into CLC matrix with helical structure, we observed the structural changes caused by the interaction the SO_2 molecules with AlN nanotubes. This change evoked the change of the step of CLC helical structure, which can be registered optically. Our studies permit to use this nanocomposite as a active material of primary transducer of SO_2 optical sensor.

3. References

[1] M. Kuratli, E. Pretsch, "Sulfur dioxide-selective optodes", Anal. Chem., Vol. **66**, pp. 85–91, 1994.

[2] J. L. Devalia et al., "Effect of nitrogen dioxide and sulphur dioxide on airway response of mild asthmatic patients to allergen inhalation", Lancet, Vol. **344**, pp. 1668–1671, 1994.

[3] J. Beheshtian, M. T. Baei, A. A. Peyghan, Z. Bagheri, "Electronic sensor for sulfide dioxide based on AlN nanotubes: A computational study", J. Mol. Mod., Vol. **18**, pp. 4745–4750, 2012.

[4] Z. Hotra, M. Vistak, Z. Mikityuk, A. Fechan, O. Sushynskyi, "Nanocomposite on the basis of the silicon dioxide doped with cholesteric liquid crystals a material primary transducers of optical sensors", Proc. SPIE, Vol. **91027**, pp. 91027F-1–91027F, 2014.

Paper No P26: Design of Structured Surfaces and Anisotropic Materials for Display and Photonic Applications

V. Bezborodov,[1] V. Zhylinski,[1] A. Chernik,[1] N. Bogomazova,[1] I. Zharski,[1] A. Smirnov,[2] A. Stsiapanau,[2] V. Lapanik,[3] and S. Mikhalyonok[1]

[1]Belarusian State Technological University, 220006 Minsk, Belarus, E-mail: v_bezborodov@yahoo.com; [2]Belarusian State University of Informatics and Radioelectronics, 220013 Minsk, Belarus; [3]Institute of Applied Physics Problems, 220108 Minsk, Belarus

Abstract

In this article, we show how inorganic and organic structured surfaces, anisotropic materials can be prepared and used for display and photonic applications. The presented results demonstrate that the design of anisotropic materials, the electrochemical formation of structured surfaces, and their combination can provide desirable variations in the anisotropic material properties; in the parameters of structured surfaces for improved satisfaction of the requirements for using them as the components for display and photonic applications.

1. Introduction

The electrochemical anodization technique of inorganic films on a glass substrate, which provide simultaneously a high optical transparency and good alignment properties for LC molecules on the substrate surface, is one of the promising solutions for the design and production of next generation of displays [1]. At the same time, different reaction possibilities for the functional groups and the cyclic fragments of the corresponding substituted cyclohexenones, isoxazolines, and similar to them intermediates allow transformations to be achieved selectively and give a chance of preparing anisotropic compounds and materials with novel combinations of the structural fragments of molecules [2]. Taking into account these results, we propose to combine the design, synthesis of anisotropic materials, conductive, and alignment structured surfaces for the creation of high efficient displays and photonic devices.

2. Results and Discussion

2.1 Formation of Structured Surfaces

One of the processes of the preparation of adoptable transparent conductors on different substrates is electrochemical anodization of thin Al layer sputtered on sodium glass. In this process, Al anodization is accompanied by the formation of porous alumina layer on metal surface, which can provide good alignment properties for LC molecules on the substrate surface [1]. The results of our investigations have shown that the nanoporous alumina layers and similar to them structured inorganic films on a glass substrate prepared by electrochemical anodization can be really one of the promising solutions for the design and production of next generations of displays, touch panels, and solar cells.

2.2 Design of Anisotropic Materials

We propose to use the substituted cyclohexenones, isoxazolines, and similar to them polyfunctional compounds [2,3] as the key intermediates for the preparation of different types of anisotropic substances and materials. It was found that anisotropic Mannich salts (**1**), UV curable substituted vinylketones (**2**), various of cyclohexene, phenylcyclohexane, biphenyl, terphenyl, or quaterphenyl derivatives, the LC compounds with negative dielectric anisotropy (**3-6**), which form, as rule, nematic phase at low temperature and in a wide temperature range and are characterized a high value of negative dielectric anisotropy ($\Delta\varepsilon = -5$-7), can be successfully prepared using this approach.

It should be noted that the anisotropic UV curable substituted vinylketones (**2**) can be easily prepared from the corresponding Mannich salts (**1**) [2].

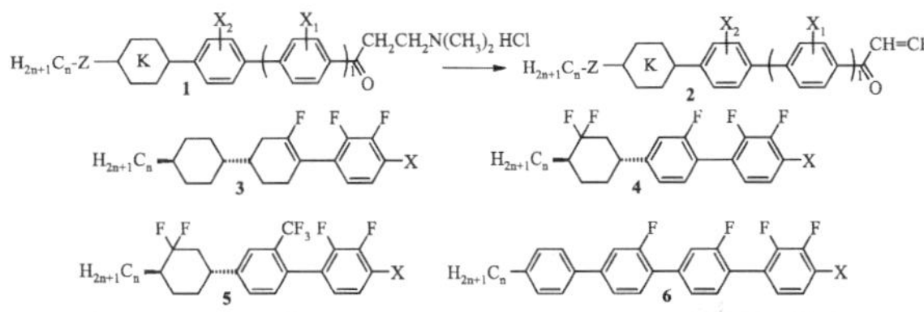

where $n = 3\text{-}11$, $l = 0-2$; $Z = CH_2$ *or* O; $X_{1,2} = H, F, Cl, CH_3$; $X = C_2H_5, C_3H_7, OCH_3, OC_2H_5$.

2.3 Combination of the Structured Surfaces and Anisotropic Materials

The prepared results demonstrate that the combination conductive and alignment structured surfaces, the corresponding host LC materials, the UV curable anisotropic substituted vinylketones can provide desirable variations of the properties and parameters of the vertically-aligned liquid crystal display (VA-LCDs). The cells, which have been prepared using the LC materials with negative dielectric anisotropy and the structured inorganic layers on glass substrate (alignment conditions) have several advantages in comparison with the cells containing commercial LC and alignment materials and possess switching time less than 3 ms and the viewing angle 170–180°.

We plan to develop new anisotropic materials and structured surfaces to assess their ability to generate the new high efficient displays and photonic devices. We hope that new results of our investigations may lead to better understanding of the nature of the liquid crystals, anisotropic, and structured alignment materials and their use for display and photonic applications.

3. References

[1] A. Smirnov, A. Stsiapanau, A. Mohammed, E. Mukha, H. S. Kwok, A. Murauski, "Combined nanostructured layers for display applications", Proceedings of SID Symposium "Display Week-2011", pp. 1385–1387, Los-Angeles, USA, May 2011.

[2] R. Dąbrowski, V. Bezborodov, "Developing synthesis of new liquid crystals", Liquid Crystals, Vol. **33**, pp. 1487–1489, 2006.

[3] V. S. Bezborodov, V. I. Lapanik, G. M. Sasnouski, S. G. Mikhalyonok, "Prospects of the development of new approaches of the preparation of anisotropic compounds and materials", 25th International Liquid crystal Conference, Dublin, Ireland, S-03.003, 2014.

Paper No P27: Optical Structure of Back Light Unit for 2-D/3-D Switchable Autostereoscopic 3-D Display With Low X-Talk Performance

Kihyung Kang, J. H. Yoon, D. K. Yang, K. B. Jeon, J. H. Lee, S. H. Son, and W. Y. Lee
Samsung Electronics, Suwon, South Korea, E-mail: kh9.kang@samsung.com

Abstract
In this article, we report a new 3-D backlight display for glasses-free 2-D/3-D switchable displays. In this type of 3-D display, 3-D works by line patterned back light unit. But light leakages from the 3-D light guide cause degrade the 3-D performance. We analyze the light leakages from light guide plate and suggest a novel backlight structure design to improve x-talk performance.

1. Introduction
There has been an increasing interest in developing glasses-free 3-D displays in recent years [1–4]. However, it is hard to find a solution to meet basic requirements such as display quality and cost. One of the basic requirements is that there must be no or minimum influence on the 2-D display quality. Several years ago, one company introduced 24 inch 2-D/3-D switchable display with using novel backlight [5]. Even though it was a good solution in terms of the material cost, the commercialization of the technology has not been successful due to the degradation of 2-D display quality and lack of effective solution to make large size 3-D light guide plate. In this work, we design a new 3-D light guide plate micro-pattern to overcome the shortcomings of the previous 3-D backlight technologies, and propose the structure of the back light unit for low x-talk performance.

2. Back Light Unit for 2-D/3-D Switchable Autostereoscopic 3-D Display
A 3-D backlight consists of light guide plate with line pattern for 3-D mode and a surface light source for 2-D mode. The 3-D backlight is located between a 2-D display panel and a 2-D backlight. The 3-D light guide plate has stripe patterns on the surface. The line patterns works as line type light source in the 3-D mode, and it forms 3-D images on the display. In 2-D mode, LEDs for 3-D light guide plate were turned off and those for 2-D light guide plate were turned on. The 2-D light guide plate generates uniform surface light and 2-D image can be seen (Figure 1).

3. Light Leakage of 3-D Light Guide Plate
The light guide plate for 3-D should generate lights only to the front for 3-D image but there are light leakages to the backward to 2-D back light unit which cause recycle of the leakage lights and increase of x-talk. We analyze the cause of leakage light of 3-D light guide and propose the structure of back light unit for 3-D display with low x-talk performance.

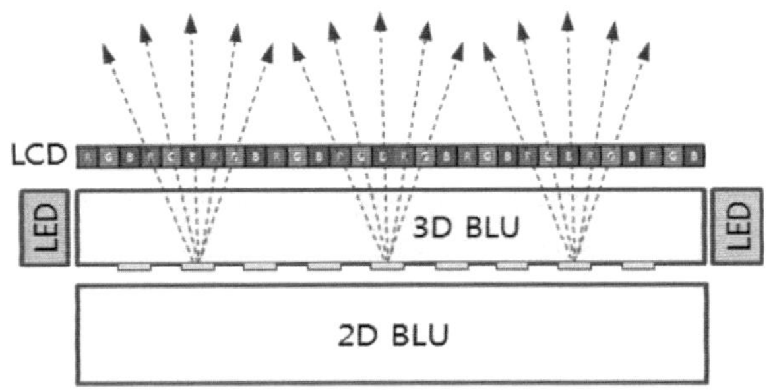

Figure 1. Configuration of 3-D display with 2-D/3-D switchable back light unit.

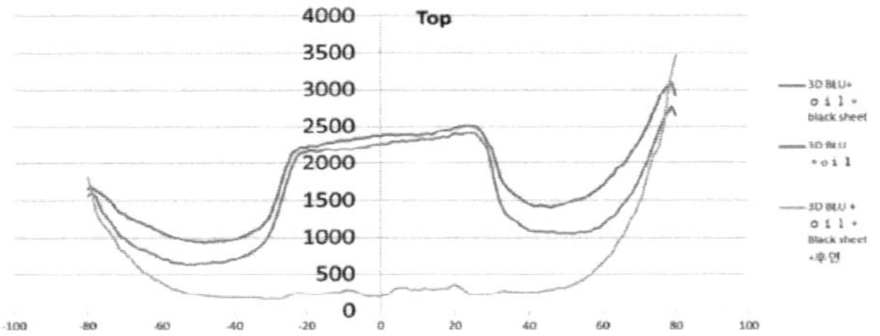

Figure 2. Angular profile of front and back ward light of 3-D light guide plate for vertical direction.

3.1. Analysis of the Leakage Light
We measure and analyze the cause of the leakage light of 3-D light guide plate on both side of front and back ward. We guess the cause of the light leakages are scattering on the surface of light guide plate, gap between pattern and substrate, bad reflective coating on pattern surface, scattering of resin material, and scattering of pattern surface.

We found the leakage light from light guide plate has large angle, which is caused by scattering on the pattered area. But the light leakage to the front side is filtered by LCD panel caused by the viewing angle characteristics of it. We should reduce the amount of the light through 2-D back light unit which the leakage light to the backward is recycled and is redirected to the front (Figure 2).

3.2. Improved 3-D Back Light Unit Structure
Generally 2-D back light unit has diffusive surface on the top of it in order to remove the moire pattern with panel and prism sheet. But the diffusive surface helps the leakage light to backward recycle and redirect to the front. We replace the diffusive surface with flat one and can reduce the recycled light. New configuration of 2-D/3-D switchable back light unit can reduce more than 10% x-talk.

4. Conclusions
For low x-talk 3-D performance, we analyzed the cause of the leakage light in 2-D/3-D switchable 3-D back light unit structure. We suggest a new configuration of 2-D/3-D switchable back light unit and it shows less than 10% x-talk performance than previous one.

5. References
[1] G. J. Woodgate, J. Harrold, "High efficiency reconfigurable 2D/3D autostereocopic display", SID Symp. Digest Tech. Pap., Vol. **34**, pp. 394–397, 2003.

[2] J. C. Schultz, R. Brott, M. Sykora, W. Bryan, T. Fukamib, K. Nakao, A. Takimoto, "Full resolution autostereoscopic 3D display for mobile applications", SID Symp. Digest Tech. Pap., Vol. **40**, pp. 127–130, 2009.

[3] S.-C. Liu, J.-F. Tu, C.-C. Gong, C.-W. Chang, "Autostereoscopic 2-D/3-D display using a liquid crystal lens", SID Symp. Digest Tech. Pap., Vol. **41**, pp. 432–435, 2010.

[4] K. Kang, S. Moon, S. Park, S. Hwang, S. Shestak, J. Yoon, D. Hwang, "Field sequential LC barrier for a full resolution auto-stereoscopic 3D display", SID Symp. Digest Tech. Pap., Vol. **42**, pp. 456–459, 2011.

[5] M. Minami, K. Yokomizo, Y. Shimpuku, "Glasses-free 2D/3D switchable display using a unique light guide", SID Symp. Digest Tech. Pap., Vol. **42**, pp. 468–471, 2011.

Paper No P28: Electric and Magnetic Fields in ORW Technology

O. A. Semina,[1,2] A. V. Dubtsov,[1,2] D. V. Shmeliova,[1,2] S. V. Pasechnik,[1,2] and and V. G. Chigrinov[3]

[1]Moscow State University of Instrument Engineering and Computer Science, Stromynka 20, 107996, Moscow, Russia, E-mail: alexanderdubtsov@gmail.com; [2]Moscow State University of Information Technologies, Radioengineering and Electronics, Vernadsky pr., 78 119454, Moscow, Russia; [3]Hong Kong University of Science and Technology, Clear Water Bay, Kowloon, Hong Kong

Abstract

In this paper, we present the results of investigation of electric (magnetic) fields action on the light induced changes of a surface orientation of a liquid crystal (LC) contacted with photoaligned surfaces. The application of the obtained results in optical rewritable (ORW) technology is considered.

1. Introduction

Photoalignment (PA) technology was originally proposed for usage in liquid crystal display (LCD) industry as a perspective tool for a perfect surface treatment alternative to the well-known surface rubbing procedure [1]. Among different variants of such technology, those based on light induced changes of molecular orientation in nanometer dye layers are of a special interest. Indeed, the initial surface orientation of dye molecules, determined by a polarization state of light wave can be further changed by the secondary illumination by light of the polarization state, different from the initial one. It is of a great importance that the mentioned above changes, take place on both dry layer's surfaces and those, wetted with LC. Such property, in turn provides the light controlled changes of surface and bulk orientation of LC that was used to propose the original optical rewritable (ORW) technology [2]. The latter technology is interesting for different applications, like bistable displays, e-paper, fiber optics, and photonics devices [3]. Usage of additional factors such as electric or magnetic fields may provide optimization of technical characteristics of LC devices based on ORW technology. The aim of the investigation, described in this paper is a study of physical backgrounds for a modification of ORW technology.

2. Experimental Results and Discussion

In our experiments, we used different types of liquid crystal cells with different surface treatment (one type for geometry A with a normal orientation of electric field, respectively, to LC layer and the second one—for geometry B with "in-plane" orientation of electric or magnetic field). In the geometry "A," both substrates of the typical sandwich like cell were preliminary treated in accordance with PA technology to provide zones of different azimuth anchoring strength (Figure 1).

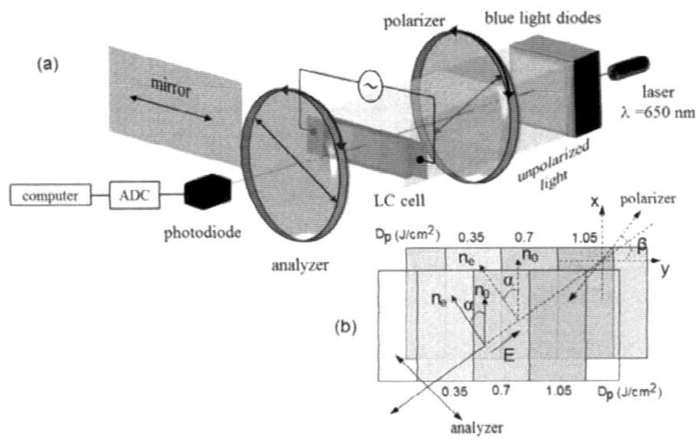

Figure 1. Experimental set-up (a) and scheme (b) of geometry A.

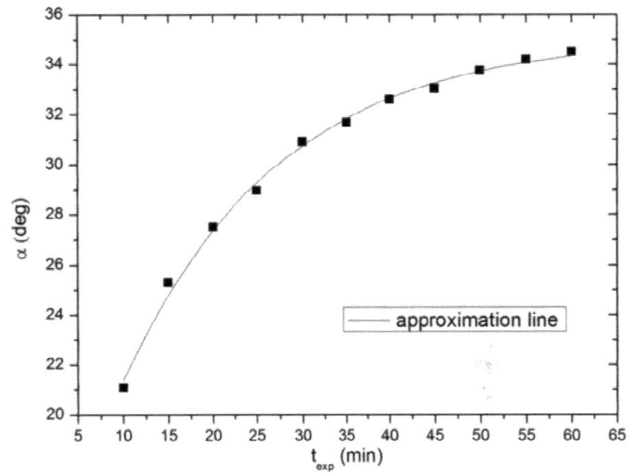

Figure 2. Dependence of the angle α on the exposure time t_{exp}.

The cells used in the geometry "B" were made in accordance with ORW technology and included both photoaligned and rubbed substrates. All the cells were filled with a standard LC (5CB) before secondary illumination by blue (450 nm) or UV (365 nm) light of a new polarization state. It resulted in a slow rotation (gliding) of an easy axis on photoaligned substrates. Usage of strong (about 1 V/μm) electric field in geometry A suppressed the optical phase delay and provided simultaneous rotation of easy axes on both substrates. It resulted in a rotation of a planar sample of LC on the angle α. The dependence of α on the exposition time t_{exp} is shown in Figure 2.

3. Conclusion

The pronounced influence of electric and magnetic fields on surface orientation induced by a secondary irradiation of photoaligned surfaces with blue or UV light was established. The light induced rotation of monodomain samples of LC was established and studied for the first time. The experimentally studied acceleration of light induced changes of surface orientation by "in-plane" electric and magnetic fields can be used for optimization of ORW technology.

4. Acknowledgements

This work was partially supported by the Ministry of Education and Science of the Russian Federation (grant No. 3.1921.2014/K, 9.1189.2014/K) and the RFBR (projects No. 14-03-31773 mol_a).

5. References

[1] V. G. Chigrinov, V. M. Kozenkov, H.-S. Kwok, Photoalignment of Liquid Crystalline Materials: Physics and Applications, Wiley, New York, 2008.

[2] A. Muravsky, A. Murauski, X. Li, V. Chigrinov, H.-S. Kwok, "Optical rewritable liquid-crystal-alignment technology", J. SID, Vol. **15/4**, pp. 267–273, 2007.

[3] V. G. Chigrinov, Liquid Crystal Photonics, Nova Science Pub Inc, New York, 2014.

Paper No P29: Examination of the Accommodation Response of Integral Photography Still Images

Sumio Yano[1] and Min-Chul Park[2]

[1]Shimane University, Matsue, Japan, E-mail: yano@ecs.shimane-u.ac.jp; [2]KIST, Seoul, Korea

Abstract

The accommodation response of the integral photography still image was examined. The result was presumed to show the coincidence between vergence and accommodation function for the integral photography still image.

1. Introduction

It is thought that integral photography (hereafter IP), which has a natural motion parallax and no-conflict between vergence and accommodation function, is different from stereoscopic and multiview image systems [1]. In this article, the accommodation response of the still image of IP and its examination are described.

2. Experimental Equipment and Conditions

2.1. Experimental Equipment

Figure 1 shows the experimental equipment used. In the development of the IP display, a 4.8 in. liquid-crystal display (LCD; Ortus Technology Co. Ltd.) was used. The LCD used the high-definition television image format, and a 55.50-μm pixel pitch. The type of lens-array is an orthogonal arrangement, 1 mm in diameter and 3.3 mm in focal length. The elemental image size was 18 × 18 dots, and the IP image size was 106 × 60 ($H \times V$) dots based on these devices. The ratio between lens diameter and the size of the elemental images was not an integer. However, degradation due to this effect was reduced as much as possible. The accommodation response was measured using a WAM-5500, which is made by Shigiya Machinery Works Ltd. The measurement eye was consisted of only a single eye, and the sampling frequency was 7 Hz.

2.2. Experimental Conditions

In the experiment, the IP display was set on the rail, and the measurement tool for the accommodation function was set before the IP display. The subject watched the IP image through the measurement tool as shown in Figure 1. The displayed IP image was of Marta Cross, which consisted of 300 × 400 dots ($H \times V$). The viewing distances were 60 and 90 cm. The IP still image was displayed maximally14 cm in the near direction, and also maximally 12 cm in the far direction from the position of IP display. The change of the IP still image is 2 cm in the near and far directions.

2.3. Experimental Results

Figure 2 shows one of the experimental results. In this figure, the abscissa axis shows the visual target's position, and the vertical axis shows the accommodation response. The black filled circle designates the position of the visual target, and the open square shows the measurement result of the accommodation response in the figure.

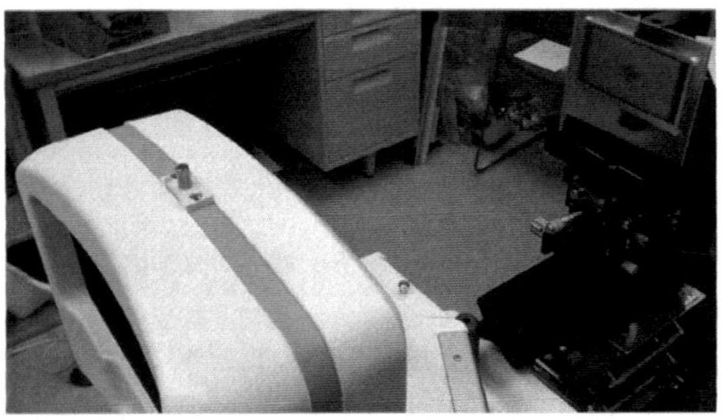

Figure 1. Experimental equipment.

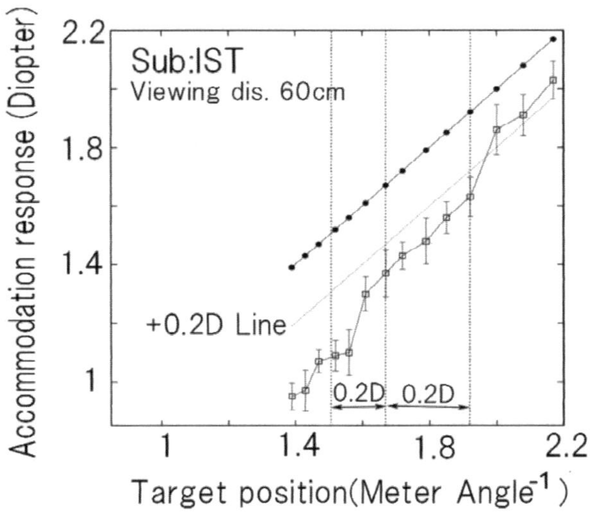

Figure 2. Experimental result.

3. Discussion

The spatial resolution S (cpr) in the depth position Z_s (m) of the IP image from the viewing distance L (m) is derived through the following Equation (1).

$$S=\min\left(\frac{L}{2P_i},\ \frac{g(L-Z_s)}{2p|Z_s|}\right) \tag{1}$$

The "min" means the minimum value in the basket. P_i represents the lens pitch, p represents the pixel pitch, and g represents the gap between the LCD and lens-array. For this reason, several of the examined points are added to the commonly considered points in the evaluation of the accommodation response of the IP image. The discrimination of depth perception and the effect of the image blur on accommodation in the IP image must be considered in evaluation of these points. The threshold of the degree of discrimination for IP image was reported as being several cpd. When the stereoscopic image was blurred, the conflict between vergence and the accommodation function was decreased, and likewise the coincidence between vergence and the accommodation function arose by the degree of less than several cpd. The coincidence between vergence and accommodation function was estimated while taking into account of these characteristics of IP still images.

3. Conclusion

The accommodation response for IP still images was measured and evaluated. The experimental result was examined from the perspective of the spatial resolution. Additional examinations will be carried from the perspective of the optical characteristics of the human visual system.

5. Reference

[1] H. Hoshino, F. Okano, H. Isono, I. Yuyama, "Analysis of resolution limitation of integral photography", J. Opt. Soc. Am. A, Vol. **15**, pp. 2059–2065, 1998.

Paper No P30: Luminance Distribution Measurements in CAVE-Type Virtual Reality Systems

Adam Mazikowski

Faculty of Electronics, Telecommunications and Informatics, Department of Metrology and Optoelectronics, Gdańsk University of Technology, Gdańsk, Poland, E-mail: adamazik@eti.pg.gda.pl

Abstract

In this article, the immerse 3D visualization lab just opened at the Gda´nsk University of Technology is presented. The effect of user "immersion," it such virtual reality systems, is largely dependent on the optical properties of projected images. Luminance distribution of screens was measured and the luminance uniformity was determined and discussed.

1. Introduction

In recent years, many scientific and industrial centers in the world attempted to develop a virtual reality laboratory [1–3]. The main idea of such laboratory is to allow the user to "immerse" into, interact with, and move in a computer-generated virtual world. This is important because of wide possible implementation of virtual reality installations: military (training pilots, paratroopers, equipment operators), professional workplaces (medicine, geology, engineering, ship or helicopter simulators), industrial (advanced prototyping), scientific (3D visualization of research results), education, virtual tourism, and entertainment. A virtual reality CAVE-type installation was also built at the Gdańsk University of Technology.

2. Immersive 3D Visualization Lab

Immerse 3D Visualization Lab (I3DVL) developed at the Gdańsk University of Technology is one of the most sophisticated VR installations in the world [2]. It is the biggest CAVE-type lab consisted of six flat screens arranged in the form of a cube. Two techniques of 3D projection were implemented: active stereo and technique with spectrum separation (Infitec). The user may be located inside a transparent sphere freely rotating inside a cube (spherical walk simulator), which allows simulation of free movement without changing the user position related to the screens. Alternatively CAVE and rotating sphere (Virtusphere) can work separately as two different virtual reality solutions [2].

High-quality equipment and components are implemented in laboratory. Projectors, rigid projection screens, and part of mechanical structure were provided by BARCO (Belgium). The integrator of the whole system was Integra AV (Poland). The view of the lab is presented in Figure 1.

3. Immersion Feeling

One of the most important aspects of virtual reality laboratory is to provide the user a high level of immersion feeling. The purpose is that the user during simulation is fully immersed and does not recognize the elements of real world: directions, door position, and borders between projection screens.

This immersion level depends on many factors: system configuration (number of screens), spatial sound, quality of mechanical fitting, type of projection (2D or 3D), and quality of image projection. From the optical point of view (projection), luminance nonuniformity may deteriorate image quality and decrease immersion feeling.

4. Luminance Uniformity Measurements

The measurements were performed for the whole working projection system (projectors and screens) taking into account the specific projection geometry (focal length of projectors, throwing angle, position of user inside the CAVE).

Figure 1. View of the immerse 3D visualization lab.

Konica Minolta luminance meter (CS-200) was implemented, mounted on a tripod with rotating head. According to recommendation of the ICDM measurement, standard measurements were taken for the following configuration: perpendicular to the screens (screens quality and differences due to projector throwing angle) and from the user point of view (influence of user position). Two different user positions were taken into account during measurements: the user in the middle of the CAVE (the best case) and the user near the corner of the CAVE (the worst case).

5. Results

Measurements show quite good luminance distribution that allows high impression level of "immersion." However, there are same luminance differences, especially for user position far from the CAVE center. Obtained results (luminance distribution) allow for further software luminance compensation for the top level of user "immersion."

6. References

[1] K. J. Fernandes, V. Raja, J. Eyre, "Cybersphere: The fully immersive spherical projection system", Commun. ACM, Vol **46**, pp. 141–146, 2003.

[2] A. Mazikowski, J. Lebiedź, "Image projection in immersive 3D visualization laboratory", 18th International Conference on Knowledge Based and Intelligent Information & Engineering Systems KES 2014, Procedia Comput. Sci., Vol. **35**, pp. 842–850, 2014.

[3] A. Mazikowski, M. Trojanowski, "Measurement of spectral spatial distribution of scattering materials for rear projections screens used in virtual reality systems", Metrol. Meas. Syst., Vol. **20**, pp. 443–452, 2013.

Paper No P31: Fast and Easy-to-Use Approach of BRDF Measurements by Use of Fixed Small Light Source and Luminance Imager

A. Marsal,[1] A. Sycev,[1] K. Blankenbach,[1] and A. Smirnov[2]

[1]Pforzheim University, Display Lab, Germany, E-mail: kb@displaylabor.de; [2]BSUIR, Lab for Information Displays and Optical Processing Systems, Belarus

Abstract

Measurements of reflection characteristic are usually done by BRDF. We evaluated successfully a method by using an imaging colorimeter and a small light source, both at fixed position.

1. Introduction

The measurement of the bidirectional reflectance distribution function (BRDF) [1] allows to acquire the reflectance properties of displays. BRDF measurement is costly and time-consuming. Our goal is to introduce and evaluate simpler alternatives.

2. Measurements Set-up

The typical BRDF measurement set-up [1,2] is shown in Figure 1 left. A movement of the point light source in steps of less than 0.1° has to be performed. Reflection measurements can also be done by gloss meters with line sensor (Rhopoint Flex20, range ±7°, 512 measurement points). Our idea (Figure 1 right) is to use a fixed luminance imager (INSTRUMENT SYSTEMS LUMICAM 1300) and a small light source (SLS) with diffuser (∅ = 5 mm); $\alpha = 0° \ldots 10°$, large distance of SLS to display.

3. Results

We measured six (four glare "G"; two matte "M") different displays and white paper. The results of our SLS measurements are shown in Figure 2 (left, right zoomed). The curves correspond to the typical characteristics of glare and matte displays (e.g., [3]). It is easy to notice that maximum reflected luminance differs in factor of 10 for the glare type displays (G1–G4).

The same displays were measured with the Rhopoint Flex20. The reflectance characteristics and the relation of their maximum reflected intensity is very similar to our SLS method. However due to an angle of 20° for θ_s and θ_d (see Figure 1 left) "double reflections" occur for G2 and G3 as shown in Figure 3; this was not observed for our SLS approach using small angles for α. This figure shows camera pictures taken of a light tube at oblique angle and the overlay of the line sensor gloss meter. It is obvious that those double peaks are less suitable for acquiring reflectance characteristics. The double reflections are probably caused by index mismatch of optical bonding material.

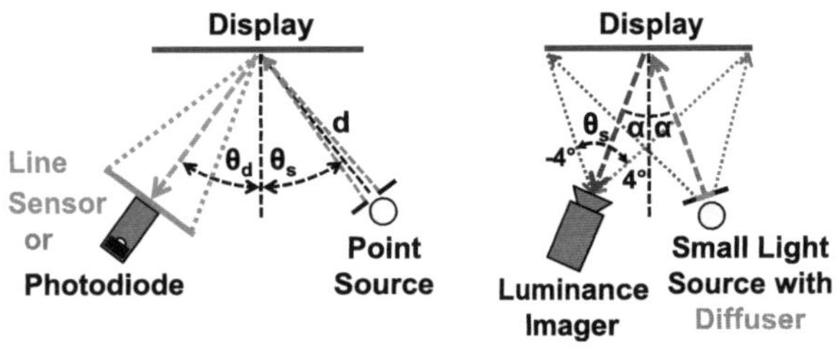

Figure 1. BRDF, gloss meter (left) and SLS set-up (right)

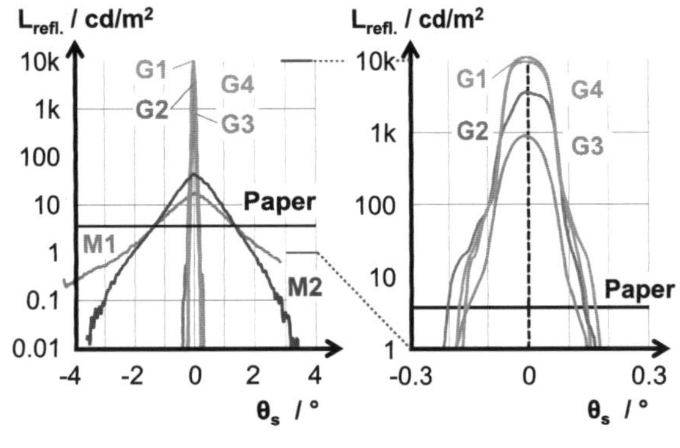

Figure 2. SLS reflected luminance (left), zoomed (right).

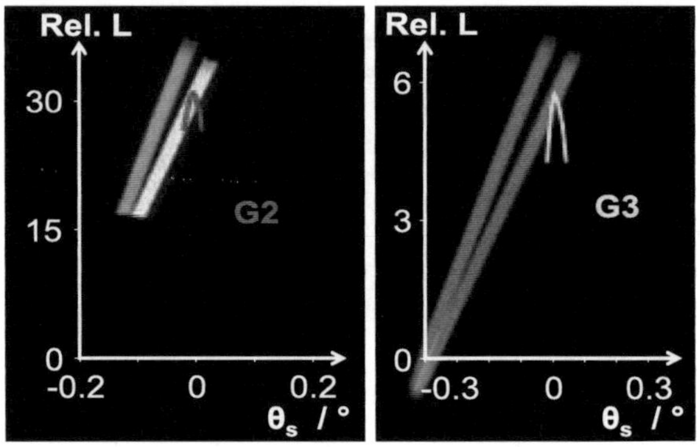

Figure 3. Double reflection measured with Rhopoint Flex20.

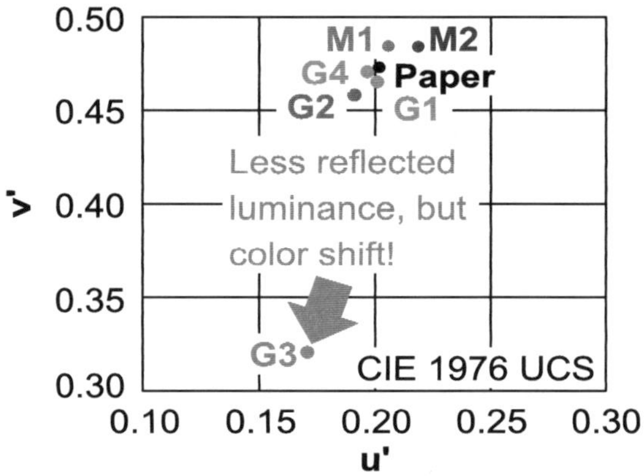

Figure 4. Color shifts of the reflected light by SLS.

Figure 4 shows the color shifts of the reflected SLS (white paper as reference). The measured and observed (by vision) color shifts were minor except for display G3. The reflected luminance of this display is a factor of 10 smaller than G1 and G4 (Figure 2 right). This highly effective AR coating shows a bluish reflection of white light.

4. Summary

We developed a simple and fast measurement method for reflection characteristics of displays compared to BRDF. Only neglectable differences were observed for several displays.

5. Acknowledgements

We thank Konica Minolta for gloss meter Rhopoint Flex20.

6. References

[1] SID, "Information Display Measurements Standard" (ICDM IDMS), Chapter 11, pp. 230–232, 2012.

[2] M. Becker, "Display reflectance: Basics, measurement, and rating", JSID, Vol. **14**, pp. 1003–1017, 2006.

[3] M. Becker, J. Laur, J. Neumeier, "Electro-optical characterization of reflective LCDs", SID Digest, Vol. **32**, pp. 322–325, 2001.

Paper No P32: Impact of Halogen Ion Size of Chemical Agent System on Electrical and Optical Characteristics of rGO Layers

V. Eskandari,[1] M. R. Fathollahi,[1] E. Mohajerani,[1] A. Fallahi,[2] and P. Tahani[1]

[1]Laser and Plasma Research Institute, Shahid Beheshti University G.C, Tehran 1983963113, Iran, E-mail: e-mohajerani@sbu.ac.ir; [2]Faculty of Polymer Sciences and Engineering, Amir Kabir University of Technology, Tehran, Iran

Read the full article at DOI: 10.1002/jsid.323

Abstract

In the current paper, we compare the effect of different hydrogen halide acid agent systems in chemical reduction of graphene oxide (GO) thin layers. We observe the large iodine ion can facilitate the reduction reaction in comparison with bromide and chloride counterpart ions. We show the sheet resistance of the graphene layer decreases by about six orders of magnitude due to efficient reduction of the graphene oxide.

1. Introduction

Indium tin oxide (ITO) is the dominant transparent conducting oxide (TCO) in the field of photo-electronic devices. Also, its fluorine-based counterpart , that is, fluorine tin oxide (FTO) has been widely used in various applications such as photovoltaic and solar cells. However, there are several drawbacks that limit the application of TCOs in optoelectronic industry, for instance the usage of indium as an expensive element; therefore there is a rising demand for replacement of TCO-based layers in photonics and electronics applications. Recently, graphene thin layer has been the focus of researches owing to its potential promising properties such as low-cost fabrication procedure and excellent electrical/optical characteristics [1–3]. In this paper, we demonstrate the efficient chemical reduction of graphene oxide (GO) layers to form thin transparent conducting graphene films. We employ a mixture chemical agent; namely, hydrogen halide acid with acetic acid to prepare conductive reduced graphene oxide (rGO). We compare the effect of different hydrogen halide acids on the characteristics of the rGO films.

2. Experiment

The scheme for preparation of the rGO films is as follows: First, we cleaned the quartz/glass substrates by following a standard procedure; namely byNaOH, acetone, isopropanol, and finally by a mixture of H_2O_2:H_2SO_4 (3:1) each for 15 min in ultrasonic bath. Then, graphene oxide solution in aqua with concentration of 5 mg/mL was spin-coated on the substrates following a sequential deposition with 400, 600, and 800 rpm each for 30 s. Next, we left the samples for 24 h in mixture of acetic acid with different hydrhalide acid for chemical reduction of the graphene oxide thin films. Afterward, we examined the optical properties of thin rGO layers by employing a USB2000 spectrometer from Ocean Optics. Also, we used a four-point probe station from Y. N. Saleh Co. and a Keithley 2400 source-measure unit to evaluate the sheet resistance of the layers. The probe station was first tested and calibrated by standard samples.

3. Results and Discussion

AcOH-HI is an efficient chemical agent for reducing GO and forming conducting rGO. We replaced the hydrhalide part in the chemical agent

Table 1. Sheet resistance of GO and rGO layers

Agent	Sheet resistance (KΩ/sq)
w/o (original GO)	$\sim 10^{+6}$
AcOH-HCl	$1.8 \times 10^{+4}$
AcOH-HBr	17
AcOH-HI	1.2

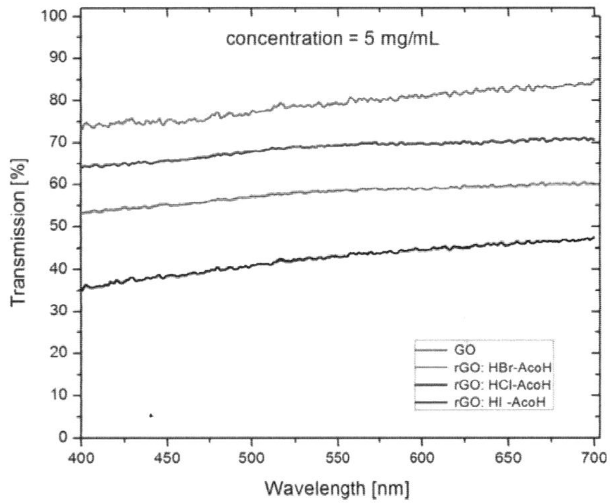

Figure 1. Transmission spectra of reduced graphene oxide layers by different agent systems.

with similar acid complex; namely HBr and HCl to investigate the reduction mechanism. In order to employ the graphene thin layers as transparent electrode in optoelectronics, the layers should possess optimal electrical and optical characteristics. Table 1 summarizes the sheet resistance of original GO layer along with GO layers which reduced by different agent systems. As seen, the sheet resistance drops by efficient reduction of the GO sheets and formation of rGO layer as the halide ion enlarges. On the other hand, Figure 1 portrays the transmission spectra in visible region for samples prepared in different acidic agent bath. We observe the transmission is decreased by reduction of the graphene layers and the formation of two-dimensional π-electron system within the flat carbon layers.

4. Future Work

We intend to investigate the effect of other reaction parameters such as agent concentration and solution mixture in the characteristics of the rGO films. Also, we will examine the thermal reduction technique in order to improve the characteristics of the final samples.

5. References

[1] I. K. Moon, J. Lee, R. S. Ruoff, H. Lee, "Reduced graphene oxide by chemical graphitization", Nat Commun, Vol. 1, Article number: 73, 2010; DOI: 10.1038/ncomms1067.

[2] S. J. Wang, Y. Geng, Q. Zheng, J.-K. Kim, "Fabrication of highly conducting and transparent graphene films", Carbon, Vol. **48**. pp. 1815–1823, 2010.

[3] Q. B. Zheng, M. M. Gudarzi, S. J. Wang, Y. Geng, Z. Li, J.-K. Kim, "Improved electrical and optical characteristics of transparent graphene thin films produced by acid and doping treatments", Carbon, Vol. **49**, pp. 2905–2916, 2011.

Paper No P33: Absorption-Scattering Based High Pitch Cholesteric Liquid Crystal (HP-CLC): 3-D Active Shutter and General Lighting Applications

Suman K. Manna, Kedar Sathaye, Samir Abbas, Stephen Le-Gall, Laurent Dupont, and Jean-Louis De Bougrenet de la Tocnaye

Department of Optics, Telecom Bretagne, 655 Avenue du Technopole, 29200 Plouzané, France, E-mail: suman.manna@telecom-bretagne.eu

Abstract

In this article, we exploit an absorption-scattering based high pitch length cholesteric liquid crystal active shutter. Using the two said fundamental optical properties, we have shown the resultant impact on optical transmission (ON & OFF state) is attracting the general lighting applications. Furthermore, the potential to be used as 3-D active optical shutter has been endorsed.

1. Introduction

High pitch cholesteric liquid crystal (HP-CLC) with its salient features such as strong and isotropic scattering ability, sunlight readability and less eye straining, no use of polarizer-analyzer, easy driving scheme and gray scale adjustability make it indispensable for general lighting applications ranging from domestic lightening to auto-vehicle and, even more exploring the potential application in polarizer free high contrast 3-D active optical shutter. In contrast to some other existing polarizer free 3-D active shutter, such as two crossed polarized dye-nematic planar cells stacking [1], dye doped polymer dispersed liquid crystal (PDLC) [2], polarization grating based diffractive liquid crystal shutter [3], etc., HP-CLC based optical shutter carries easy fabrication steps, low cost, high performance and more specially not being used of UV in the processing steps, it is not also limited from bulk production.

2. Principle of Light Scattering in CLC

The underlying principle is by increasing the helical pitch length, and the birefringence of the liquid crystal, the effective domain size of the focal conic state can be optimized to have enhanced scattering [4]. Further, this optimized chiral nematic mixture once added with few percentage of black dye the blocking state optical transmission can be reached sufficiently high. However, the optimization of the dye concentration is

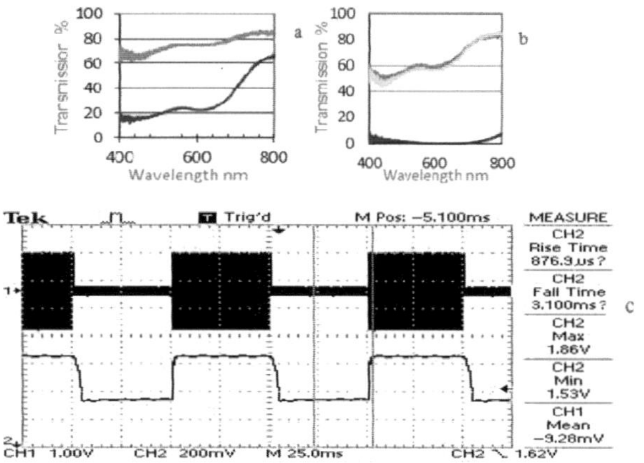

Figure 1. ON state and OFF state optical transmission spectra (a) without black dye (b) with black dye (c) response time 3 μs fall time and applied field 5 Vp-p/μm.

Figure 2. Bulk optical shutter for various applications based on HP-CLC with black dye: (a) SLM (10 × 10 cm^2) ON & OFF states (b) 3-D goggle (c) application as a white diffusing screen (26 × 12 cm^2) and showing some projected image over that.

done with respect to the required ON state transmission within the miscibility range of the dye in liquid crystal.

3. Sample Preparation

In order to have high birefringence, we use liquid crystal E-44 (Δn=0.28,Merck), which is mixed with 7 wt% (optimized with respect to maximum scattering) of chiral molecule R-811 (Merck). The above mixture is further mixed with 3wt% (optimized w.r.t. ON state transmission) black dye (Nematel). Final mixture is mixed homogeneously at isotropic temperature of liquid crystal (65°C) and finally filled in the conventional liquid crystal cell for characterization.

4. Results

5. Acknowledgements

We thank to LC-Tech for designing the 26x12 cm^2 panel and Eyes3Shut for providing the 3-D glasses. Mixture has been optimized in clean room of Telecom Bretagne.

6. References

[1] M. Schadt, "Liquid crystal materials and liquid crystal displays", Annu. Rev. Mater. Sci., Vol. **27**, 305–379, 1997.

[2] P. S. Drzaic, "Liquid Crystal Dispersions", World Scientific, Singapore, 1995.

[3] J. Chen, P. J. Bos, H. Vithana, D. L. Johnson, "An electro-optically controlled liquid crystal diffraction grating", Appl. Phys. Lett., Vol. **67**, 2588–2590, 1995.

[4] D. Coates, "Handbook of Visual Display Technology", Springer-Verlag, Berlin, 2012

AUTHOR INDEX

AUTHOR INDEX

AUTHOR INDEX

AUTHOR INDEX

John Wiley & Sons
111 River Street
Hoboken, NJ 07030-5774

CURRAN ASSOCIATES INC.
proceedings.com

ISBN 978-1-5108-3310-4
9 781510 833104